GW00458989

THE HUNGRY

Published 1997

The Institute of Irish Studies
The Queen's University of Belfast
and the Centre for Emigration Studies
at the Ulster-American Folk Park

© The Authors and editor

© Foreword, Sir Peter Froggatt

All rights reserved. No part of this publication may be reproduced, stored in a retrieval system, or transmitted in any form or by any means, electronic, photocopying, recording or otherwise, without the prior permission of the publishers.

British Library Cataloguing-in-Publication Data. A catalogue record for this book is available from the British Library.

ISBN 0 85389 677 1 hardback
ISBN 0 85389 674 7 paperback

Cover design by Dunbar Design
Printed by Nicholson & Bass Ltd, Belfast

THE
HUNGRY STREAM

ESSAYS ON EMIGRATION AND FAMINE

•

EDITED BY
E. MARGARET CRAWFORD

FOREWORD BY
SIR PETER FROGGATT

PROCEEDINGS OF THE CONFERENCE HELD AT THE
ULSTER-AMERICAN FOLK PARK 1995

THE CENTRE FOR EMIGRATION STUDIES
ULSTER-AMERICAN FOLK PARK
AND
THE INSTITUTE OF IRISH STUDIES
THE QUEEN'S UNIVERSITY OF BELFAST

Acknowledgements

The Ulster-American Folk Park gratefully acknowledges the sponsorship and assistance received from the following organizations: Allied Irish Banks, the American-Ireland Fund, the Australian-Ireland Fund, United States Information Service, Cultural Traditions Group, Northern Ireland Tourist Board, Omagh District Council, Department of Education Northern Ireland, Western Education and Library Board and Nicholson & Bass Ltd.

Contents

Notes on Contributors

Donald Harman Akenson, Professor of History at Queen's University, Kingston, Ontario, Canada.

Lawrence Bickford, Computer co-ordinator at the Hopkinton High School in Contoocook, New Hampshire, United States of America.

Evelyn Cardwell, Education Officer at the Ulster-American Folk Park, Mellon Road, Castletown, Omagh, County Tyrone, Northern Ireland.

Brenda Collins, Research and Publications Officer at the Linen Centre and Lisburn Museum, Lisburn, County Antrim, Northern Ireland.

E. Margaret Crawford, Senior Research Fellow at The Queen's University of Belfast, Northern Ireland.

Patrick J. Duffy, Associate Professor of Geography at St Patrick's College, Maynooth, County Kildare, Ireland.

Patrick Fitzgerald, Assistant Curator at Ulster-American Folk Park. Mellon Road, Castletown, Omagh, County Tyrone, Northern Ireland.

David Fitzpatrick, Professor of Modern History at Trinity College, Dublin, Ireland.

Peter Froggatt, Vice-Chancellor of The Queen's University of Belfast, Northern Ireland 1976–1986. Chairman of Scotch-Irish Trust of Ulster and of the Ulster-American Folk Park Management Committee.

Jim Grant, formerly lecturer at St Mary's College, Belfast, Northern Ireland.

Sophia Hillan King, Assistant Director, Institute of Irish Studies, at The Queen's University of Belfast, Northern Ireland.

Donal P. McCracken, Dean of Arts and Professor of History at the University of Durban-Westville, Durban, South Africa.

Frank Neal, Professor of Economic and Social History at the University of Salford, European Studies Research Institute, England.

Janet Nolan, Associate Professor at Loyola University of Chicago, United States of America.

Edward O'Donnell, Assistant Professor at Hunter College, City University of New York, United States of America.

Trevor Parkhill, Keeper of History at the Ulster Museum. Formerly archivist with the Irish Manuscripts Commission, Dublin and the Public Records Office of Northern Ireland.

Michael Quigley, founding member and Historian/Publicist on the Executive of the Toronto-based Action Grosse Île, Canada.

Robert J. Scally, Professor of History at New York University and Director of the Glucksman Ireland House, New York, United States of America.

Foreword

'We stop the Press with very great regret to
announce that the potato Murrain has unequivocally
declared itself in Ireland . . . where will Ireland be in
the event of a universal potato rot?'

Editorial by Dr John Lindley,
Gardeners' Chronicle and Horticultural Gazette,
13 September 1845

JOHN LINDLEY'S ANNOUNCEMENT heralded the Great Irish Famine, and his rhetorical question was soon to be brutally answered by the horrific events of the 'universal potato rot' whose effects on all aspects of Irish life and attitudes to the present day have been the subject of extensive dissection and debate. The bare statistics are mind-numbing. In the years 1846–51 some one million people died and at least an equal number emigrated *over and above* the 'normal' pre-Famine experience, and all from a population in 1846 of some 8.5 million. Small wonder that the Great Famine is seared into the national conscience as deeply as into individual ones at home and among the extensive Irish diaspora and has had such enduring consequences.

The Ulster-American Folk Park decided to mark the sesquicentenary in 1995 of the Great Famine by holding an international conference close to the 13 September – the date in 1845 of Lindley's editorial – and focused on the Famine emigration: the publication in 1997 of the Proceedings of this conference fittingly marks the sesquicentenary of the Famine's darkest days. The Park was an ideal venue. It is extensive (66 acres or 27 hectares) and is developed around its original exhibit – the Mellon homestead from where in 1818 the five-year-old Thomas Mellon started his journey of emigration ultimately to found the great Pittsburgh banking dynasty. It is thematically dedicated to emigration from Ireland (mainly Ulster) to North America. It boasts appropriate exhibitions, vernacular buildings, structures and artifacts. Its proprietary Trust, the Scotch-Irish Trust of Ulster, was founded in 1967 on the initiative of the late Dr Matthew Mellon, great-grandson of Thomas, to foster a deeper understanding of such emigration and its consequences. Above all, it houses the Centre for Emigration Studies, the largest and best-resourced of its type in Ireland, and recognised by The Queen's University of Belfast as a teaching and research institution for its degrees.

The conference, aptly entitled 'The Hungry Stream', was held on 7th-9th September 1995. On behalf of the Trustees and of the Management Committee of the Park I am pleased to express their indebtedness to all those whether or not on the staff of the Park who made the conference a success not least Mr John Gilmour (Director) and Mr John Walsh (Head of Museum Services) who so ably shouldered the major burden of the conference organisation and administration and Mr Eric Montgomery (Executive Secretary, Scotch-Irish Trust) who ensured the energetic involvement of so many. Generous sponsorship and assistance from a number of organisations ensured the viability of the conference and underwrote the *Proceedings*: AIB Group; the American-Ireland Fund; the Australian-Ireland Fund; the United States Information Service; the Cultural Traditions Group (of the Community Relations Council); the Northern Ireland Tourist Board; the Omagh District Council; the Department of Education (Northern Ireland); the Western Education and Library Board and the Trust itself.

We were fortunate to have the support of the Institute of Irish Studies of The Queen's University of Belfast and of its Director, Dr Brian Walker, in the publication of the conference *Proceedings*: while no amount of thanks and praise would be adequate for the skilful and dedicated editing by the Irish famine historian, Dr Margaret Crawford, who also contributes a chapter and the Introduction. The process of editing a collection of papers takes time and patience, and our thanks also go to Mrs Anne Rodgers for assisting the Editor in this task.

Ultimately, however, the enduring value of the conference depends on the quality and impact of the contributions, and we thank all the contributors whether from the podium or the floor, who did so much to ensure it.

Sir Peter Froggatt
(Chairman, Scotch-Irish Trust of Ulster and of the
Ulster-American Folk Park Management Committee)

Introduction: Ireland's Haemorrhage

E. Margaret Crawford

THE ESSAYS THAT FOLLOW deal with a major theme in the history of modern Ireland: emigration. They range widely but can be grouped, loosely, into four sub-themes: the vocabulary of Irish emigration history; the mechanisms of migration; destinations; and its legacies, at home in Ireland, abroad and in the collective memory.

The words we choose to discuss emigration are crucial, for language does more than describe merely events; it also conveys meaning and is loaded with value judgements. The very title of this volume, 'Hungry Stream' carries its own interpretative baggage. 'Hungry' may be thought obvious, although not every emigrant was hungry; the really starving scarcely progressed beyond their townlands. But what of 'stream'? The image here is of an outpouring, not merely of people but of a nation's life blood, a process that I have hinted at by the choice of 'haemorrhage' in the title of this introduction.

The great starvation is what persuaded hundreds of thousands to abandon Ireland and seek pastures new. Several authors – David Fitzpatrick, Patrick Fitzgerald, Janet Nolan, Edward O'Donnell and Robert Scally – allude to the Famine exodus in such terms although the image is less doleful than the language Akenson discusses. His contribution emphasises the power of vocabulary. Selecting 'galut', 'exile' and 'diaspora', as key words in the lexicon of emigration studies, he examines their origins and appropriateness in the context of the Irish exodus during the Famine years, and in a cautionary tone urges sensitivity in our choice of language. Throughout this collection we find authors striving to find the language appropriate to express the horrors of the Great Famine and its sequel.

The mechanisms that were employed to move the Irish population to new countries are the concerns of Patrick Fitzgerald, Trevor Parkhill, Patrick Duffy and Robert Scally. Fitzgerald delves back several centuries, identifying the migration responses to earlier subsistence crises when, as during the Great Famine, Irish men and women wandered within the country, travelled across the Irish Sea and, from the early eighteenth century, made the hazardous journey to North America in search of a better life. Departure from the country of their birth was not a new phenomenon in the nineteenth century. Countless numbers had migrated across the Irish Sea to Britain as permanent or seasonal migrants for at least two centuries.

Prior to the Great Famine, a significant number of emigrants financed their own passages. When blight ruined the subsistence crop in three seasons out of four after 1845, many people lacked the resources to pay their own way out of the country. Emigration, therefore, was assisted by a number of organizations.

Parkhill examines the poor law scheme by which unions could siphon off some of their increasing numbers of 'deadweight' paupers – single mothers, deserted wives and orphan children – to Australia and Canada.

Duffy reveals in his study of the Shirley estate in County Monaghan, a well-oiled and efficient organization for aiding passages to North America and Australia. The financial outlay was considerable, and although the estate emigration scheme was based on economic considerations, nevertheless, the approach was also benevolent in character. The benevolence did not however, survive into the folk memory; on the contrary the landlord and his agent, William Steuart Trench, have been remembered as oppressive and unjust. Both poor law and estate-assisted emigration served only a tiny fraction of those who left Ireland. We know that estimates of landlord and poor law-assisted migration accounted for under 10 per cent of total emigration. James Grant's essay touches on a further institutional response to the Famine, the work of local relief committees, in alleviating distress. They were not, however, offering emigration as a solution, rather attempting to relieve the starving at home.

Scally illustrates migration links by the example of Liverpool, which was the main conduit through which a mass of Irish migrants flowed. The well-established trade routes from Irish ports to Liverpool, and from Liverpool to America provided the infrastructure in which people moving westwards replaced goods – cotton and grain – moving in the opposite direction. As quickly as the cotton cargoes for Manchester's mills were unloaded in Liverpool the self-same boats were refitted to accommodate a human cargo of Irish migrants.

While some migrants had the practicalities of travelling organized for them others had to make their own arrangements. Their experiences were harrowing and their reception at their destinations uninviting, and indeed at some locations hostile. Many got no further than Britain, disembarking at Glasgow, Liverpool, Cardiff, Swansea and Newport. Liverpool bore the brunt of the mass famine migration from Ireland. It is upon this group, the poorest of the emigrants, that Frank Neal and Margaret Crawford concentrate. Neal examines the strain on public resources which the influx of thousands of hungry, impoverished Irish imposed, and describes the means by which the authorities used their legislative powers, small though they were to cope. While it was the wealthier ratepayers who bore the cost of the hungry stream from Ireland, the social price affected all levels of society. This is demonstrated in Crawford's piece on the 'unseen baggage' of the Irish – typhus, relapsing fever and dysentery. Rich and poor, old and young, English and Irish all fell prey to 'fever'.

Far-off fields may have looked green, but many emigrants exchanged poverty in one country for poverty in another, at least in the short term. In Britain Irish families crowded into dirty, disease-ridden tenements, and worked in the poorest paid jobs. They clustered in the towns and cities of Lancashire, in Glasgow, Edinburgh, Dundee, London and South Wales. Brenda Collins' essay discusses the 'push' and 'pull' forces that regulated the movement of Irish linen workers to Dundee. Emigrants crossing the Atlantic rarely found the streets paved with gold. Some died on the journey, others at point of entry. The appalling mortality at the quarantine station of Grosse Île in Canada is the subject of Michael Quigley's essay. The number who died on Grosse Île will never be known precisely though the figure reached many thousands. Neither did survivors of the journey and of quarantine find a welcoming hand when they reached dry land. Irish arrivals at New York were met with hostility both from the Irish community and Americans. Emigrants presented an ever increasing burden on an already hard-pressed community and were seen as a dangerous, unassimilable, seditious, and utterly undesirable group. Their lack of occupational skills and capital was a disadvantage.

America, Canada, Australia and South Africa, nevertheless, offered a new start and a new opportunity. The reception the migrants received at the different destinations was conditioned by their skills and education. Edward O'Donnell traces the assimilation of the Irish into New York society, Janet Nolan examines the experience of women emigrants in America, while Donal McCracken focuses on 'the land the Famine Irish forgot', South Africa. Only a small fraction of Ireland's exiles arrived in South Africa. They were different from their American-bound counterparts. Male migrants exceeded females, whereas family groups were common among those migrating to America. The religion of the Irish-American travellers in the 1840s was primarily Roman Catholic; in South Africa there were as many Protestant as Catholic Irish. Occupational skills were greater and educational ability higher among those who tried South Africa. The selectiveness of the white community in South Africa and the lack of established Irish networks made South Africa a difficult destination for all but the determined.

The majority of emigrants found low-paid menial jobs; their sweated labour made a major contribution to America's industrial and commercial wealth. As in Britain the Irish in New York lived in ghettos of poor housing and suffered great deprivation and discrimination. O'Donnell outlines the strategies used by the Irish to strengthen their position within their adopted city, and emphasises that with luck and hard work some migrants were able to prosper. Women were primarily employed in domestic service in the homes of middle and upper classes. Nolan explains how the skills they acquired in their American jobs and the refined environment in which they worked, provided a model to aspire to. In the countries of destination women became wage-earners, wives and mothers. Second generation Irish women were better educated, more assured and enjoyed an urban prosperity far distanced from the rural poverty of their mothers.

What have been the legacies of this mass Famine migration? Several authors explicitly or implicitly refer to the short and long-term consequences. The social world that the migrants left behind was the setting for the works of William Carleton – the subject of Sophia Hillan King's essay. The women who stayed behind were left in a changing post-Famine Irish society. Janet Nolan points out that their opportunities for early marriage and their previously well-defined functions within the household economy were diminished. Surplus single females, therefore, sailed away to grasp both jobs and husbands in a new country. Their remittances were used to aid yet other members of the family to travel abroad, or to supplement the household income at home. The broader economic and social conditions in Ireland are highlighted by Fitzpatrick's analysis of letters sent from Ireland to Australia. To the writers of these letters emigration appeared more as an escape from difficulties than an infliction imposed on a suffering society.

The legacies of migration have not faded with the passing of the generations. On the contrary, they have endured and grown to the present day. The Great Famine is part of the education of children. As examples, we have included two contributions which deal with programmes offered to pupils on both sides of the Atlantic. Both projects attempt to reconstruct the experiences and thereby provide students with opportunities of sampling the flavour of nineteenth-century migration. At higher educational levels, Irish emigration studies are strong and vibrant courses in universities and colleges. But the most poignant legacy, is the memory of Grosse Île.

We have come full circle. The legacies of the Great Famine and the emigration flows that it accelerated, are preserved in how our schools and colleges teach history, how we commemorate the Famine, and the language we use. 'Stream', 'haemorrhage', 'diaspora', 'exile', are all metaphors striving to give meaning to the spread of Ireland's population over half the world.

A Midrash on 'Galut', 'Exile' and 'Diaspora' Rhetoric

Donald Harman Akenson

ONE OF IRELAND'S FEW truly original social critics has described faminism as the belief that a catastrophe has occurred and that the causes thereof are: public indifference, especially among the official class; English greed; and the *Sunday Independent*. Of course Eamon Dunphy is here referring to the Great Famine in Irish international football fortunes, but there is more than a little resonance in what he says.

Today, indeed, we have faminists – people who make their professional careers (or at least major portions of those careers) – by studying and curating and writing about the Great Famine. One of the most surprising developments in Irish historiography in the last fifteen years is the way in which a virtual scholarly vacuum on the Famine has been filled (previously we had only *The Great Hunger* by Cecil Woodham-Smith (1962), and *The Great Famine: Studies in Irish History, 1845–52*, edited by R.D. Edwards and T.D. Williams (1956), as attempts at full, or fullish, scholarly histories) and now we have literally scores of studies, some local, some regional, others national or international in scope. Mostly that is to the good.

There is, however, a less attractive, slightly rancid side to the business, and this is that a lot of people have relearned the truth of the proverb, 'It's easy to travel on another man's wound.' A species of what can only be called famine-pornography has emerged, in which the standards of historical scholarship are replaced by those of the illicit *frisson*. Skilful practitioners of this new form have immediately recognized a basic law of Newtonian economics: the more lurid the depiction of the victims, the simpler the picture, the greater their own fees. Sometimes this is called popular history.

Because one of our collective duties as responsible scholars is to protect the graves of the dead from their looting by the living, I believe that one of the most important tasks that must be accomplished in the next fifteen years is to assay the products of this present era – this era of ambiguous 'celebration' of the Famine – and, first, to help the meritorious drive out the meretritious and, second, to try to come to terms with the literature as a very special, very confusing entity in itself, as a form of thinking.

I

Many of us know to some degree what we think about the Great Famine. However, I hope we can reflect on *how* we think. In the long run, this is more important. In particular, I hope that we can reflect upon the unspoken attitudes and beliefs that are part of the presumptive software of our modes of thought: for the unspoken grammar of how we think often determines what we think.[1]

I should like to approach this matter in a very gentle fashion, through the time-honoured employment of midrash. This is quite different in style and, especially, in tone, from traditional academic argument. Usually, a midrash is a meditation upon the Tanakh – the Hebrew scriptures – and most commonly upon an item in the Torah. It involves both exegesis – a punctilious analysis of text – and eisegesis: it is homiletical in purpose, but not stridently so. The biblical message is adapted to suit contemporary needs. The key, though, is tone: it often is tinged with bemused observation and the application of these observations is through implied or direct analogy.[2]

The texts that I wish to consider all relate to three concepts, namely 'galut', 'exile' and 'diaspora', matters that lie at the heart of mid-nineteenth-century Irish emigration. In being concerned with these matters, nineteenth-century Irish historians are not being parochial. 'Diaspora' has become one of the most fashionable of terms in the present decade. Recently, the International Committee of Historical Sciences was held in Montreal. There, the world's leading historians were asked to focus their attention upon three major topics, determined to be the most important for the present decade and the start of the next century: one of these was 'peoples in diaspora.' Thus, although some of us may have reservations about the use of the term 'diaspora' quite as widely as it is employed, that concept and the related ones I am touching on will be part of the standard international vocabulary of historical discourse for at least the next generation.

At a conference in Montreal, Mark Cohen defined the concept of 'galut' efficiently:

> In biblical Hebrew *galut* means 'exile,' that is, forced removal from the homeland to a foreign place. It also denotes the place to which the Israelites had been exiled, hence, for example, *galut bavel*, 'the Babylonian Exile' . . . From the time of the Babylonian Exile on, Jews maintained that God had cast them out of their land, dispersing them among the gentile nations because of their sins. Thus is galut a weighty negative term, denoting a state of degradation and punishment, to be ended at the time of the messianic redemption. It connotes a structural state of alienation, of the Jew from his surroundings, of the host society from the Jew.[3]

The three overlapping concepts – and they are not identical – with which we are dealing are very old. 'Diaspora' stems from the third century before the Common Era and was popularized by the Septuagint. 'Galut', much older, comes from the deportations of the leaders of Judah to Babylon in the early sixth century BCE. 'Exile' is sometimes used in English for each, although it has modern connotations of its own.[4]

Essentially, therefore, the historical profession will be dealing in the twenty-first century with certain very complex social phenomena, employing concepts determined roughly two and a half millennia earlier. In Irish history, I suspect, we will continue to view the Famine of the nineteenth century through the lens of the sixth century before the Common Era. Now, that is not bad, but we should be aware of the reality. Granted, it is possible to argue that we are not using ancient constructs, since we are using them now, and therefore, are investing them with our own agreed meanings. That has a certain theoretical fashionability but, as historians, we should at least meditate on two points. One of these is that if words are continually reinvented (and thus forever new and never old) it is very striking that one could substitute the term 'galut' for 'exile' in much of the writing at present being done concerning diasporas and not have much change of meaning. Certainly, one could write a book called, imaginatively, *Emigrants and Galut* concerning the nineteenth-century Irish diaspora and many scholars would accept it as gospel. Thus, one begins to suspect that the ancient concept of exile has as much power over our thinking as we do over it.

To consider this possibility may require more humility than we normally muster in our trade, but there are two face-saving reasons we can accept this possibility. The first of these is that the concept of exile is enhulled in the single greatest, most powerful, and most extensive metaphor the human mind has yet constructed, the ancient Hebrew covenant with Yahweh. And, second, it comes to us – 'galut', 'exile' and 'diaspora', considered as a whole – from inside the cultural primer of the English-speaking world. Specifically, one refers to the miraculous sequence begun by William Tyndale. Before his martyrdom by strangulation and burning in 1537, he had managed not only to translate the Christian scriptures from Greek, but while still on the run, taught himself Hebrew and translated the Torah. He kept translating from the Hebrew until his unfortunate end. Tyndale's translation of the 'Books of Moses' was largely assimilated into the Geneva Bible of 1560, and expanded. This was the first English-language Bible to be widely available in England. It was from this version that John Bunyan and William Shakespeare learned the Bible stories and acquired a sense of the English language. Even more important, from the 'King James Bible' (also called the 'Authorized Version') of 1611 (90 per cent of whose New Testament portions are from Tyndale, and its Old Testament, from Tyndale and the Geneva Bible, for the most part), the English-speaking world learned to read and, perforce, to think about certain major social issues. As the novelist and critic Robert Stone has noted, 'the greatest vehicle of mass literacy in the English-speaking world has been the King James Bible. It has been the great primer.'[5] So, if the concepts of 'galut', 'exile' and 'diaspora' have great power over us, there is a very good reason for it: they are part of the cultural bedrock upon which our own recent bits of intellectual architecture rest.

II

Now, let us take a look at some texts so that, quite literally, we can know where we are coming from. If it is possible that the concept of exile, as used in the historiography of nineteenth-century Ireland actually stems from the Babylonian Exile of the Nation of Judah, then a modest glance at that exile might be in order. I am viewing this with you in the same spirit that some of us viewed those first satellite photographs of earth: with the thought that we can see ourselves accurately only by sometimes getting very far away from the mirror we so often hold close to our face.

This possibility is particularly interesting because the matter of the Babylonian Exile is one of the few issues on which one catches the scriptures lying. I do not mean contradicting themselves, because that happens hundreds of times and, far from being an indication of mendacity or bad faith, these contradictions are an indication of the faithfulness of the Tanakh's compilers. When they encountered variant versions of traditions, the redactors acted like the good historians they were: when they could not make up their minds about two alternate sources, they presented both of them. For this sound historical practice, they took a good deal of criticism from nineteenth-century sceptics. Such intentionally-preserved contradictions are not what we are here talking about. But, every once in a while, the record is intentionally falsified, and one of these instances involved the central matter of exile.

Here, a bit of background is in order. We find the relevant information that established the concept of 'galut' or 'exile' in two separate bodies of text, and it is the dissonance between these two textual entities that is of probative value. The Tanakh, we must realize, is not structured in the same way as is the Christian Bible. Christian scholars made a bit of a mess of things in their arrangement of the Hebrew scriptures. The foundation of the Tanakh is a set of nine sequential books: the Pentateuch and Joshua, Judges, Samuel and Kings. (If you are familiar with the Christian Bible, you will note certain divergencies. Ruth, a much later work, was wrongly inserted in this sequence and, in both the Jewish and Christian canons, Samuel and Kings, each of which was originally a single book, were divided in the middle ages.) The primary narrative of the Tanakh – the books of Genesis through Kings – is both the oldest and the most important part of the Hebrew scriptures. It provides a coherent, compelling history of the Chosen People, from creation to the Babylonian Exile of 587 BCE. This primary unit contains a story of exile that contrasts considerably with a set of texts produced much later. A second tale of exile is found in the Book of Ezra-Nehemiah (a single book until the early middle ages) and Chronicles (again, a single book). Some scholars think these are by the same author, but that matter is not important here, for they come from the same era and the same mindset. Their impetus comes from a period roughly 140 years after the Babylonian Exile and they almost certainly were written before the Hellenic conquest of Palestine. (Again, the Tanakh has, for quite specific reasons, a different order of presentation of these texts than does the Christian Bible. In the Tanakh they are found at the very end. This is done for ideological advantage, for there they assume a privileged position, rivalling, but not quite equal to, that assumed by the Genesis-Kings unity which opens the scriptures.)

The report of the Babylonian Exile – the beginning of 'galut' and of diaspora – that one finds in the book of Kings, near the conclusion of the fundamental building block of the Hebrew (and Christian) scriptures, is either by an eye-witness or by one of the second-generation – that is, one of the children of the exile. It is based on good solid historical information. The salient point is how undramatic, how factual, the report of these events was – given, of course, that they were perceived as tragedy.

Although later chroniclers were to dramatize the physical and social dimensions of the 'Babylonian captivity', it was not, by the standards of the Ancient Near East (or even by the standards of the twentieth century) a particularly nasty conquest and the editor-writer of Kings knew this. Only a minority, at most 10 to 20 per cent, of the population was actually sent into exile. The 'poorest sort of the people of the land' were left behind (II Kings 24:14) to be farmers and to tend the vineyards. Their life in a war-levelled land must have been bleak, the more so because the skilled artisans such as carpenters and blacksmiths, who could have rebuilt the city, were taken away. But even this was moderated by the Babylonian official who was in charge of Judah: he gave land and vineyards to the poor – probably an indication that some of the lands of the exiled elite were redistributed to the poor (Jeremiah 39:10). No new national or ethnic group was introduced into Judah. It was not colonized in any formal sense, but rather was a tiny, poor satrapy. The key to understanding the Babylonian captivity is to see it from the vantage point of Babylonian *realpolitik*. The standard Babylonian practice was to strip conquered territories of their political and religious elites. This removed most of the potential trouble makers, the local leaders, but there was more: the very top men in the conquered societies were brought to the capital, and were treated well, while they were indoctrinated in Babylonian learning which, in some areas, such as astronomy, was prodigious.[6]

Thus, King Jehoiachin, who had been on the throne of Judah in 597, was taken to Babylon with his family and treated well. He was still alive in 562 when Nebuchadnezzar died, and members of his family took a leading role not only in the exiled community of Babylon, but also in Judah after the exile ended. Admittedly, King Jehoiachin's successor, and the last of King David's line, the puppet King Zedekiah (597–586/7) was treated horribly. His sons were killed before his eyes and then he was blinded and incarcerated until he died (Jeremiah 52:10–11). This, however, was not routine policy. Zedekiah was punished because he had taken an oath of loyalty to the Babylonian king and had broken it by treating with the Egyptians. That was unusual: for the most part, the Babylonians treated the departed elites well, and probably used many of them, those who were not artisans, as what would today be called middle-level civil servants.

The displaced Judaeans were given considerable religious toleration and were not dispersed. In addition to those who lived in Babylon proper (located in what is today the suburbs of Baghdad), another concentration of diaspora Judaeans lived in 'Tel Aviv', an ancient Babylonian location of some debate, and not to be confused with the modern city of that name.[7] There they may have been engaged in reclaiming land, a form of manual labour which must have been anathema to a soft-handed elite. The key, however, is that even there the Babylonians permitted sufficient concentrations of Judaeans to coalesce, to preserve their language and their literary and religious traditions. Eventually, in 538, Cyrus of Persia allowed the Judaean religious elite to return to Jerusalem. The Babylonian Exile was over.

Why, then, is the exile imprint so strong in the Judaeo-Christian tradition? Why does the image in Psalm 137 of a people weeping by the waters of Babylon have such resonance?

Because that earlier, realistic bit of reporting in Kings was erased, or as close as one was permitted to do so with ancient Judaean religious writing. Here, some simple arithmetic illuminates the process. In the Book of Kings, written within easy living memory of the Babylonian captivity, the editor-writer gives some very realistic estimates of how many persons were taken prisoner. Almost all were males, except in the case of princely families. A total of 10,000 persons were taken to Babylon, the editor-writer estimates. Of these, 7,000 were soldiers and 1,000 were craftsmen and blacksmiths. Those numbers are schematized – 'rounded off', as it were – but they are not unrealistic or exaggerated. There is no wailing in this report, just a straight-faced historical tone. Using those estimates, one infers that the total of princely families and retainers and of scribes (both civil and religious) and priests was only 2,000 persons. Assuming even a moderate number of princely exiles, the number of scribes and priests taken away can have been no more than 1,750 persons (II Kings 24:14-16).

Consider what this must have meant fifty years later when the religious elite was permitted by Cyrus to return to Jerusalem: they must have been woefully short of manpower. Given that only men were deported (except for female members of the royal family), there had been no women of the proper religious background for the Judahite elite to marry. Either they had to intermarry with Babylonians – and thus effectively drop out of the Judahite cause – or import women from the old homeland or from Egypt (or remain without issue). Whatever the prevailing choice, the number of trained and enthusiastic and physically resilient Judahite religious leaders had to be greatly reduced between 587 and 538. If there were 1,000 exiles and their sons and grandsons to straggle back to Jerusalem, it would have been surprising. And, further, we know that not all the exiled Judahites returned. So few and so weak were those who did that it was almost twenty years before they began to rebuild the Temple, the centre-piece of their religion. Even then, it took a major external intervention in the 450s before the religion of Yahwah triumphed in Jerusalem. In other words (1) the exile was not particularly brutal and (2) the return was inglorious.

That brings us to a second set of numbers. These are found in the books of Chronicles and in Ezra-Nehemiah. Both the book of Ezra and of Second Chronicles rewrite the estimate of the editor-writer of Kings, a man who, at minimum, was in contact with many eye-witnesses to the Babylonian deportation, and replace the earlier estimates with ones that are less realistic historically and make a different story. According to Ezra (2:1-65), some 4,363 priests and levites, accompanied by 128 religious singers and 139 temple porters led the return to Babylon after Cyrus' decree – in total, 42,360 persons, plus 7,337 servants (presumably of foreign origin). This was a great band of the previously-exiled Chosen People. Crucially, in Chronicles (the companion volume to Ezra-Nehemiah), the eye-witness based reports of the Book of Kings are rubbed off the page. Whereas the editor-writer of Kings made it clear that the lower-caste majority of the population of the former Kingdom of Judah remained in the homeland and was not exiled (see also Jeremiah 39:10), the author of Chronicles introduces the new – and certainly historically inaccurate – myth that everyone in Jerusalem was either killed or carried away to Babylon and that the land experienced a 'sabbath of desolation' for seventy years, that is, from 587 to the rebuilding period, 520-515 (II Chronicles 36:20-21).

Where the material in the Book of Kings, balefully accurate though it may have been, was faulty from an ideological point of view, was that it explained all too well the failure, for a period of nearly three generations, of the Judahite religion to win over the people of Jerusalem and of the surrounding countryside: the number of returnees was too small, their character was insufficiently authoritative and the local majority, which had been left behind, had developed religious institutions which resisted successfully the No-Way-But-Yahwah sloganeering of the Judahite returnees. In other words, the numbers provided in the Book of Kings concerning the deportees to Babylon and the majority that had been left behind had to be erased because they provided all too accurately an historical explanation of why the Judahite re-taking of Jerusalem for the religion of Yahwah had failed for so long. Thus was the concept of 'galut', 'exile', 'diaspora' formed as a result of an ideologically-dictated judgement that the real story was not sufficiently lurid and was insufficiently simple. In other words, for the purposes of propaganda. That origin might bear reflection.

III

If 'exile' has come to incorporate the concept of degradation and alienation inherent in 'galut', the term 'diaspora' in our own time has had its own path. Briefly, I wish to trace for you the concept's evolution in the twentieth century, for that evolution is a text in itself.

The effective motive force for the modern use of 'diaspora' came from the field of Black Studies. The first book to use the term 'African diaspora' in its title was published in 1976. The editors of that volume, Martin Kilson and Robert Rotberg, noted:

> The application of the Greek word for dispersion, *diaspora*, to this process of Jewish migration from their homeland into all parts of the world not only created a term which could be applied to any other substantial and significant groups of migrants, but also provided a concept which could be used to interpret the experiences (often very bitter experiences) of other peoples who had been driven out of their native countries by forces similar to those which had dispersed the Jews: in particular, slavery and imperialism.[8]

This idea, that there were parallels between the Jews and Black Africans had been suggested, Kilson and Rotberg noted, as early as 1802 by the English author William Movor in a volume entitled *The History of the Dispersion of the Jews, of Modern Egypt, and of the other African Nations* and had been taken up several times during the nineteenth century by writers on Africa.[9] It was only during the 1960s, however, that the word 'diaspora' began to enter the working vocabulary of Africanists and of historians of Black history world-wide. At the International Congress of African Historians held at University College, Dar-es-Salaam, in 1965, Joseph E. Harris and George Shepperson each gave papers in various aspects of the African diaspora. Shepperson's 'The African Abroad, or the African Diaspora' was especially important, for it attempted simultaneously to indicate the breadth of the topic and to impose a significant limitation. The breadth came from an estimate Shepperson cited for the year 1946, that in the western hemisphere alone there were 41 million people of African descent. The limitation was this: 'it must be emphasized that not all migration from Africa comes within the bounds of the concept of the African diaspora which is the study of a series of reactions to coercion, to the imposition of the economic and political rule of alien peoples in Africa, to slavery and imperialism.'[10] That limitation introduced a major problem into the study of the African diaspora: should it involve only the study of those persons, and their descendants, who were forcibly moved from their African homeland? Work done in the 1970s and early 1980s emphasized the futility of the concept of diaspora and, though it focused overwhelmingly on forced migration and its results, it left open the theoretical possibility of non-forced voluntary migration being of some consequence.[11]

Things changed sharply in the late 1980s, with the introduction of a strong feminist perspective[12] and with the increasing recognition of the magnitude of pre-slavery mobility of the African population and of the degree of voluntary migration since slave times. 'A balanced appreciation of the Diaspora must note that many Africans were dispersed globally by choice, through adventure, long before Columbus went to the New World and inaugurated the trade in human cargo.'[13] And an immense amount of voluntary migration by Africans and persons of African descent had occurred since the ending of most forms of slavery. As Roy Bryce-Laporte forcibly argued: 'With regard to Blacks, the term 'diaspora' too often operates against the background of a yet pervasive but incorrect present-day orientation which presents them as a dominated, confined and immobile people in closed, segregated conditions. But in fact, an important and understudied aspect of the Black Experience is the historical and ongoing geographical mobility of its people, which indeed carries us back to the very genesis.[14]

If the concept of diaspora could be applied to the dispersal, both voluntary and involuntary, of the African peoples, it could also be employed by white groups, at least those whose cultural history included an epochal tragedy comparable to slavery. Thus, the 'Armenian genocide' of 1915 becomes a fulcrum upon which the idea of an Armenian diaspora pivots. The exact extent of this displacement and slaughter of Armenians during the last days of the Ottoman empire is a matter of some controversy, but in the two decades before the First World War perhaps 200,000 Armenians were killed and, beginning in the spring of 1915, as many as a million were killed, deported, or simply scattered. The United States and Canada became their chief new homelands, but Armenians and their descendants are found all over the Middle East and Europe, as well as South Africa. The Armenians have maintained a strong cultural identity. As one generation has folded into another and yet another, the single motif that more than any other elicits loyalty is the genocide of 1915.[15]

Yet, must a group be as severely persecuted and oppressed as were the Jews, the Africans and the Armenians in order for 'diaspora' to be applicable? Apparently not. Take three examples. The first of these is the phenomenon known as the 'Sikh diaspora', a process that has been in train for at least a century. The heartland of this diaspora, the Punjab, today holds roughly one-third of the world's population of 13 to 16 million Sikhs. Although far from wealthy in their homeland, the Sikh diaspora has no mythic event equivalent to slavery or the holocaust in its story. The Sikhs migrated world-wide, by choice, and with considerable economic and social acumen. They have been particularly effective in filling middle-class roles in places where the pluralist societies that evolved under British hegemony occurred – ranging from the Malay Peninsula, to East Africa, to Canada.[16] A second diaspora, that of the Chinese, is of major proportions statistically and culturally, but it too arose not out of systemic oppression but from the prudent calculations of opportunity by several million individuals. The number of ethnic Chinese in south-east Asia alone is roughly 15 million and, when one adds the uncounted (and probably statistically uncountable) ethnic Chinese in the western Indian Ocean and in North America, one is probably dealing with a total ethnic diaspora that is larger than the entire population of Canada.[17] A third diaspora, that of the Koreans in the last half-century, is particularly notable in North America, especially the United States. This population movement occurred after, rather than during, the fearful oppression the Koreans experienced at the hands of the Japanese. It was the removal of the bonds of Japanese imperialism, rather than its experience, that permitted large-scale Korean migration. The Korean émigrés to the United States have been particularly successful entrepreneurs, first as small business persons and, increasingly, as large-scale venture capitalists.[18]

The point about the diasporas of the Sikhs, the Chinese, and the Koreans is that they force one either to say that, no, these are not true diasporas, since they did not occur as the direct result of extensive oppression, but were largely voluntary migrations; or that, yes, these are indeed instances of true diasporas. To choose the first alternative is to exclude from our purview some of the most important population movements of the past century, and to do so on the grounds of perceived pain – that is to say that unless some quantum level of social oppression was experienced, the phenomenon is not worth study as a diaspora. That, besides being operationally impracticable (who is to say how much 'oppression' is sufficient to qualify?), would lead to inane contests in relative victimhood ('My group suffered more than yours, so my group is a true diaspora, yours is not').

So one admits the Chinese, the Sikhs, the Koreans, and similar groups to the collective umbrella. But where does one stop? The term 'diaspora' threatens to become a massive linguistic weed. One can find, for example, serious studies on aspects of the Russian diaspora,[19] the Greek diaspora,[20] and even the Cornish diaspora.[21] What does the term diaspora exclude?

Here, again, the purpose of a midrash is to promote reflection. Is the concept one of any real fecundity, or is it a mere renaming of old ideas, such as 'emigration' and 'cultural transfer'? I have found the concept useful, but can easily see how competent scholars could, in good faith, reject its use entirely.

IV

'Galut', 'exile', and 'diaspora' are all terms we acquired from ancient Judah, and each can be used with some degree of value. Each helps to determine how we think, especially, in this case, about the Irish Famine and its subsequent human outflow. How each scholar will use these terms – or if he or she will use them – is a matter of personal judgement.

One word, however, is not open to our usage. This is a word that is not in the title of my talk, but which one sees with increasing and alarming frequency related to the Famine. This is the term 'holocaust'. When you see it, you know that you are encountering famine-porn. It is inevitably part of a presentation that is historically unbalanced and, like other kinds of pornography, is distinguished by a covert (and sometimes overt) appeal to misanthropy and almost always an incitement to hatred. In Ireland, such an incitement is perforce an invitation to violence. For those reasons alone, we should not use holocaust in relation to the Great Famine. However, equally important is the fact that our use of the term is deeply offensive to members of the Jewish community. And properly so. *Ha Shoah* is their tragedy, and theirs alone. It involved a degree of programmatic racism and planned genocide which have no counterpart in the Irish experience.

It is customary for a midrash to contain at least one direct halachak determination, and mine is this: let us not travel on other people's wounds – not on those of the dead of Ireland – and, emphatically, not on those of the people who have taught us how to think about exile, in all of its pain and ambiguity.

References

1   For a discussion of how unspoken hegemonic assumptions interact with the real world, see Ian S. Lustick, 'What Gives a People Rights to a Land?', *Queen's Quarterly*, 102 (Spring 1995), pp. 53–68.

2   For definitions of midrash, see Geza Vermes, *Scriptures and Tradition in Judaism* (Leiden, 1961) pp. 6–8, and Jacob Neusner, *A Midrash Reader* (Minneapolis, 1990), pp. 1–4.

3   Mark R. Cohen, 'Diaspora, Galut, Alienation: The Jews of the Islamic Middle Ages' (paper delivered at the Eighteenth Conference of the International Committee of Historical Sciences, Montreal, September 1995), p. 1.

4   A second diaspora occurred after the Romans razed the Second Temple and, indeed, most of Jerusalem, in 70 CE. The term 'diaspora' covers this phenomenon accurately.

5   Robert Stone, 'The Reason for Stories: Toward a Moral Fiction', *Harper's Magazine* (June 1988), p. 72.

6   Niels Peter Lemche, *Ancient Israel. A New History of Israelite Society* (Sheffield, 1988), p. 179. For general background, see D.J. Wiseman, *Nebuchadnezzar and Babylon* (Oxford, 1985).

7   Ezekiel 3:15 speaks of one group of captives 'at Tel-abib, that dwelt by the river of Chebar . . .' The juxtaposition of water – as in Waters of Babylon – and the place of exile are significant.

8   Martin L. Kilson and Robert I. Rotberg (eds), *The African Diaspora: Interpretative Essays* (Cambridge, Mass., 1976), p. 2.

9   Kilson and Rotberg, *The African Diaspora*, p. 2.

10 George Shepperson, 'The African Abroad, or the African Diaspora,' in T.O. Ranger (ed.), *Emerging Themes of African History: Proceedings of the International Congress of African Historians* (Nairobi, 1968), p. 153.

11 Graham W. Irwin (ed.), *Africans Abroad: A Documentary History of the Black Diaspora in Asia, Latin America, and the Caribbean during the Age of Slavery* (New York, 1977).

12 Rosalyn Terborg-Penn, Sharon Harley and Andrea Rushing (eds), *Women in Africa and the African Diaspora* (Washington, D.C., 1987).

13 Aubrey W. Bonnett and G. Llewellyn Watson, 'Introduction', in *Emerging Perspectives on the Black Diaspora* (Lanham, 1989), p. 3.

14 Roy S. Bryce-Laport, quoted ibid., p. xiii.

15 Lorne Shirinian, *The Republic of Armenia and the Rethinking of the North American Diaspora in Literature* (Lewiston, 1992).

16 N. Gerald Barrier and Verne A. Dusenberry (eds), *The Sikh Diaspora: Migration and the Experience beyond Punjab* (Delhi, 1989).

17 On the Chinese diaspora, see Huguette Ly-Tio-Fane Pineo, *Chinese Diaspora in the Western Indian Ocean* (Port Louis, 1985); Joseph Harry Haines, *Chinese of the Diaspora* (London, 1965). A model local study is Leonard Blussé, 'Batavia, 1619–1740: The Rise and Fall of a Chinese Colonial Town', *Journal of Southeast Asia Studies*, 12 (1981), pp. 159-78.

18 See Hyung-chan Kim (ed.), *The Korean Diaspora: Historical and Sociological Studies of Korean Immigration and Assimilation in North America* (Santa Barbara, 1977).

19 Aiden Nichols, *Theology in the Russian Diaspora: Church, Fathers, Eucharist in Nikolai Afanasev 1893-1966* (Cambridge, 1989).

20 George Kanarkis, *Hellenic Letters of the Greek Diaspora since the Mid-Nineteenth Century* (Sidney, 1985).

21 Gill Burke, 'The Cornish Diaspora of the Nineteenth Century', in Shula Marks and Peter Robinson (eds), *International Labour Migration: Historical Perspectives* (London, 1984), pp. 57-75.

External Forces in the Famine Emigration from Ireland

Robert Scally

IT IS NO SURPRISE THAT North Americans have been more interested in Irish migrations than in the *internal* history of Ireland itself. The United States and Canada are, one might say, a migration in progress, changing year after year as emigrants from all parts of the world continue to land on their shores. But they are especially the creation of the great European migrations of the nineteenth and early twentieth centuries, which account for a good part of both countries' folklore and founding mythologies.

At the heart of North American folklore is the image of free and independent individuals, choosing their own fate and making their own history. Nowhere is that myth more deeply embedded than in the image of the immigrant as a voluntary agent, making the free and rational choice of escaping from the oppression of the Old World for the personal freedom and opportunity of the new. Compared to the Old World, the American world view has given very little thought to the idea of submitting to history or to the limits on individual choice imposed by the past and the impersonal forces of history. That is probably one reason why we Americans, brought up with the conceit of unfettered control over our fates, sometimes get Irish history a little wrong. This is especially common when the issue is emigration from Ireland because the myth of the 'Golden Door' demands that the emigrant be portrayed as a voluntary traveller, notwithstanding the Irish-American counter-myth of exile so ably dissected by Kerby Miller and others.

I was reminded of this peculiarity of American thinking during the international conference on hunger held at New York University's Ireland House in May 1995, where a variety of distinguished scholars from Asia, Africa and Europe presented very different views about the history of hunger and migration in other parts of the world. One of the lessons they offered was that the American concept of the emigrant as a free agent is very much a minority view in the world.

Another tacit consensus became increasingly clear as the conference progressed: that in most instances large-scale migrations and food crises have been parts of a single historical phenomenon and cannot be understood separately. This is a truism in the case of nineteenth-century Ireland, at least to the degree that most studies include the migration of 1845 and after as an integral part of the Great Hunger, a result of the potato blight. But the most obvious connection between famine and migration, that populations suffering from hunger inherently tend to flee in search of relief, may also be the most misleading route to follow in studying migrations because it leads us to think that mass movements of people are merely spasmodic responses to sudden natural catastrophes, like fleeing from an avalanche or volcano.

There is general agreement among the Famine scholars that the rise in emigration from Ireland in the nineteenth century was certainly neither a sudden nor spasmodic phenomenon but one that originated in the previous century and had established a dramatically rising pattern in the 30 years before the Famine and, indeed, had become an intrinsic part of the dynamics of Irish history. Nevertheless, most famine studies still rely on the cause and effect axiom of hunger and flight and thereby reinforce the flawed theory of famine as a natural phenomenon and the flight from it merely the victims' reflex response to an empty stomach. This persistent view of the Famine migration trivializes the historical process that produced the victims' vulnerability in the first place and overlooks their efforts to resist it, often for generations before the calamity finally came upon them.

In his groundbreaking work of the past 20 years, Amartya Sen has demonstrated that *hunger*, rather than *famine* or migrations brought on by famine, remains the central mystery. Unlike relatively short-lived crises, like drought, floods or the potato blight, all of which have produced sudden flights of people, hunger can only be understood as part of a prolonged process of erosion of what he calls 'entitlements', established traditional methods of maintaining access to subsistence from year to year and of surviving exceptional crises in the supply of food. In this perspective, the nineteenth-century Atlantic migrations of Germans, Poles and southern Italians may be seen as part of a like process in which marginal agrarians were forced to the edge of subsistence and shaken from the land through commercialization and the intrusion of market forces into the countryside. In the case of India, this erosion begins with the expansion of colonial rule through the nineteenth century, especially in its encroachments on local food production and commercial development, separating marginal producers, small tenants and labourers from access to their accustomed local sources of food.

A political corollary of this thesis is that famines and the migrations which follow them are not to be found in democratic societies, in which the *alienation* of ruler and ruled has been bridged by democratic institutions and in which public entitlement to the basic necessities of life approaches a right of citizenship, a 'right to life' even if only on a precarious level. With all of its horrors and abuses, the English poor law recognized the entitlement of all parish residents to this protection at the expense of the community. But it is precisely this right, the right of the citizen, that is missing or curtailed in colonial and other undemocratic societies, so this argument goes, producing hunger amid plenty by denying the rights of the citizen and undermining the means of resistance by law and military force.

It is open to debate whether this perspective on famine migration applies well to Europe or other areas outside the colonial world, in particular to Ireland in the mid-nineteenth century, where Catholic Emancipation was quite recent and the popular franchise still severely limited. But at least one consensus that emerged from the Ireland House Conference does seem to encourage this approach universally: that there is a persuasive correlation between the incidence of famines (and famine migrations) and the presence of authoritarian or corrupt regimes. This was certainly the case, for example, in Russia in the 1930s, China in the late 1950s and in the Sudan in the mid-1980s. The research presented at the conference on France and England in the eighteenth century and Germany in the

1920s also agreed that the experience of hunger in western Europe cannot be understood without reference to some concept of progressive 'disentitlement', the intrusion of the marketplace and market forces into the countryside, distancing vulnerable sectors of the population from direct access to food. The rich scholarship on eighteenth-century food riots generally takes this approach, especially that of the 'moral economy' school created by E.P. Thompson in the 1960s. But what is instructive about these examples is that one finds chronic hunger throughout early modern Europe, *but not famine* in France or England at any time *after* the eighteenth century, that is, after the foundation of elementary democratic institutions in those societies.

Applying a similar approach to Britain and Ireland in the nineteenth century confronts a number of problems, however, some peculiar to the history of these islands and some of an ideological nature. The two come together in the question of whether Ireland was a 'colony' or a 'kingdom' at the time of the Famine and therefore whether its political status reduced the access of the Irish population, or large parts of it, to the food supply as compared to that of the English, the French, the Dutch and other peoples of the European democracies – or for that matter to the peoples of the post-colonial societies in the Americas who had acquired the rights of citizenship by that time. This issue revolves around the embattled history of the potato in Ireland and has been argued endlessly. But there are still no answers to the question of why the blight produced famine and death in Ireland and the Western Highlands of Scotland but not in the other provinces of western Europe where it had also become a staple of the diet. For most of the poor of Europe these were the 'hungry forties' but they were not the 'famine forties'.

Where a process of progressive disentitlement has been seen outside of Ireland, particularly in the former colonial world, it is accompanied by the erosion of some form of 'old regime' on the land – not necessarily a benevolent, prosperous, or even less a democratic regime as nationalist ideologies often portray the pre-colonial past, but one in which some degree of food entitlement existed or in which mere isolation from the international market tended to prevent local shortages from becoming general catastrophes. If this pattern applies to colonial societies, it does not seem to apply as well to most of western Europe in the colonial period. The generally accepted process there has the 'last subsistence crises' *ending* with the industrial and commercial revolutions with their networks of transport and cash economies reaching further and further into the countryside, speeding the flow of food through the marketplace from areas of plenty to areas of dearth. Of course, the premise for this solution to the age-old curse of famine is that its former victims were now *consumers* in the national and international market and part of the cash economy. It should be noted, too, that the bulk of the literature on this 'process of modernization' finds that it was achieved largely through coercion and against stubborn resistance from below.

I found plentiful evidence of this resistance in my own work on Irish townlands of the pre-Famine period. By the 1840s the commercialization of Irish agriculture and its integration in the international, largely English, market was also very much in progress. Yet, 'modernization' in Ireland did *not* protect the bulk of the people from famine. That at least suggests that the Irish case differs in some essential way from that of western Europe, that 'entitlements' had been stripped away but without having transformed the rural population into true consumers, since when the potato failed the majority were still unable to purchase their relief through the marketplace. In Amartya Sen's construction, this economic 'alienation' would seem to place Ireland squarely in the category of a colony within Europe. That status seems also to be confirmed by the complacency of the Peel and Russell governments towards the spectacle of starvation and death in the country and even on the streets of English cities, especially those of East Lancashire. Such spectacles brought down governments in France and would certainly have caused turmoil in Britain in the Chartist years had the starving been seen as 'true born Englishmen'.

Not all of the sources of the incomplete modernization of rural Ireland before the Famine were external. But because the British economy was without doubt the most international of any in the mid-nineteenth century, it is probably safe to say that the Irish peasantry was more decisively affected by external forces than any other in Europe at the time. And in no other respect more than in the pattern, the timing and the volume of emigration were these external forces more decisive. The main conduit through which these forces penetrated Ireland and the lives of the Irish peasantry was the great Atlantic port of Liverpool.

I have written a good deal, in a recent book, *The End of Hidden Ireland: Rebellion, Famine, and Emigration* (1995), and elsewhere, about what I call the 'Liverpool System' and its influence on Irish emigration. Liverpool offers the best focus to study the historical relationship between migration and hunger not only in Ireland but in nineteenth-century Europe generally. This is so because one of the greatest human migrations in history was a seaborne migration spanning more than a century in which some 40 million people crossed the Atlantic. It was certainly greater in numbers than the westward land migration which had created Europe from the ruins it had made of Rome a millennium before. The once great port of Liverpool, a drab, depressed and almost irrelevant place at the end of this century, had by far the most potent influence on this great trans-Atlantic movement of people. Its influence directed the flow of millions toward destinations of its own choosing, through a global maritime network of commercial ties and routes which it had been developing for more than a hundred years before the migration approached its peak in the 1840s and 1850s.

Slavery and cotton were two of the main reasons for Liverpool's rise to power in the Atlantic – it had cornered the slave trade before abolition and was the principal receiver in Europe of the cotton of the Old South, the endless flow of 500 lb. bales towed by slaves to the levees of New Orleans, Savannah and Charleston and there lugged aboard ship by immigrant labour, increasingly by the immigrant Irishmen of those towns. These ships, when they were not American, were most often Liverpool ships, owned and chartered by brokers and factors who had learned their accounting from their fathers in the slave and cotton trades. The cotton was bound via Liverpool for East Lancashire, especially Manchester, where the Liverpool merchants' ties were long-established and where an increasingly Irish population of immigrant 'operatives' were on hand to turn the bales into cotton cloth, a great deal of which was to be worked and then sold in populous, cotton-wearing India. There, as Gandhi knew well, it helped destroy the ancient native cotton industry and in doing so also helped to reduce access to food sources among the affected parts of the native population.

This world economic system has been well-known and studied for years, although Liverpool's key place in it has not always been recognized. Even more surprising is the mostly anecdotal place that Liverpool has been given in the various histories of the migration from Ireland. Even at their best, as in Herman Melville's *Redburn* (1924) or Terry Coleman's *Passage to America* (1972), these chronicles have dwelt on the horrors and criminality of the port city in the Famine years. There have been a number of detailed accounts of the emigrant trade of Liverpool, the ticket frauds, the crimps and runners, the overcrowded cellars and fever sheds and, especially, the infamous 'coffin ships', most of which sailed from Liverpool. Liverpool dominated the movement of emigrants from Ireland throughout the nineteenth century and shipped at least three out of four of all the Famine emigrants to all points out of Europe, in all more than a million before the Famine ended. Perhaps another quarter of a million passed into England through Liverpool in these years or went no further than the slums and alleys surrounding its great docks. Because of its dominant place in the emigration, Liverpool was to become the most Irish city outside of Ireland and the first great city in the experience of most Irish emigrants, whatever their ultimate destination.

For those who stayed or those who boarded the emigrant ships, there was a great deal of suffering in the 'Liverpool system' during the Famine years. The ordeals suffered in its docklands and in the steerages were as much a part of the Irish Famine experience as the stench of rotting fields or the sight of swollen bellies back in the townlands of Ireland. But Liverpool is not usually counted among the *causes* of the Famine in Ireland. The reason for this has been partly a matter of rival perspectives, the tendency on one hand to look for causes in rapacious landlordism and hostile policy emanating from London or, on the other, in the inherent flaws of Irish character and culture. From a more distant perspective encompassing the European peasantry in general in this era, the Irish experience appears less exceptional and less intentional than this while the impersonal force of political economy, through which the Liverpool world system exercised more control over the lives and options of the tenant farmers of Ireland than did Her Majesty's ministers, looms larger among the causes of the calamity. For it was Liverpool that controlled the lion's share of the Irish food trade, or more accurately, the system of food extraction that was at the heart of the colonial relationship between England and Ireland in the nineteenth century. To support this system, a network of middlemen, wholesalers, factors and shippers had grown throughout Ireland by 1845, and the trade in food followed routes bent toward the Merseyside and from there to all points outward. The great emigration of the next half century merely followed these pre-paved routes and could not have chosen the directions it did had the 'Liverpool system' not been ready to accommodate it.

It was into the maw of Liverpool and its massive warehouses that the cargoes of grain, meat and dairy goods denied to the starving Irish countryside flowed unceasingly from the Irish ports in the holds of a vast fleet of ferries, steamers and barges that made the Irish Sea one of the busiest waterways in the world – a fleet much larger in number than any that later sailed to Dunkirk or to the Normandy beaches and one sailing daily back and forth for decade after decade. Had this 'Liverpool system' not been in place by 1845, the exodus of two million people of the next eight years would have been impossible. Indeed, the exodus should be seen as the natural extension of the food trade, with Irish labour moving outward as supercargo along the same routes and in the same hulls as the exported food.

First slavery and cotton, then the Irish food trade had become the foundation of Liverpool's maritime empire by the time of the Famine, especially the foundation of its dominance over the movement of vessels and people around the Irish Sea. The network of power, commerce and internal influence in Ireland played a far more decisive and direct role in producing and exacerbating the food crisis of 1845 to 1853 than had any policy made in London, more than the Gregory Clause and perhaps even more than the Act of Union. By 1845, this 'Liverpool system' had a humming operational network of routes and middlemen in Ireland which formed the infrastructure of the food-export trade. When the Famine flight began, it was through this existing system that the bulk of the emigration had to pass, for all intents oblivious to the individual choices of most emigrants, since it dictated the available routes out of the countryside, the terms and times of departure, the costs and conditions of travel, as well as the principal destinations of the emigrants. As one Liverpool witness described this great migration,

> The Exodus still continues. With what eager rapidity one
> multitude follows another. They have no king, yet their muster
> is prompt and their march is regular. The great army moves on,
> its footsteps leading to the sea . . .

There is a striking similarity between this scene and others enacted on the docklands of North America, on the lower East Side of Manhattan Island or on New Orleans jetties. Indeed, they are two glimpses of the same migration, linked by the emigrant ships. The leaderless army moved on with great losses. Many moved randomly on landing, but most reached their appointed places. In a resourceful adaptation of mercantilism, Liverpool had cornered the business of exchanging labour for cotton, timber and tobacco in the Atlantic. In this context, the pull from the west was that of just one pole of a 'distant magnet' and Liverpool the other, pushing millions outward along well-worn routes toward established destinations. At eye level the movement seemed chaotic, filled with accident, random cruelty and bewilderment, the experience of individuals often seeming purposeless as in most other historic events that affected millions. But order and direction are unmistakable in the impersonal forces that drove the migration through time and space.

One of the great strokes of nineteenth-century America's luck, on top of its Eldorado of natural resources and providential isolation from European power, was that the small farmers and manual labourers of Europe were being forcibly 'loosened' from the land at precisely the time that the New World needed both habitual agrarians and migrant hand and back workers. More suddenly than anywhere else, this demand was met by the copious supply of refugees from the Famine in Ireland.

Old classic works on this migration of labour, like Brinley Thomas' *Migration and Economic Growth* (1954) and Arthur Redford's *Labour and Migration in England 1800-50* (1926) rely like Bentham and Smith on a thesis presupposing the ability of large populations of people to make 'independent' and informed decisions in response to the international market over the long term. Thomas' rational ebb and flow of voluntary labour across the Atlantic in synchronized tides of supply and demand seems to offer a more satisfying theory for Irish emigration than the idiosyncrasies of the Irish land system and the potato. But, while his view may fairly apply to those European emigrants already integrated into the market system and its informational network, it is fundamentally flawed when applied to peasant migrants like those of rural Ireland in the mid-nineteenth century. As I tried to show in *The End of Hidden Ireland*, the great majority of Irish cottiers and labourers of the 1840s, even those in close proximity to busy market towns, had neither the information, the cash nor the aspiration to make such calculated responses to market forces which very few of them understood or respected.

E.P. Thompson, a far more imposing figure and synthesizer of primal popular movements, stands as one of the most merciless critics and satirists of this 'invisible hand' historical view. Yet even he, perhaps the most eloquent mouthpiece in the English language of history's inarticulate majority, speaks of the Irish migrant labourer in a language reserved for colonials. The emigrant Irish labourer appeared as if on cue in industrial England and America, he thought, not only because he was cheap to hire but because he was temperamentally and even *physically* suited to the mindless back-breaking tasks that history had assigned him in the historical process.

It is probably inevitable that all such general theories distort the human realities of history to some degree. But history without theory runs the risk of becoming history without meaning. In the case of the Famine emigration, that would be a very sad result of an historians' work. Even without the disaster of the Famine, and all the rancour and dispute that subject still raises, there could hardly be any doubt that millions of Irish rural labourers would certainly have migrated to much the same places as they did in the 1840s and 50s, whether willingly or not. Therefore, I agree with the effort to put Irish emigration in a context that includes as broad a range of comparable human experiences in other parts of the world, that is, to move away from the conceit that Irish history, including the Famine and the Famine exodus, is somehow an exception to the human experience of the poor. As part of the history of mid-nineteenth-century Europe the terrible experience of Ireland in the 1840s *should* then be seen as an event propelled by historic transformations elsewhere, in Lancashire, India and the American South, in the West Midlands of England, in London, in the Hudson, Delaware and New England Valleys, and thereafter far beyond.

One might object that giving primacy to these distant and impersonal forces in the Irish emigration experience tends to erase most human agency from the picture along with the human tragedy and adventure that the Atlantic migration of 150 years ago also was. But it also helps to mute and refocus the question of *blame* in the debate over the Famine itself. At this late date, I regard this as a blessing to the historian and an opportunity to put some of the restless dogs of both nationalism and colonialism to sleep for good. It is certainly a more defensible way to review the tragedy than to pretend either that it never happened or to enlarge or diminish its horrors in the heat of a political debate.

In a recent issue of the *Irish Reporter* there appeared a short article entitled 'Towards The Concept of Famine Criminals'. In a reference to the export of food from Ireland during the Famine, the author claims that, 'At the very time when Bob Geldof and his other Band Aid associates were airlifting goods to the Sudan, Sudanese grain was being exported to feed the Saudi camel industry!' The writer aims his 'criminal' charges at a particular Sudanese bank manager, who presumably is still living and breathing and who may indeed bear some responsibility for the suffering of his countrymen.

Such profiteers undoubtedly exploited chances offered by the Famine in Ireland. But, however many individual villains may have been responsible for the human suffering, they are *all* now returned to the dust. So, perhaps it is time, after 150 years to invoke a statute of limitations on the bones of both the guilty and the blameless.

Grosse Île: 'The most important and evocative Great Famine site outside of Ireland'[1]

Michael Quigley

IN BLACK 47 the shipping season in the St Lawrence opened as usual with the thaw in mid-May. The first ship to arrive, the *Syria*, left Liverpool on March 24 carrying 241 passengers. She anchored at Grosse Île on 15 May. Nine people aboard the *Syria* died on the voyage, and 84 fever victims were immediately admitted to hospital. The first recorded Famine victim at Grosse Île in 1847 was four year old Ellen Kane, 'legitimate daughter of John Kane, weaver, and Bridget McNally of the parish of Kilmore in the county of Mayo',[2] who died the day she arrived in the New World. Six days later, 202 passengers from the *Syria* were ill. The quarantine hospital on the island, built for 150 patients, could barely accommodate 200, and was already filled to capacity. Already 'the catastrophe had taken place, and was beyond control'.[3]

Despite its name, Grosse Île is a small island, barely one and a half miles long by half a mile wide, lying mid-stream in the St Lawrence river about 30 miles downstream from Quebec City. Much of it is densely wooded with stands of oak, maple, pine and birch; migrating ducks and geese rest on the beaches on its south shore. A pretty place, it was a favourite picnic spot for officers in the Quebec garrison in the early nineteenth century. Robert Whyte, who arrived at Grosse Île in July 1847, called it 'a fairy scene', 'the distant view of which was exceedingly beautiful' but, he added, 'this scene of natural beauty was sadly deformed by the dismal display of human suffering that it presented'.[4]

The western end of the island is haunted by the physical presence of that suffering. A broad meadow lies in a dip below the rocky outcrop known as Telegraph Hill. This meadow has a corrugated surface, a regular series of ridges, which inevitably remind the visitor of lazy beds, the old Irish ridge-and-trench manner of cultivating potatoes. On Grosse Île, too, the ridges are man-made, for they mark the mass graves where the Irish Famine victims of 1847 were buried, 'stacked like cordwood'.[5]

Alexander Buchanan, Chief Emigration Agent at Quebec, believed as many as 3,000 people died on board the coffin ships at sea, in the first two months of the shipping season; in the same period (15 May-17 July), he reported, 2,069 people died at Grosse Île.[6] Among those who survived the passage, thousands were desperately ill, driven half-insane by starvation, and fever, and distraught with bereavement as they watched their loved ones die before them. Many may have wandered away from the reception sheds, dying along the shore and in the woods.

Chosen because it is isolated in mid-river but still close to Quebec City, Grosse Île was first designated as a quarantine station in 1832, in response to well-founded Canadian fears of the cholera epidemic which had swept westwards across Europe from India since 1826. Grosse Île was to be 'the centre of an outer defence to prevent the disease reaching Quebec City'.[7] Dr Griffin and a party of soldiers under the command of Captain Ralph Alderson took possession of the island on May 1, 1832 and began to set up hospital sheds, tents and a bakery.

The partial failure of the potato harvest in Ireland in 1831 engendered hunger and physical debilitation which proved a fertile breeding ground for cholera, with the result that almost all the carriers and most of the victims of the trans-Atlantic cholera epidemic of 1832 were Irish. The rudimentary standards of the quarantine system, at the beginning, are best illustrated by the fact that when the cholera reached Quebec City, on 8 June 1832, aboard the brig *Carricks* from Dublin, the *Quebec Mercury* ascribed the cause to 'some unknown disease'. Indeed, before the end of June most ships simply sailed past Grosse Île to Quebec.[8]

The doctors and attendants on Grosse Île were overworked and underqualified to treat a disease many of them had never seen; the diagnosis, treatment and epidemiology of cholera were all a mystery to them; the hospital facilities on the island, still incomplete, were overwhelmed; the numbers of sick from the ships arriving in the river kept mounting. By early June, when 15,000 people had been examined at Grosse Île, the Canadian authorities stopped trying to detain and inspect all vessels, only requiring full quarantine of the ships arriving from Irish and British ports. 'At times', says Mitchell, 'over thirty vessels were present in the anchorage. In a word, the capacity of the station was insufficient to deal with the vessels bearing infected immigrants'.[9]

In 1832, the unavoidable failure to manage the quarantine station adequately resulted in some 7,000 deaths as the cholera epidemic swept down the St Lawrence valley from Quebec to Montreal, Kingston, Toronto and Hamilton, Buffalo and Detroit. 'By September 30, the newspapers reported the "official burials" at Quebec City at 3,292. More than that had died at Grosse Île'.[10] The Irish dead of 1832 on Grosse Île were buried in mass graves. Oral tradition reports that the original burying grounds were at low tide in Back Bay, whence the location became known as Cholera Bay.[11]

The contrast between 1832 and 1833 is remarkable: it is the difference between normal and extraordinary circumstances at the quarantine station. In 1833, 22,000 people were examined at Grosse Île but only 27 deaths occurred among the 239 people who were admitted to the island's hospital; again, in 1841–46 only 224 deaths were recorded at Grosse Île, out of a total of 170,683 people who landed at Quebec.[12] What happened in the summer of 1832 was a foretaste of the disaster which overwhelmed Grosse Île in 1847.

I

In 1846, after the first blast of blight but before the full fury of the Famine swept Ireland, nearly 33,000 people, mostly Irish, entered Canada at Quebec City. Already the effects of the Famine in Ireland were evident in Dr Douglas's report that twice as many people as usual were admitted to the hospital on Grosse Île.[13] The Canadians were aware of the circumstances in Ireland; they did not know the full dimensions of the horror, but they knew a crisis was at hand.

In February 1847, before the year's first emigrant ships arrived, Dr George Mellis Douglas, Medical Superintendent, warned the Legislative Assembly that the approaching season would bring 'a greater amount of sickness and mortality' and that the closure of American ports would 'augment the number of poor and destitute who will flock to our shores'. Little had changed on the island since 1832: its establishment consisted of a hospital shed, two chapels, a bakery, a barracks and the doctor's house. Douglas asked for £3,000 to expand the quarantine facilities to cope with the expected increase in numbers; he was given £300 with which he managed to acquire 50 extra beds and extra straw for bedding. But even Dr Douglas was utterly unprepared for the reality.[14]

Dr Douglas was astonished by the 'unprecedented' 'state of illness and distress' on the coffin ships; he had 'never contemplated the possibility of every vessel arriving with fever as they do now', all of them carrying passengers 'in the most wretched state of disease'. In the first few days after the arrival of the *Syria*, seven more emigrant ships arrived; they carried 2,778 passengers; 175 passengers had died at sea, 341 were ill. On 23 May, he reported between 50 and 60 deaths per day. By 24 May another 25 ships had arrived; 260 of the 5,600 passengers had died en route, and another 700 were ill. Douglas was resigned to the prospect that many more would fall sick and require treatment but, he told the authorities, 'I have not a bed to lay them on or a place to put them in'. As a result, he was obliged to flout the quarantine law and confine all passengers, healthy and sick alike, on board the ships at anchor in the river.[15] Before the end of May, 36 coffin ships were at anchor in the river. The hospital space on the island was entirely overwhelmed, and the ships at anchor were all full of passengers, close to 12,500 altogether, the healthy and the sick, the dying and the dead sharing grossly overcrowded quarters, packed as human ballast in the holds of vessels built not as passenger ships but to carry Canadian lumber to England.[16]

On 29 May, Buchanan blamed the problem on the laxity of the British shipping regulations and the greed of the shipowners: 'Much of the present disease and sickness is, I fear, attributed to the want of sufficient nourishing food'.[17] This was a diplomatic understatement; all the eyewitnesses that summer agreed that conditions on the coffin ships, even the best of them, were unspeakably Hobbesian.[18] British shipping regulations provided for the barest minimum as rations for emigrants; ship owners and captains seldom provided more. Too often, the crews were callous, brutal, capricious and avaricious.[19] Profiteering ship's chandlers supplied mouldy food and water that was unfit to drink, and many shipping agents in Ireland and Liverpool made a point of warning passengers to take aboard their own food supplies, an impossible demand on people who were already starving and destitute. Those who landed at Grosse Île tended to be the poorest of the Famine refugees: passage to Quebec was half the going rate to American ports, cheap enough for those who scraped together their last few shillings and a powerful attraction as well for landlords who offered the invidious choice of assisted emigration or eviction, such as Mahon at Strokestown and Palmerston in Sligo. Steerage passengers, accommodated between decks in hastily constructed, rudimentary bunks, were allotted less space than British regulations had defined as adequate for the transport of slaves from Africa.[20]

One of the more interesting witnesses at Grosse Île in 1847 was Stephen De Vere, who was anything but an ordinary emigrant. Scion of a noted Anglo-Irish family from County Limerick, landlord, magistrate and social reformer, he took passage on an emigrant ship in order to provide a firsthand report to the Colonial Office. His account of conditions on the ship which, he was assured, was 'more comfortable than many' is a funeral dirge.

> Hundreds of poor people, men, women and children, of all ages from the drivelling idiot of 90 to the babe just born, huddled together, without light, without air, wallowing in filth, and breathing a foetid atmosphere, sick in body, dispirited in heart . . . the fevered patients lying between the sound in sleeping places so narrow, as almost to deny them a change of position . . . living without food or medicine except as administered by the hand of casual charity, dying without spiritual consolation and buried in the deep without the rites of the church.[21]

Robert Whyte was untypical too, a cabin passenger rather than one of the huddled masses in steerage, but his account of conditions below decks mirrors De Vere's. Whyte also told the instructive story of the German immigrants who reached Grosse Île a couple of days after him. One of the assistant medical officers, Dr Jacques, boarded the German ship, and inspected the 500 passengers who had embarked at Bremen, 'all of them (without a single exception) comfortably and neatly clad, clean and happy. There was no sickness among them and each comely fairhaired girl laughed as she passed the doctor to join the robust young men who had undergone the ordeal'. Later that day, as it passed upstream to Quebec, the ship's 'deck was covered with emigrants who were singing a charming hymn, in whose harmony all took part . . .'[22] This description of the normal quarantine procedure at Grosse Île is invaluable, not least because it casts the Irish experience in such sharp contrast.

As the summer wore on, the Canadians confronted shipload after shipload of malnourished, diseased and even naked people. On 25 June, the Legislative Assembly voted to urge the British government to ameliorate the conditions mandated by the shipping regulations, calling specifically for more space per passenger, more food and better medical facilities.[23] Among those who wrote, with growing anger, to the Colonial Office in London were Adam Ferrie, chairman of the Legislative Assembly's Emigration Committee and the Common Council of the City of St John, New Brunswick, who called the conditions of the Irish emigrants 'as bad as the slave trade'.[24]

On 31 May, forty vessels were at anchor in the St Lawrence, in a line stretching two miles downstream. More than a thousand fever cases were on the island, the overflow from the hospital housed in hastily erected sheds and tents and in the chapels; as many again were on the ships waiting to come ashore. The death toll was appalling: 900 deaths had been recorded in the two weeks since Ellen Kane's. Dr Douglas's reports to the Legislative Assembly became peevish with good reason. He complained that he and his staff were unable to carry out even one minimal daily inspection of the passengers still held on the ships. Conditions on the island were unbearable; he and his assistants, medical, clerical and lay, were worn out and oppressed by the disease and mortality all around them. Douglas himself contracted typhus but survived, as did dozens of nurses, orderlies, servants and several of the priests. A poignant symbol of the epidemic is the case of Dr John Benson, from Castlecomer, County Kilkenny, a physician with experience in the fever hospitals in Ireland, who arrived on the *Wandsworth* on 20 May, volunteered to assist Dr Douglas, contracted typhus and died within a week.[25]

On Buchanan's recommendation, the Governor General, Lord Elgin, appointed three physicians, Drs Painchaud, McDonnell and Campbell, as a Medical Commission to examine the crisis at Grosse Île. On 5 June, when they arrived at the island, 21,000 emigrants were at Grosse Île and the daily death toll had tripled: 150 people were buried that day.[26] On arrival, the commissioners discovered the sick on the island 'in the most deplorable condition, for want of the necessary nurses and hospital attendants', while on board the ships in the river they found 'corpses lying in the same beds with the sick and the dying'. The hardship was compounded by the demoralisation of the victims: 'common sympathies being apparently annihilated by the mental and bodily depression produced by famine and disease'. The commissioners echoed Buchanan's criticism of 'the crowded manner in which vessels were allowed to leave the British Ports'. On the central issue of the management by Dr Douglas of the quarantine station, they wrote:

> We entirely disapprove of the plan of keeping a vessel in Quarantine for any period, however prolonged, whilst the sick and healthy are congregated together, breathing the same atmosphere, sleeping in the same berths, and exposed to the same exciting causes of contagion. This year's melancholy experience has in many instances proved that the number attacked and the mortality of the disease increased in direct ratio with the length of time the ship was detained under such circumstances. As an evidence of the truth of the above statement, we may be permitted to instance the case of the ship *Agnes* which arrived about 16 days ago, with 427 passengers, out of which number not more than 150 are now in a healthy condition, the remainder being dead, or sick on board, or in Hospital.

They were, however, unable to offer any concrete remedies for the problem beyond instructing Dr Douglas to comply with the regulations which was, by this stage, no longer possible.[27]

De Vere's description of the hospital sheds on the island echoed and amplified the Medical Commissioners' remarks:

> They were very miserable, so slightly built as to exclude neither the heat nor the cold. No sufficient care was taken to remove the sick from the sound or to disinfect and clean the beddings. The very straw upon which they had lain was often allowed to become a bed for their successors and I have known many poor families prefer to burrow under heaps of stones, near the shore, rather than accept the shelter of the infected sheds.[28]

Fr Bernard McGauran, who led the first group of Catholic priests on the island that year, put the same point more graphically, when he told the Select Committee, 'I have seen in one day thirty-seven lying on the beach, crawling in the mud and dying like fish out of water'.[29]

In July, when the temperature reached 37°C, more than 2,500 sick people, suffering from typhus, dysentery and simple starvation, were on the island, and the conditions had not appreciably improved. The Legislative Assembly appointed a Special Committee 'to inquire into the management of the Quarantine Station at Grosse Isle'. The Special Committee's report, released on 28 July, consisted solely of oral and written evidence, without recommendations. The witnesses testified unanimously to the awful situation on the island: the sheds, tents and other buildings were overflowing; the beds, such as they were, were shared by as many as three people; many fever victims were lying on bare planks or on the ground, the more fortunate on a bedding of straw. 'Six men are constantly employed', said Douglas, 'digging large trenches from five to six feet deep, in which the dead are buried'. The dead were buried two or three deep. So many were interred and so close to the surface, Douglas had to arrange to bring soil from the mainland to cover the dead; even so, rats came ashore from the ships to feast on the cadavers.[30]

Testifying on 13 July, Fr William Moylan, parish priest of St Patrick's in Quebec City, told of seeing corpses left lying overnight in the bunks in the hospital 'even when they had a companion in the same bed'. He confirmed the Medical Commission's observations, saying 'the sick would have been better ashore under tents, having medical attendance close at hand, and besides would not have affected the healthy Emigrants confined in the holds of the vessels with them'. He estimated the mortality as a result of confinement on the ships was 'at least twice as great as on shore'.[31]

Fr Bernard O'Reilly from Sherbrooke blamed the British government for the conditions on the emigrant ships, but he also warned the Canadians that unless they acted quickly they would 'choose to consent to the wholesale murder of thousands who are just now on the ocean or preparing to leave home for Canada'. His evidence, given on 23 July, balanced praise for Dr Douglas's unstinting efforts with reiteration of criticism of the policy of keeping people on board the ships.[32]

De Vere, however, criticised the quarantine system, saying both 'medical attendance and hospital accommodations were inadequate'. Because the doctors were overwhelmed, the 'medical inspections on board were slight and hasty' which produced a 'twofold ill effect': 'Some were detained in danger who were not ill, and many were allowed to proceed who were actually in fever'.[33]

Even those who escaped confinement in the holds of the ships were not safe. Fr Jean Baptiste Antoine Ferland, Director of the College of Nicolet, reported that 'in the greater part of the sheds on Grosse Île, men, women and children are found huddled together in the same apartment . . . many who have entered the shed without any serious illness, have died of typhus, which they have caught from their neighbours'.[34]

The *Agnes*, cited by the Medical Commission, was not extraordinary. The *Larch* sailed from Sligo with 440 passengers; 108 died at sea and 150 had the fever on arrival. The *Lord Ashburton* brought tenants evicted by Lord Palmerston; 107 of the 477 passengers died at sea, 60 were ill. The *Sir Henry Pottinger* left Cork with 399 passengers; 106 died and 100 were sick. The ships carrying people from the Mahon estate at Strokestown, County Roscommon, earned a particularly unsavoury reputation. Major Denis Mahon acquired notoriety as a tyrannical clearing landlord, and a place in history as one of the handful of landlords assassinated in 1847. He left behind, also, an unadorned summary of the landlords' economic point of view. 'I think', he wrote to his agent, 'the first class for us to send is those of the poorest and worst description, who would be a charge on us for the Poor House or for Outdoor Relief, and that would relieve the industrious tenant'. Like scores of other landlords, Mahon undertook large scale eviction – the Bishop of Elphin reported that Mahon had evicted 3,006 people from his estate – but he also provided assisted emigration to about 1,000 of his tenants. But even this apparently humane part of the process was fraught with squalor and indignity. Medical inspection of the prospective emigrants was hasty and rudimentary, they were sent to Liverpool to squalid lodging houses where fever was already rampant, and they took passage to Canada (the cheaper destination) in the holds of unsanitary, overcrowded merchant ships.[35]

The outcome, recorded in early August, was the first of Mahon's ships to arrive at Grosse Île, whose condition struck Dr Douglas as noteworthy even after weeks of unrelieved horror:

> The *Virginius* sailed from Liverpool, 28 May, with 476 passengers. Fever and dysentery cases came on board this vessel in Liverpool, and deaths occurred before leaving the Mersey. On mustering the passengers for inspection yesterday, it was found that 106 were ill of fever, including nine of the crew, and the large number of 158 had died on the passage, including the first and second officers and seven of the crew, and the master and steward dying, the few that were able to come on deck were ghastly yellow looking spectres, unshaven and hollow cheeked, and, without exception, the worst looking passengers I have ever seen; not more than six or eight were really healthy and able to exert themselves.[36]

Nineteen more passengers died while the *Virginius* was at anchor, and 90 died in the sheds. As he was writing this report, two more ships commissioned by Mahon arrived. On the *Naomi*, Dr Douglas said, 'the filth and dirt in this vessel's hold creates such an effluvium as to make it difficult to breathe'; 196 of her 421 passengers died before she reached Quebec. The *Erin's Queen* sailed with 493 people – 136 died at sea; on arrival at Grosse Île, the ship's master had to bribe his crew, at the rate of a sovereign per corpse, to remove the dead from the hold.[37]

Although they disapproved of the quarantine arrangements, neither the Medical Commissioners nor other witnesses were able to provide an alternative. There were no resources available and the flood of Famine refugees was simply too great. It fell again on the shoulders of Dr Douglas to seek a remedy. In the first half of July, before testifying at the Special Committee hearings, Douglas attempted to address the critical problem of the admixture of sick and healthy on board the ships at anchor. Starting from the eminently sound medical principle of preventing the spread of disease by segregating the healthy from the sick, he instituted a new form of triage. He began by setting up a tent camp at the eastern end of the island where the healthy could be sheltered while remaining in quarantine. This new hospital area was made permanent by the rapid construction of a dozen wooden hospital sheds, prefabricated in Quebec and assembled on the island. By August, the hospital sheds and tents could accommodate some 2,000 sick people, 300 convalescents and as many as 3,500 people deemed healthy but held in quarantine. By the end of the year, the summary report of public works effected on the island listed a total of 22 hospital sheds.[38]

Unfortunately, the difficulties of diagnosis and epidemiology which had been evident in 1832 remained, and were compounded by the sheer size of the task. Despite good intentions, segregation was at best a palliative measure. At worst it exacerbated the situation, spreading the disease even more widely. Fr O'Reilly told the legislative inquiry that he had given the last rites to 50 people, on one July day, among the so-called healthy in the east-end tents. On July 20, when more than 2,500 fever cases were housed in the island hospitals, Bishop Mountain of Montreal described 'scenes of loathsomeness, suffering and horror, in the holds of the ships and in the receptacles for the patients'.[39] The extent of the problem was underlined by a report of 27 deaths among the healthy on 31 July, and a month later when the *Montreal Gazette* reported 88 deaths in one week among the healthy at the east end of the island. A month later, as the shipping season drew to a close, there were still 14,000 people held in quarantine on board the ships at anchor off Grosse Île. Twelve hundred of the sick were transferred to the hospitals at the east end of the island on 13 September, to allow Douglas and his staff to fumigate the sheds and tents at the western end. As late as 16 September, the *Quebec Mercury* reported a large number of dysentery cases among the healthy. In the first three weeks of October, the parish register of St Luke's church on the island recorded 97 anonymous burials. At the end of October, after the first snowfall of the winter, the final 60 patients on the island were transferred to hospitals at Quebec and Montreal and the Grosse Île quarantine station closed for the winter.[40]

II

The implications of failure of the quarantine system were clearly recognised by several witnesses. As early as Tuesday, 8 June, Douglas had written to Buchanan warning of the imminent danger of the spread of disease throughout the colony:

> Out of the 4,000 or 5,000 emigrants who have left this island since Sunday, at least 2,000 will fall sick somewhere before three weeks are over. They ought to have accommodation for 2,000 sick at least at Montreal and Quebec, as all the Cork and Liverpool passengers are half dead from starvation and want before embarking; and the least bowel complaint, which is sure to come with change of food, finishes them without a struggle. I never saw people so indifferent to life; they would continue in the same berth with the dead person until the seamen or captain dragged out the corpse with boat hooks. Good God! what evils will befall the cities wherever they alight. Hot weather will increase the evil. Now give the authorities of Quebec and Montreal fair warning from me. I have not time to write, or should feel it my duty to do so. Public safety requires it.[41]

Six weeks later, Fr O'Reilly told the inquiry, 'those who are healthy, if sent up as hitherto to Montreal, must bring with them the seeds of sickness . . . while out of the numbers who can leave Montreal for a further destination, the large majority are pre-doomed to expire on the wharves of Kingston or Toronto, and to carry with them whithersoever they direct their steps, the dreadful malady that now hangs over the country like a funeral pall'.[42] Looking further ahead, Robert

Whyte anticipated more deaths, as his fellow passengers 'wandered over the country, carrying nothing with them but disease, and that but very few of them survived the severity of the succeeding winter, ruined as their constitutions were, I am quite confident'.[43]

These gloomy predictions were all too accurate, but it took some time for Douglas's fair warning to be heeded. In Montreal, the Irish were initially housed in the sheds erected in 1832, in the centre of the city. The growing danger of further contagion – the death toll in Montreal reached thirty people a day in June – led to demands for what was effectively a second quarantine station. After considerable debate, Point St Charles was chosen as the site; hospital sheds and open-sided shelters for the healthy were built. The new establishment formed 'a large square with a court in the centre where the coffins were piled, some empty waiting for the dead, some full awaiting burial'.[44] Twelve years later, when the site of the fever sheds and mass graves at Point St Charles was cleared to begin construction of the Victoria Bridge across the St Lawrence, the workers, mostly Irishmen downed tools and refused to continue until a proper memorial was built. They dredged a huge black stone out of the river and had carved on it this inscription: 'To preserve from desecration the remains of 6,000 immigrants who died from ship fever AD 1847-48 this stone is erected by the workmen of Messrs Peto, Brassey and Betts employed in the construction of the Victoria Bridge AD 1859'.

The Montreal experience was repeated as the epidemic swept down the St Lawrence from Quebec to the western end of Lake Ontario. In Quebec, Montreal, Kingston, Toronto and Hamilton, the emaciated, starving, destitute and febrile Irish brought disease and misery with them. They caused alarm and fear but, for the most part, generosity outweighed xenophobia in the Canadian response. Indeed, the story of 1847 is as much one of Canadian heroism as it is Irish suffering. In the face of unspeakable horror, hundreds of Canadians demonstrated remarkable generosity of spirit. Fever sheds were built, the victims were hastily segregated, and they were tended – tirelessly and heroically – by clergy and laity in each community, but still they died, in their thousands.

Some of the Canadian heroes are well-known, but most remain anonymous. At the end of the year, Dr Douglas raised a monument at the mass graveyard at the western end of the island, to mark the sacrifice of the four doctors, Benson, Pinet, Malhiot and Jameson who 'died of typhus fever contracted in the faithful discharge of their duty upon the sick'. The monument also bears this inscription: 'In this secluded spot lie the mortal remains of 5,424 persons who fleeing from Pestilence and Famine in Ireland in the year 1847 found in America but a Grave.'

Although only a minority, perhaps 10 per cent, of the Irish emigrants in 1847 were non-Catholic, the Anglican Bishop of Montreal, George Jehoshaphat Mountain, worked tirelessly that summer, travelling back and forth between Montreal, Quebec and the island, which he visited twice, spurring on his flock to the charitable work of offering assistance to the Famine victims. In all, 17 Anglican clergymen volunteered to serve on Grosse Île; two of them – Rev. Richard Anderson and Rev. Charles Morris – died of fever contracted from those they helped, as did two other Anglican priests: Rev. William Chaderton in Quebec and Rev. Mark Willoughby in Montreal. Similarly, four of the 42

Catholic priests who tended the sick at Grosse Île paid with their lives for their charity: Frs Hubert Robson, Pierre Roy, Felix Severin Brady and Edouard Montminy. Fr Hugh Paisley died in Quebec City. In addition, Dr Douglas reported 34 other deaths on Grosse Île: stewards, nurses, orderlies, cooks, policemen, carters and servants.[45]

In Montreal, as elsewhere, the 'ocean plague' exacted its price among the Canadians. Tending the sick fell largely to the Catholic Church. The Order of Grey Nuns provided nurses, almost all of whom became ill; Fr Hudon, Vicar-General of the diocese of Montreal, died in August as did eight other priests. In November, John Mills, the Mayor of Montreal whose energy and magnanimity ensured relatively safe and healthy conditions for the Famine victims, caught the fever at the sheds and died. Toronto's first Catholic Bishop, Michael Power, tended the sick in that city and fell victim to the fever.

Like other witnesses, Bishop Mountain was particularly touched by the plight of the hundreds of children left orphans by the epidemic. Among the dozens of miserable waifs, a couple particularly caught his attention: a dying child, huddled under a pile of rags in one of the tents; and the body of a little boy who was walking with his friends, sat down to rest under a tree, and died.[46] It fell, however, to Fr Moylan and to Fr Charles-Félix Cazeau, 'priest to the Irish' and future Vicar-General of the diocese of Quebec, to ensure the future of the children. In Quebec, the Catholic Ladies' Charitable Society took charge of 619 children, and the priests went on the circuit of parishes in Quebec urging the faithful to adopt the orphans. One priest, Fr Thomas Cooke of Trois Rivières, wrote that his parishioners were arguing over the right to adopt the orphans. In addition to the 619 children recorded in Quebec, many more orphans – Lord Elgin reported another thousand children in Montreal – were welcomed into Quebecois families. Even more remarkable than the adoptions of all these orphans was the generosity of spirit which allowed them to retain their Irish names. To this day, the number of Irish family names, in purely francophone communities in Quebec, is part of the legacy of that summer of sorrow at Grosse Île.[47]

III

In light of Don Mullan's assertion that Grosse Île is the 'most important and evocative Great Famine site' outside Ireland, the critical question may be posed. How many Irish men, women and children are buried in the mass graves at Grosse Île? A completely accurate answer is not within our grasp. It was in the interests of many – the British government and politicians, English landlords and, apparently, the colonial administration in Canada – to minimise the extent of the Irish disaster of 1847. Moreover, it is clear that the statistics for 1847 are muddled, incomplete, internally inconsistent and contradictory. The best we can do is reach an approximation.

In March 1848, the British government reported that 258,000 people, the vast majority of whom were Irish, set sail in 1847 from British and Irish ports: 143,400 for the U.S. and 106,812 for British North America. Norman Anick, citing the same report, gives 138,000 passengers bound for the U.S. Coleman, citing yet another parliamentary paper, gives 109,680 people embarking for Canada.[48] Whether it was 106,000 or 109,000, the number is an underestimate, by as much as 10 per cent, for two reasons. First, a number of the ships destined for

American ports were turned away on arrival and made their way to Halifax, St John or Grosse Île.[49] Secondly, the official manner of reckoning passengers counted 'statute adults' as defined in the British shipping regulations; in other words, one person over the age of 14, or a mother and dependent child under one year, or two children between one and 14 years old. So, for example, the master of the *Greenock* was legally correct to declare he carried only 633 'statute adults', though his vessel was crammed with 816 persons: 528 adults, 210 children between the ages of one and fourteen and 78 infants.[50]

In his first report, Alexander Buchanan, the Canadian Emigration Agent, said 97,002 people arrived at Quebec City from British, Irish and Canadian ports by 31 October, 1847. The report approved in December 1847 by the Committee of the Executive Council gives 98,106 as the total number of immigrants landing at Quebec. While this document specifies a figure of 54,329 as those who sailed from Irish ports, this fails to take into account the obvious fact that virtually all of the 134,524 people who embarked at Liverpool were Irish. Another account by Buchanan, also written in December 1847, reduced the number of Irish immigrants to 89,738, of whom 5,293 died before arriving, leaving only 84,445 who actually reached Canada. Finally, a year later, in his annual report for 1848, Buchanan had lowered the number again to 82,713 or 82,694 emigrants who had arrived at Quebec in 1847 from Irish or British ports.[51]

Approaching the matter from Grosse Île itself is no more helpful. The officials, doctors, priests and lay attendants were so overwhelmed they lost count of the dead within the first month. Deaths and burials were recorded at 50 per day very soon after the first ship arrived; on 5 June, 150 people were buried. The mass grave at the western end of the island, where six men dug trenches, occupied an area of six acres. In his official report to the government, at the end of the year, Dr Douglas gave a total of 3,238 deaths on the island, but plainly carved on the monument he erected overlooking the mass grave is the statement that it contained the remains of 5,424 people. Meanwhile, Buchanan reported 3,452 deaths at quarantine.[52] Again, the best we can say about these figures is they approximate the truth.

It is clear that the records on the island are both fragmentary and internally contradictory. An entire month's records of burials (as well as baptisms and marriages) is missing from the register of the Catholic parish of St Luke (20 May-15 June).[53] Among the excerpts reproduced by O'Gallagher is a notation by Fr Philippe Jean that he buried 21 people on 23 June; the summary of burials, from the same St Luke's parish register, however, says 112 people 'whom it was not possible to name' ('*sans qu'il ait été possible de mentionner les noms*') were buried that day. Similar, albeit less radical, discrepancies between these two documents occurred throughout the months of June-August. The summary of burials records a global figure of 2,900 people buried between 16 June and 20 October. The preceding four weeks, from 20 May, when at least 1,050 deaths occurred, are unrecorded.

The confusion about the number of people buried in the mass graves at the western end of the island is compounded by the even more fragmentary evidence of other grave sites. Dispute exists about the cemetery at the eastern end of the island, identified by the Canadian Parks Service as divided into 'Catholic' and

'Protestant' sections (following later practice). In light of the evidence of substantial numbers of deaths among the so-called healthy accommodated first in tents and then in the hospital buildings erected in July 1847, this area also probably contains the remains of Famine victims. The alternative explanation – that the bodies of those who died at the east end of the island, of fearsome contagious fevers, were transported across the island for burial south of Cholera Bay – is illogical and unreasonable. Moreover, oral tradition tells the story of the bulldozer driver, employed by the Canadian Department of Agriculture in 1964 to grade the land for an airstrip, who uncovered human bones. Unlike the main mass grave site at the west end of the island, this area is less well-known and, despite clear evidence of its existence and extent in the archives, it is only grudgingly acknowledged by the Canadian Parks Service in its most recent publications.[54]

When all the pieces of this puzzle are assembled, the best point of departure for estimating the importance of Grosse Île as a Great Famine site is the difference between the most realistic number of Irish Famine refugees who actually came up the St Lawrence in 1847 – about 110,000 – and the number reported as arriving, alive, in Canada. Given the contradictions in the primary sources, the latter number is also an estimate – and 90,000 is the most generous round number that best accords with the estimates offered by Buchanan, Douglas and others. In other words, at a minimum, the death toll in the coffin ships and at Grosse Île must be reckoned at about 20,000 Irish men, women and children. It must be emphasised that this number does not include the thousands of others who, having survived Grosse Île, reached Quebec City, Montreal, Kingston, Toronto and Hamilton, only to die there in fever hospitals and emigrant sheds.

We shall never know exactly how many Irish people are buried at Grosse Île. Early accounts, by J. F. Maguire and Béchard, estimated the number of Irish people buried on the island in 1847 at 12,000; a later local history put the figure at 11,000.[55] In the end, it is undignified and disrespectful to squabble about the numbers. It is certainly less important to reach a definitive number than it is to acknowledge the sanctity of the site.

IV

The special significance of Grosse Île for the Irish community, in Canada, the United States and, increasingly, in Ireland itself, was first demonstrated over 80 years ago. On 15 August 1909, a 46-foot high Celtic Cross, built of Stanstead granite, was unveiled on Telegraph Hill, the highest point on Grosse Île, 140 feet above the river. It faces west, towards Quebec City and the new life the thousands who died there never saw. The Irish inscription on the panel on the eastern face of the cross declares:

> Cailleadh Clann na nGaedheal ina míltibh ar an Oileán so ar dteicheadh dhóibh ó dhlíghthibh na dtíoránach ngallda agus ó ghorta tréarach isna bliadhantaibh 1847–48. Beannacht dílis Dé orra. Bíodh an leacht so i gcomhartha garma agus onóra dhóibh ó Ghaedhealaibh Ameriocá. Go saoraigh Dia Éire.

Which translates into English as:

Children of the Gael died in their thousands on this island

having fled from the laws of foreign tyrants and an artificial
famine in the years 1847–48. God's blessing on them. Let this
monument be a token to their name and honour from the Gaels
of America. God Save Ireland.

This monument was paid for by public subscription raised by the Ancient
Order of Hibernians in Canada and the United States. The opening ceremony
drew 9,000 people from all over North America. The cross was unveiled by the
Papal Legate to Canada, Mgr Antonio Sbaretti; sermons were delivered by Mgr
Sbaretti, Archbishop (later Cardinal) Louis-Nazaire Bégin, and Fr A.E. Maguire,
chaplain to the AOH. Among those present at the ceremony were Fr McGuirk,
the last survivor of the 42 priests who tended the victims of 1847, and Madame
Roberge, one of the many children orphaned that year and adopted by a local
family. In addition to spokesmen for the AOH, the dignitaries included Canada's
Chief Justice, Sir Charles Fitzpatrick and Secretary of State Charles Murphy, as
well as members of both the federal and provincial parliaments.[56]

In August 1989, at a ceremony marking the eightieth anniversary of the
unveiling of the High Cross, His Excellency Dr Edward J. Brennan, Ireland's
Ambassador to Canada, recalled the Famine as 'Ireland's holocaust . . . [which]
condemned the Irish to be the first boat people of modern Europe'.[57] Dr
Brennan's words were echoed again in 1994, by Mary Robinson, President of
Ireland, who chose Grosse Île as the first stop on her visit to Canada. She noted
that while the failure of the potato was a 'natural disaster' across Europe, 'in
Ireland it took place in a political, economic and social framework that was
oppressive and unjust'. Speaking to some 400 people gathered on the island to
commemorate the victims of 1847, she said, 'Grosse Île – Oileán na nGael – l'île des
irlandais – is special. . . This is a hallowed place'.[58]

The catastrophe of 1847 was both an extraordinary chapter in the history of
the Grosse Île Quarantine Station, and a benchmark. The facilities on the island
never again faced a similar challenge, but the experience of 1847 led to tighter
regulations and stricter enforcement. The cost of the effectiveness of the
quarantine station's subsequent 90 years was the Irish 'summer of sorrows'. For
that reason, above all, the dreadful events of 1847 stamped a particularly Irish
character irrevocably on the island's story.

References

1 Don Mullan, Director, Great Famine Project, Action from Ireland, *Public Consultation: Briefs presented in Montreal* (Quebec, 1992), pp. 2-3.

2 Register of the Parish of St Luke, Grosse Île, reprinted by Marianna O'Gallagher & Rose Masson Dompierre, *Eyewitness Grosse Île 1847* (Quebec, 1995), p. 69.

3 Cecil Woodham-Smith, *The Great Hunger: Ireland, 1845-49* (London, 1962), pp. 219-20.

4 Robert Whyte, *The Ocean Plague* (Boston 1848), reissued as *Robert Whyte's 1847 Famine Ship Diary* (Cork, 1994), pp. 62, 67.

5 Testimony of John Wilson, Shipping Agent at Quebec, Report of the Special Committee appointed to inquire into the management of the Quarantine Station at Grosse Île, *Journals of the Legislative Assembly of the Province of Canada*, 1847, Vol. 6, Appendix RRR (no pagination).

6 *Journals of the Legislative Assembly of the Province of Canada*, 1847, Vol. 6, Appendix RRR.

7   Chas A. Mitchell, 'Events leading up to and the Establishment of the Grosse Île Quarantine Station', *Medical Services Journal*, Canada, 1967, p. 1436.

8   Marianna O'Gallagher, *Grosse Île Gateway to Canada 1832-1937* (Quebec, 1984), p. 24.

9   Mitchell, 'Grosse Île Quarantine Station', p. 1443.

10 O'Gallagher, *Grosse Île*, p. 26.

11 Suzanne Kingsmill, 'Isle of Irish Despair', *Canadian Geographic* (1992), p. 80.

12 O'Gallagher & Dompierre, *Eyewitness*, p. 384; O'Gallagher, *Grosse Île*, p. 40; Norman Anick, 'Grosse Île & Partridge Island Quarantine Stations', *Historic Sites & Monuments Board of Canada Agenda Papers* (Moncton, 1984), pp. 83-4.

13 O'Gallagher & Dompierre, *Eyewitness*, p. 384.

14 Donald MacKay, *Flight From Famine: The Coming of the Irish to Canada* (Toronto, 1990), p. 263; Woodham-Smith, Great Hunger, p. 218.

15 Letters (21 & 24 May) from Dr G. M. Douglas to Provincial Secretary, Dominick Daly, *Journals*, App. L.

16 Terry Coleman, *Passage to America* (1972, reissue: Quebec, 1991), p. 84; Marianna O'Gallagher, 'Island of Sorrows', *Irish America*, April 1991, p. 27; Woodham-Smith, *Great Hunger*, pp. 222-30; MacKay, *Flight from Famine*, pp. 198-99.

17 *Journals*, App. L.

18 Whyte, *Ocean Plague*; Coleman, *Passage*; De Vere cited in MacKay, *Flight from Famine*; Medical Commission and Select Committee in *Journals*.

19 Coleman, *Passage*, Chapter 6: 'Hard-driven Ships & Brutal Crews', pp. 82-99 *passim*; MacKay, *Flight from Famine*, pp. 198-215.

20 Coleman, *Passage*, Appendix A, pp. 324-32.

21 Stephen De Vere, cited by Woodham-Smith, *Great Hunger*, p. 226.

22 Whyte, *Ocean Plague*, pp. 76-7 and *passim*.

23 Padraic O Laighin, 'Grosse Île: The Holocaust Revisited', in Robert O'Driscoll & Lorna Reynolds, eds., *The Untold Story: The Irish in Canada* (Toronto, 1988), v. I, p. 85.

24 Woodham-Smith, *Great Hunger*, pp. 228-29.

25 *Journals*, App. L; O'Gallagher & Dompierre, *Eyewitness*, p. 76. A minor mystery attaches to Dr Benson. Dr Douglas's report of deaths for the week of 23-29 May gives Dr Benson's age as 60, but the register of the Anglican parish of St John the Evangelist on Grosse Île says he was 'about forty or forty-five years of age'. Even more curious is the report of another researcher that Benson's name appears in a list of persons evicted from an estate in Castlecomer, confirming a comment by Dr Douglas that Benson had arrived with the 'tenants from the estates of William Wandesford' (O'Gallagher & Dompierre, *Eyewitness*, pp. 373-4). How did a doctor become an evicted tenant? (personal communication from Anthony Lorraine, 1994).

26 *Morning Chronicle* (Quebec), 10 June 1847, cited O Laighin, 'Holocaust Revisited', p. 84.

27 Report of the Medical Commissioners, *Journals*, App. L.

28 Stephen De Vere, cited in Whyte, *Ocean Plague*, Appendix III, p. 114; Anick, 'Grosse Île & Partridge Island', p. 85.

29 Report of the Select Committee, *Journals*, App. RRR; cited by MacKay, *Flight from Famine*, p. 269.

30 Report of the Select Committee, *Journals*, App. RRR; Coleman, *Passage*, p. 150.

31 Report of the Select Committee, *Journals*, App. RRR.

32 Report of the Select Committee, *Journals*, App. RRR.

33 Cited by MacKay, *Flight from Famine*, p. 267; Anick, 'Grosse Île & Partridge Island', p. 85.

34 Report of the Select Committee, *Journals*, App. RRR.

35 Stephen J. Campbell, *The Great Irish Famine* (Strokestown, 1994), pp. 40-42; Woodham-Smith, *Great Hunger*, pp. 324-25.

36 B.P.P., *Colonies – Canada*, Vol. 17, p. 385, cited O'Gallagher & Dompierre, *Eyewitness*, p. 365.

37 O'Gallagher & Dompierre, *Eyewitness*, p. 380; Coleman, *Passage*, p. 160.

38 *Quebec Mercury*, 7 August 1847; Christine Chartré, *Chronologie des Aménagements de Grosse-Ile, 1796-1990*, [Chronology of Development at Grosse Île, 1796-1990] (Quebec, 1992), pp. 39-51; Anick, 'Grosse Île & Partridge Island', p. 86.

39 Report of the Select Committee, *Journals*, App. RRR.

40 Report of the Select Committee, *Journals*, App. RRR; *Montreal Gazette*, 20 August 1847, cited by Woodham-Smith, *Great Hunger*, p. 222; *Quebec Mercury*, 31 July 1847 and September 16 1847, cited by Chartré, *Chronologie*, pp. 43, 48.

41 Cited by MacKay, *Flight from Famine*, p. 265; Coleman, *Passage*, p. 149.

42 Report of the Select Committee, *Journals*, App. RRR.

43 Whyte, *Ocean Plague*, p. 84.

44 Cited by Woodham-Smith, *Great Hunger*, p. 235.

45 O'Gallagher & Dompierre, *Eyewitness*, p. 385; O'Gallagher, *Grosse Île*, pp. 88-9; Coleman, *Passage*, pp. 160-61.

46 Cited by Woodham-Smith, *Great Hunger*, p. 222.

47 O'Gallagher, *Grosse Île*, pp. 56-7, 115-43; Coleman, *Passage*, pp. 156-7.

48 *Report of the Select Committee of the House of Lords on Colonization from Ireland*, v. 5, p. 42; Anick, 'Grosse Île & Partridge Island', p. 81, citing ibid. p. 55; Coleman, *Passage*, p. 161, citing *Reports of Colonial Land & Emigration Commissioners*, 1848 and 1873.

49 Woodham-Smith, *Great Hunger*, pp. 239-40.

50 *Colonies – Canada*, v. 17, p. 422, cited by O Laighin, 'Hidden Holocaust', p. 89.

51 *Colonies – Canada*, v. 18, p. 449; ibid. v. 17, p. 384; ibid. p. 4; v. 18, pp. 463-69; *Journals*, 1849, App. EEE: see Anick, 'Grosse Île & Partridge Island', p. 84; O'Laighin, 'Holocaust Revisited', pp. 88-9; Coleman, *Passage*, pp. 160-61; cf. Commission on Emigration and other Population Problems, 1948-54, *Reports* (Dublin: Stationery Office, 1954), Statistical Appendix, pp. 314-20.

52 *Colonies – Canada*, v. 17, pp. 383-87.

53 O'Gallagher & Dompierre, *Eyewitness*, p. 69.

54 Christine Chartré, *Rapport synthèse sur les aménagements de Grosse-Ile 1832 à nos jours*, [Outline Report of Development at Grosse Île, 1832-present](Quebec, 1992), pp. 61, 116, 196, 328, 348, 360; Pierre Dufour et al., *Inventaire sommaire du patrimoine architectural de la Grosse-Ile*, [Summary Inventory of the Architectural Heritage of Grosse Île] (Quebec, 1983), pp. 9899; *Grosse Île: Development Concept and Supplement* (Quebec, 1992) – the Supplement says the cemetery at the east end of Grosse Île was not opened until 1848 or at the earliest 'the end of 1847', pp. 13-17.

55 John Francis Maguire, *The Irish in America* (London, 1868); A. Béchard, *Histoire de l'île-aux-grues et des îles environnantes* [History of Crane Island & Surrounding Islands] (Quebec, 1879); J. A. Jordan, *The Grosse Île Tragedy* (Quebec, 1909); Damase Potvin, *Le Saint-Laurent et ses îles* [The St Lawrence & Its Islands] (Montreal, 1940) – cited by Coleman, *Passage*, pp. 150-56; see also Padraic O Laighin, 'Grosse Île: The Irish Island', *Public Consultation: Briefs presented in Montreal* (Quebec, 1992), note 5.

56 O'Gallagher, *Grosse Île*, pp. 85-88.

57 Ireland Fund of Canada, *Journal*, 1992, p. 14.

58 'Address by the President, Mary Robinson, at Grosse Île on 21 August, 1994', pp. 1-2.

The Land the Famine Irish Forgot

Donal P. McCracken

The South African-Irish

IN THE ANNALS OF THE IRISH DIASPORA one region of the British empire has, until the present generation, been largely ignored.[1] The experience of the Irish who ventured to the British colonies of the Cape of Good Hope and of Natal, and to the Boer republics of the Transvaal and the Orange Free State, even today remains a closed book to many Irish historians. Their story, however, is not without interest or without significance to the student of the Irish diaspora. The Irish did come to South Africa – more men than women, as many Protestants as Catholics (urban rather than rural-based), the skilled and semi-skilled rather thán the destitute and the desperate.[2] They gravitated towards specific occupations, such as the colonial police forces, the railways, retailing and the mines, their concentration in these fields creating an impression of greater numbers than actually existed.[3] In addition the British army, the Catholic church and the colonial services, including the judiciary, each had a noticeable Irish element.[4]

A good sprinkling of Irish governors arrived at the Cape, not always to the delight of citizens of Cape Town. There was an Irish prime minister of the Cape (Thomas Upington) and of Natal (Alfred Hime) and from 1839 to 1865 an eminent Irish Cape attorney general (William Porter).[5] Later in the nineteenth century a fair number of Irish merchant princes made good, the most successful being John Orr from Armagh and William Cuthbert from Dungiven.[6] As is well known, at the turn of the century two rival Irish commandoes fought for the Boers in the second Anglo-Boer war.[7] But their numbers were not great – perhaps between 400 and 500 – and their significance lies in their propaganda value for advanced Irish nationalism back home in Ireland. The fact that nearly 30,000 Irish soldiers in the British army fought against them has been conveniently ignored and even the great Boer war memorial in St Stephen's Green in Dublin is today a nameless landmark to most Dubliners, its earlier tag, 'the traitors' gate', having been long forgotten.[8]

By the time the Boer war had ended in 1902 there were perhaps some 60,000 people in South Africa who would have termed themselves 'Irish'. In his excellent primer Professor Donald Akenson speaks of viewing the Irish diaspora as a spectrum with America at one end of the range of possible patterns that Irish emigration could take. At the other end was South Africa. South Africa, he asserts in his *Occasional Papers*, received the 'best' of the Irish emigrants if one uses their economic background in Ireland as the criterion.[9] This statement is true but needs to be treated with caution, especially given South Africa's immediate past. As a general rule the Irish who came to South Africa in the nineteenth century were not wealthy. The Orrs, Cuthberts and Hendersons walked up the

Heerengracht in Cape Town for the first time with little money in their pockets. But they did differ from the huddled masses yearning to breathe free as they shuffled up the queue on Ellis Island. First, more often than not Irish emigrants to South Africa, their family or sometimes their prospective employer had paid a full passage for them. Second, they often arrived without the encumbrance of debt, family or obligation to anyone in their new home. Third, because South Africa was not on the 'exiles' route', it took an adventurous spirit to risk an African odyssey. By implication, this meant that the young and healthy came to Africa. It is true that the highveld gained a justifiable reputation for being good for sufferers of tuberculosis, but this was later and was generally confined to the artisan and middle classes. In the nineteenth century the mindset of most Irish immigrants to South Africa was positive. They looked to the future and they did not hold grudges from the past. It is significant that there are few sentimental exile songs of the South African-Irish. That there are also few surviving South African-Irish emigrant letters also points to a new-start mentality.

The Famine

The British first captured the Cape in 1795, finally occupying it in 1806, thanks in large part to the 83rd Regiment (Royal Irish Rifles). In 1842 the 27th (Inniskilling) Regiment withstood the siege of Port Natal, allowing for the annexation of Natal. Thus before the Irish Famine was underway there were two large areas in southern Africa, both controlled by the British, both interested in encouraging British immigration and half the sailing distance from the British Isles to Australia.

A few years before the Famine, in May 1840, William Porter, speaking in the Cape legislative council, was reported as saying:

> With regard to the great question of Emigration, as an Irishman, coming from a country where he had seen the utmost excess of misery arising from the circumstances of there being more hands than can possibly obtain employment, to a country where he found there was such great difficulty in obtaining hands, and such inconvenience and diminution of happiness experienced from the want of persons to act as servants, he should surely be as much disposed as any man to adopt measures which would yield relief to the one class, while they would bring prosperity to another.[10]

Nothing came of the suggestion.

Realisation that all was not well in Ireland filtered through slowly to South Africa. By February 1846 the *South African Commercial Advertiser* was carrying reports of distress in Ireland taken from British newspapers. In August an editorial observed sanguinely: 'In Ireland the arrangements made to avert the threatened Famine seem to have kept the miseries of the people down to, if not below, the average of Irish woe.'[11] However, by October the reality of the situation was becoming plain: 'Reports of the potato crop that reach Dublin from all parts of Ireland are of the very worst kind. The disease seems to have attacked the growing plants in all quarters.'[12] On St Patrick's day 1847 the *Commercial Advertiser* carried the comment from the *Morning Chronicle* that, 'A social revolution is palpably and rapidly going forward in Ireland' .

At the beginning of April 1847 a subscription list was opened in Cape Town for the relief of the destitute in the highlands and islands of Scotland. A week later, on 9 April, under the secretaryship of William Porter, a subscription for the 'Starving Irish' was opened.[13] Donations once collected would be sent to the Dublin 'Trustees of the Calcutta Fund'. In his appeal for help Porter wrote that:

> all hope of preserving life in a multitude of men, women and children must either be totally abandoned or sought, under God, in the united exertions of the imperial parliament, of the comparatively affluent in Ireland itself and of those throughout the extended dominions of the Crown who recognise the law of human brotherhood . . . Horrors, enough to sicken every heart, might be accumulated without number from provincial papers and private letters.[14]

Porter's committee consisted of some of Cape Town's most prominent citizens: R. Crozier (born Ireland), postmaster-general; Edward Eagar; Hon. William Field (born Ireland), collector of customs; Rev. Robert Lamb; T.J. Mathew; J.A. Merrington; Hon. William Porter (born Ireland), attorney general; Hon. Hamilton Ross (born Ireland), merchant and member of legislative council; Howson E. Rutherford; James Searight.

At the next meeting of the committee it was agreed to send a circular letter soliciting co-operation to all the civil commissioners, resident magistrates and ministers of religion in the colony. Already £203 had been subscribed including £25 each from Porter and Galway-born merchant prince and politician, Hamilton Ross. One donation was for three guineas, being half a day's pay from the Cape Town police.[15]

How long collecting lasted is not known. By July 1847, when lists of subscriptions cease to appear in the press, a total of £2,809 had been raised.[16] As well as the wealthy and prominent; small sums came in from overseers, masons, constables, 'a maid servant' and a 'Malay collection'. Churches which gave proportions of their collections to the 'Starving Irish Committee' included the Tulbagh evangelical church, a Lutheran congregation and several Dutch reformed congregations, including one at Malmesbury. Thus rich and poor, Irish and non-Irish, English speaking and non-English speaking, white and people of mixed race, all were touched by the plight of the Famine Irish and subscribed to their relief.[17]

Most of the subscriptions came from the western Cape, but in the eastern Cape, where the Inniskillings were then stationed, there was also concern about Ireland. The *Graham's Town Journal* recorded: 'the people of this town and neighbourhood are not behind any other part of the Colony in their practical expression of sympathy towards those who are dying from the pangs of hunger, and enduring the sufferings of penury in their most aggravated form.'[18]

And in the colony of Natal, where the settler population and especially the Irish component of it was much smaller than in the Cape, the *Natal Witness* by mid-1847 was recording details of the Irish Famine. In one edition, under the headline 'To the Irishmen residing in Natal', the following appeared:

> Gentlemen
> It appears from recent accounts that our countrymen are in a state of starvation; I know it is only to mention it, and you will

come forward to assist them. A subscription list lies at my store, whatever amount may be received will be forwarded to the Hon'able Wm Porter, Esq, Her Majesty's Attorney General, Cape Town.

I am Gentlemen

Yours very obediently

W.L. Higginson.[19]

Two months later the paper announced that Rev. J.L. Doehne of the Dutch Reformed church in Pietermaritzburg would deliver a sermon in Dutch, when a collection would be made in aid of the destitute in Ireland and the highlands of Scotland.[20]

Why the Famine Irish did not come to South Africa

The words of sympathy were genuine and given the fragile economies of the two colonies, the charity generous, but the realities of colonial life, especially in Cape Town, were that mass immigration was impracticable. Two wars on the Cape's eastern frontier, one lasting from 1846 to 1847 and the other from 1850 to 1852 proved very expensive for the colony. There just were not the funds to finance large-scale immigration. The only form of immigration which the imperial authorities proposed and nearly enforced – transportation – was unacceptable to Cape Town's white society.

In September 1849 a prison hulk, the *Neptune*, sailed into Table Bay with 288 ticket-of-leave men on board. Most of them were Young Irelander revolutionaries, including the Young Ireland leader, John Mitchel. These ticket-of-leave men were meant to be widely distributed in the colony, where they could find paid employment. They would report at regular intervals to the police.

This scheme was viewed with horror in Cape Town. Convicts were to be dumped on the colony and allowed freedom to prey on the colonial community. Worse still, they were Irish rebels: 'avowed and determined enemies of the constitution, who are not infrequently possessed of great talent, energy and enterprise.'[21]

The arrival of a party of 20 young girls from Irish workhouses in November did not help dispel the impression that the 'dregs of Irish society were being dumped on the Cape'. William Porter found himself in a difficult position, having some sympathy with the protesters, but realising that the political implications of the agitation whipped up by the Anti-Convict Association would be far reaching. Convicted criminals and revolutionaries were not the Irish who Porter wanted for the Cape. In February 1850 the *Neptune* was ordered to set sail for Tasmania, thus effectively closing the Cape for mass white settlement with a substantial Irish component.[22]

The convict crisis was an unfortunate incident in many respects, for in colonial minds it connected Irish immigration with criminal activity and trouble-making. This attitude was reinforced by the Cape's experience of some limited Irish settlements in the early 1820s. In 1820 about 350 Irish settlers had been brought in under an imperial government emigration scheme. But instead of being sent to the eastern Cape with the rest of the '1820 English settlers', the Irish were directed to the semi-arid region around Clanwilliam in the northern Cape.

Not surprisingly they protested and so loudly that most were eventually moved to the eastern Cape.[23]

Three years later, in 1823, John Ingram brought in 352 destitute people from Cork. Described as 'very ignorant and illiterate' and 'much given to drunkenness', these immigrants merely served to confirm colonial reservations about poor Irish settlers.[24]

The final nail in the coffin of mass Irish immigration to South Africa was to come in the two decades after the Famine. There were more disasters, such as the scandal over the 46 single Irish women who arrived in Table Bay in 1851 on the *Gentoo* having 'mixed freely' with the crew on the voyage. All gratuities were withheld except to one steward.[25] The arrival of 153 single Irish women in the eastern Cape in 1857 on board the *Lady Kennaway* was more successful.[26]

Mrs E. Bull has estimated that between 1858 and 1862 nearly 5,000 Irish arrived at the Cape by way of emigration schemes. The various Cape immigration boards had great problems with many of these. Permits granting a passage and settlement at the Cape appear to have been sold or exchanged in Ireland. False names were used, stated occupations falsely given and the number of children understated. The Irish were accused of being dirty and unco-operative on board ship and new employers at the Cape frequently complained about the Irish labour supplied to them. In 1860 the Cape's immigration agent in London was instructed to suspend Irish immigration, though permits where the emigrant had a sponsor in the Cape were still valid. It is little wonder given the anti-Irish prejudice in the Cape that some of these unfortunate and impoverished Irish people moved on to Australia.

Mrs Bull has estimated that between 1823 and 1900 a mere 14,000 poor Irish came to the Cape under various emigration schemes.[27] This is a small number compared to the hundreds of thousands who fled Ireland for England, Scotland, North America or Australia. But the point must be made that South Africa was not a mass-destination for any emigrant in the nineteenth century.[28] In 1875 the Cape had only 28,200 first-generation immigrants, of whom the Irish were 13 per cent and in 1911 the Irish were the fifth-largest immigrant group in South Africa.

To blame the Cape's colonial population and the Cape authorities for the failure of the Famine Irish to make their way to South Africa is not wholly fair. It is true that those Irish who did come in under emigration schemes were generally looked upon with little sympathy. But it can equally be argued that there were other parts of the world where the Irish went where they were not welcomed with open arms. In essence, the Famine Irish by-passed South Africa because they specifically wanted to go elsewhere. They did not want adventure; they wanted a new life surrounded by their own people. By the time the mineral revolution took place in South Africa in the last quarter of the nineteenth century and jobs were readily available, the Irish had already established their patterns of emigration. They had family and cultural ties and support networks well developed in America and Australia. Why go into the unknown?

For some, the treatment of Irish immigrants to the Cape in the 1820s may have been a deterrent It was said in 1825 that some of the 1823 Irish settlers wrote home: 'giving a bad account of the Colony . . . that the colony was in a state of starvation and that the former emigrants only wished the government to send them to Van Dieman's Land, or some other place out of the colony.'[29]

It is, however, doubtful that this memory survived into the immediate post-famine era. By the 1850s few Irish peasants contemplating emigration would have even thought of South Africa. The *Natal Times* noted in 1852: 'The Celtic population has almost vanished from the face of the soil . . . the cry of "Ireland for the Irish" . . . is now changed to "America and Australia for the Irish!" '[30]

A quarter of a century later nothing had changed and South Africa remained *terra incognita* for the post-famine generation. The *Cape Town Daily News* put the matter in a nutshell when it concluded:

> We are afraid we could not induce the Irish labouring classes to come to this colony in anything like sufficient numbers. They know nothing of it beyond having a dim idea that it is associated with Kaffir wars; but they know all about America and Australia, or think they do, having heard them talked about from their infancy by those who had friends there – and away they pour across the Atlantic, sometimes to a glutted labour market, where they find themselves worse off than at home. There is much in a name.[31]

References

1   Recent publications on the Irish in South Africa include: D.H. Akenson, *Occasional papers on the Irish in South Africa*, (Grahamstown, 1991); D.P. McCracken (ed.), *The Irish in Southern Africa, 1785-1910*, volume 2 of *Southern African-Irish Studies* (Durban, 1992) and D.P. McCracken (ed.), *Ireland and South Africa in Modern Times*, vol. 3, *South African-Irish Studies* (1996).

2   D.P. McCracken, 'Irish settlement and identity in South Africa before 1910, *Irish Historical Studies*, 28, no. 110 (1992), pp. 134-49.

3   D.P. McCracken, 'The Irish in South Africa: The police, a case study', *Familia*, 2, no.2 (1991), pp. 40-6.

4   For the Irish in the British army in South Africa, see S. Monick, *Shamrock and Springbok* (Johannesburg, 1989).

5   To date no lives of Upington or Hime have been written. For Porter, see J.L. McCracken, *New Light at the Cape: William Porter. the father of Cape liberalism* (Belfast, 1993).

6   N.D. Southey, 'Dogged entrepreneurs: Some prominent Irish retailers', in *SAIS*, 2 (1992), pp. 163-78.

7   D.P. McCracken, 'The Irish Transvaal Brigades, *SAIS*, 2 (1992), pp. 54-72.

8   M. Staunton, 'Boer war memorials in Ireland', in *SAIS*, 3 (1996), pp. 290-304. See also D.P. McCracken, *The Irish Pro-Boers, 1888-1902* (Johannesburg, 1989), p. 167.

9   D.H. Akenson, *The Irish diaspora: A primer* (Toronto and Belfast, 1993), chapter 5; and Akenson, *Occasional papers*, p. 41.

10 *The Porter speeches* (Cape Town, 1886), pp. xli-ii.

11 *South African Commercial Advertiser*, 29 August 1846.

12 *South African Commercial Advertiser*, 17 October 1846.

13 *South African Commercial Advertiser*, 3 April 1847.

14 *South African Commercial Advertiser*, 10 April 1847.

15 *South African Commercial Advertiser*, 14 April 1847.

16 *South African Commercial Advertiser*, 17 July 1847.

17   *South African Commercial Advertiser*, 24 and 28 April and 1, 3, 15 May 1847.

18   *Graham's Town Journal*, 1 May 1847.

19   *Natal Witness*, 28 May 1847.

20   *Natal Witness*, 23 July 1847.

21   *British Parliamentary Papers*, 1849, xliii (217), p.22; and A. F. Hattersley, *The convict crisis and the growth of unity* (Pietermaritzburg, 1965), p. 13.

22   Ralph Kilpin, *The romance of a colonial Parliament* (London, 1930), pp. 69-70.

23   G. B. Dickason, *Irish Settlers to the Cape: A history of the Clanwilliam 1820 settlers from Cork Harbour* (Cape Town, 1973).

24   George Theal, *Records of the Cape Colony*, xviii, 186-8, 199, 256 (1824); xxi, 262, 435 (1825); xxvi, 316, 363, 421 (1826).

25   E. Bull, 'Aided Irish immigration to the Cape, 1823-1900'. *SAIS*, 2 (1992), p. 271.

26   K. P. T. Tankard, 'The Lady Kennaway girls', *SAIS*, 2 (1992), pp. 278-86.

27   These figures do not include those Irish emigrants who paid their own passage to South Africa.

28   Further proposals for Irish emigration to Natal in 1855 and 1857 came to nothing. See KwaZulu-Natal Archives, Ladysmith magistrate letterbook, 1854-62, 1/LDS; 3/1/1/4, .ff. 260-3.

29   Theal, *Records of the Cape Colony. April-June 1825*, vol. xxi, p. 452.

30   *Natal Times*, 19 November 1852.

31   *Cape Town Daily News*, 2 February 1876.

'The Scattered Debris of the Irish Nation': The Famine Irish and New York City, 1845–55

Edward O'Donnell

> We regret to have to state that we have had communications
> from more than one well-informed correspondent, announcing
> of the appearance of what is called 'cholera' in the potatoes in
> Ireland, especially in the north. In one instance the party had
> been digging potatoes-the finest he had ever seen-from a
> particular field . . . up to Monday last. On digging in the same
> [field] on Tuesday he found the tubers unfit for the use of man
> or beast. We are most anxious to receive information as to the
> state of the potato crop in all parts, for the purpose either of
> allaying unnecessary alarm, or giving timely warning.

THUS DID THE PEOPLE of New York City receive, in the 4 October 1845 edition of the *Tribune*, the first indication of Ireland's impending disaster. As more information regarding the failure of the potato crop reached New York City, it quickly became apparent that the 'alarm' was not 'unnecessary'. As for the prospect of giving 'timely warning', the size and scope of the Famine devastation rendered any such effort virtually meaningless. No amount of warning could have prepared Ireland for what lay ahead in the coming 'hungry years'.

The same must be said for the societies which experienced the profound secondary effects of the Famine: cities like Liverpool, Boston, and New York which took in the millions of Irish fleeing starvation and death in their native land. As the steady stream of immigrants from Ireland became a torrent, then a deluge, these receptive cities experienced far-reaching social, cultural, political and economic change. By the mid-1850s it became clear to many that neither New York, nor its new Irish residents, would ever be the same again.

The focus of this paper is the impact of the Famine immigration on the largest metropolis in North America, New York City. No city in the nineteenth century, let alone the Famine years, received more emigrants from Ireland. Though the great majority moved on from New York to other parts of the nation, hundreds of thousands remained, making New York City by mid-century not simply America's most Irish city, but the *world's*, with an Irish-born population (203,000) in 1860 greater than that in Dublin or Cork or Belfast.[1]

It should go without saying that given the sheer volume of the Famine immigration, New York City was forever changed. The scope, nature and significance of that change constitutes the heart of this paper, though not its sole purpose. For just as the Famine emigration had a lasting impact on the city, so too did the city have a profound impact upon the Irish and the long-term American perception of them.

I

Perhaps the most significant fact regarding New York City on the eve of the Famine is that in 1845 it already was an 'Irish City'. Although New York's history as a colony is marked by the presence of a few notable figures of Irish ancestry, the beginnings of a recognizable pre-Famine Irish community can be dated to 1798. The ill-fated rising of that year produced a significant number of refugees to New York City, among them leaders like Dr William James MacNevin, William Sampson, and Thomas Addis Emmet, brother of the legendary martyred nationalist Robert Emmet.[2] Together they worked to develop a series of social, charitable, religious, and ethnic institutions dedicated to assisting the fledgling Irish community which grew appreciably after the cessation of the Napoleonic Wars. The city's first Irish newspaper, the *Shamrock* or *Hibernian Chronicle*, appeared in 1810 providing news from Ireland and practical advice to the Irish living in New York City. In 1814 the Irish Emigrant Society opened to offer assistance to the newly arrived. The following year the newly established Catholic diocese of New York opened its first cathedral, named in honour of Ireland's patron saint St Patrick. Other agencies like the Society of the Friendly Sons of St Patrick, founded in the late eighteenth century, grew in this period to assume a wide range of charitable activities.[3]

In contrast to those who would arrive at mid-century, many of the Irish who came during these first decades of the nineteenth century found New York City a place of optimism and opportunity, even if tempered by the melancholy of exile. Unlike those who would flee Ireland during the Famine, these emigrants arrived to find a smaller, less tumultuous New York City. They also brought with them greater capital and occupational skills – fully 48 per cent of Irish arrivals in 1826 were artisans (versus 28 per cent unskilled). 'As yet it's only natural I should feel lonesome in this country, ninety-nine out of every hundred who come to it are at first disappointed', wrote John Doyle to his wife in 1818. '. . . Still, it's a fine country and a much better place for a poor man than Ireland . . . and much as they grumble at first, after a while they never think of leaving it.' Doyle never did and went on to develop a prosperous career as a book seller.[4]

Emigration from Ireland to New York grew steadily through the 1820s as British free trade policies crushed Irish craft industries, most especially linens and textiles, and high rents and land enclosures drove many peasants off the land. Increased trade between Ireland and New York and Liverpool and New York encouraged emigration by lowering the cost of passenger travel. As more and more Irish arrived, they began to make a visible impact upon the city's economy. 'Is not this city prospering and growing by the labour of the poor Irish,' queried William Sampson, 'who swell the capital of our rich proprietors by their hard and daily work? Do they not help to dig our canals, and to erect our works of defence?' Even among those who disliked the Irish, the evidence of the latter's positive impact upon the city's economy was undeniable.[5]

In the 1830s the number and character of Irish immigrants to the city changed markedly. Whereas in previous decades most emigrants from Ireland were Protestants of modest means from Ulster, the overwhelming majority thereafter arrived as poor Catholics mainly from the South and West of Ireland.[6] Over 200,000 Irish emigrants landed at the Port of New York in the 1830s, pushing the city's Irish population to nearly 50,000 by the early 1840s.[7] By that time the institutional network of the Irish community included two newspapers, the Emigrant Aid Society, the recently founded Ancient Order of Hibernians (1836), one notable Irish theatre (Niblo's), and the ten Catholic parishes with affiliated schools, orphanages, and temperance societies. Thus, from an institutional standpoint, it would appear that New York's Irish community was well established on the eve of the Great Famine.[8]

Yet social history that relies on measures of institutional growth is both superficial and misleading. Closer analysis of the Irish community of New York on the eve of the Famine makes clear the fact that the poverty and discrimination faced by the majority of pre-Famine Irish immigrants rendered their charitable, ethnic, and religious institutions barely able to cope. Cast as poor, mostly illiterate, rural people into the swirling, expanding cauldron that was New York City, a large proportion of the pre-Famine Irish found themselves forced to take the lowest-paying and hardest work. Unable to afford decent housing and seeking the comfort of familiar faces, they crowded into Manhattan's lower wards where disease, crime, violence, and mortality rose to unheard of rates. Cholera epidemics claimed the lives of thousands in 1837 and 1842. Riots, at the centre of which were the Irish, broke out in 1834, 1835, 1837, and 1844.[9]

By 1840 a particularly treacherous section of the Sixth Ward, the Five Points, achieved a national reputation. Indeed, it became notorious *internationally*, for when he visited New York in 1842 on his tour of America, Charles Dickens insisted on taking a guided tour of the area, accompanied by a police escort. He recorded his observations in a travelogue entitled *American Notes*, published the following year.

> There is one quarter, commonly called the Five Points, which in respect of filth and wretchedness, may be safely backed against Seven Dials, or any other part of famed St. Giles . . . These narrow ways, diverging to the right and left, and reeking everywhere with dirt and filth. Such lives as are led here, bear the same fruits here as elsewhere. The coarse and bloated faces at the doors, have counterparts at home, and all the wide world over. Debauchery has made the very houses prematurely old. See how the rotten beams are tumbling down, and how the patched and broken windows seem to scowl dimly, like eyes that have been hurt in drunken frays. Many of those pigs live here. Do they ever wonder why their masters walk upright in lieu of going on all-fours? And why they talk instead of grunting?[10]

The horror and contempt expressed by Dickens for the poor Irish of New York was shared by a great many of the city's native-born inhabitants. On occasion this sentiment led to violence against the Irish, as in 1831 when a mob set fire to St Mary's Church, built only five years before and symbolic of the city's growing Irish and *Catholic* presence. Soon the city's vast publishing network began producing some of the best-selling literature of the era – salacious accounts of murderous priests, seduced nuns, and papal plots to send the Irish as the advance guard in a planned invasion of America. One of the leading practitioners of this genre was Samuel F.B. Morse, a man far better known for his career as an artist and perfecter of the telegraph.[11] In 1842 the Irish and their leaders clashed with city officials over the presence of an anti-Catholic curriculum in the public schools and the possible use of public funds for parochial schools.[12] Two years later James Harper was elected Mayor as a staunch advocate of municipal reform, a programme which included establishing a professional police force, mandating regular street cleaning, the prohibiting of wandering pigs from the streets, and ridding the city of the Irish. That election, coupled with word of a deadly riot against the Irish in nearby Philadelphia which left eighteen dead and two churches destroyed, brought tensions to the breaking point. Archbishop Hughes, self-appointed defender of the Irish Catholic flock challenged Harper to rein in his nativist supporters declaring that 'if a single Catholic church is burned in New York, the city will become a second Moscow.' These were chilling words for those who remembered that only thirty years earlier Moscow burned to the ground before Napoleon's invading legions. The message was clear: all that we ask is to be left alone; but if provoked we will fight back and the results will be grave.[13]

Thus even before the first refugees from the Famine debarked at the Port of New York, they faced two formidable problems: one, an Irish community already hard pressed to provide social services and relief to its less fortunate numbers, and two, a hostile host society that had all but fixed its opinion of the Irish as a dangerous, unassimilable, seditious, and utterly undesirable group.

Then in 1845 'the blight' struck Ireland's potato crop, opening one of the most harrowing chapters in recent human history.[14] Many Irish in New York learned of the crisis from local newspapers, both Irish and American. Doubtless, however, most gained such knowledge through letters from loved ones back in Ireland. 'My dear brother I suppose you have heard of the very great failure of Ireland,' wrote John Frazer to his brother in New York in 1847. '[Y]ou cannot compare it to anything more properly than the seize of Jerusalem[;] people are dying so fast with perfect hunger that we cannot attend to see them perfectly inter[r]ed [.T]he crops failing in Ireland this season has left it in the greatest distress.'[15] Not surprisingly, the Irish of New York responded immediately, sending over $800,000 to relatives in 1846 alone. Still, more than a million perished and an equivalent number fled their native land as immigrants, some to England, Canada, Australia, and Latin America, but most to America and its first city, New York.[16]

A brief recitation of the figures is sufficient to convey the magnitude of the Famine emigration to New York. Whereas, Irish immigrant arrivals in 1840 numbered 25,000, they soared in 1847 to roughly 53,000, 113,000 in 1849, and 163,000 in 1851 as shown in Table 1. All told nearly 850,000 Irish entered America through the port of New York between 1847 and 1851, and the numbers continued to average more than 60,000 per annum up to 1860.

Table 1: Irish Arrivals at the Port of New York, 1847–60

Year	Number	Year	Number
1847	52,946	1854	82,302
1848	91,061	1855	43,043
1849	112,591	1856	44,276
1850	117,038	1857	57,119
1851	163,306	1858	25,075
1852	118,131	1859	32,652
1853	113,164	1860	47,330

TOTAL : 1,100,034

While most Irish moved on almost immediately, those that stayed contributed to a demographic revolution in the nation's largest city. It is not enough to say that New York's Irish-born population rose to 175,000 by 1855. That figure becomes magnified in significance when one realizes that it represented 28 per cent of the city's population. Quite suddenly then, the largest city in America had been transformed, from a metropolis in 1840 which was approximately 15 per cent Irish and 25 per cent Roman Catholic, to one in 1855 that was approaching one-third Irish and 50 per cent Roman Catholic. And one must bear in mind the fact that the former figure is for Irish-born residents, and does not include the tens of thousands of persons born in the city of Irish parentage who appear in the census as 'American'.[17] 'There are portions of New York,' noted one visitor in 1860, '. . . where the population is as thoroughly Irish as in Dublin or Cork.'[18] Perhaps, thought many a New Yorker by the mid-1850s, Morse's warnings of a secret papal plot to take over America seemed not so far-fetched after all.

As with the large pre-Famine immigration, the impact of the Famine-era Irish in New York City is only barely conveyed by the raw numbers. A more intensive examination of the Famine Irish paints a vivid picture of a population that would have been hard pressed to survive in New York even if they had emigrated without the dreadful effects of the Famine all too apparent.

Perhaps the most striking feature of the Famine Irish in New York is the remarkable degree to which they – as a people fleeing starvation – arrived so ill-equipped to earn a living. That situation was not of their making, but rather the logical result of taking masses of pre-industrial rural peasants with little or no knowledge of the world outside their village in Connacht and depositing them pell-mell into an environment not only distant and foreign, but also urban, capitalist, and dynamic.

Specifically, the Irish arrived in New York City to an alarming extent bereft of the two essential ingredients for economic success: occupational skills and surplus capital. Whereas only 28 per cent of Irish immigrants arriving in 1826 were unskilled labourers, sixty per cent were by 1836, a figure which grew in the next decade.[19] This general characteristic of the Famine Irish as a whole was made more extreme in New York City by the fact that those who *did* possess money and/or skills were the most likely to move on. 'The pith and marrow of Ireland', commented the *Irish-American* in 1849, 'averaging between 100 and 5,000 dollars per family, have arrived within the past two years, in our seaboard cities. These emigrants do not stop in cities to spend their money and fool away their time. They go directly into the interior to seek out the best location as farmers, traders, and so forth.' Other contemporary assessments echoed similar, if less judgemental, conclusions, noting that 'Irish emigrants of the peasant and labouring class were generally poor, and after defraying their first expenses on landing had but little left to enable them to push their way into the country in search of such employment as was best suited to their knowledge and capacity.'[20]

Those who remained in New York City enjoyed few occupational choices. By the mid-1850s, fully 60 per cent of Irish-born men and women in New York worked either as unskilled labourers or in domestic service, occupations that paid very little and, in the case of men, often suffered from seasonal or quixotic disruptions. Furthermore, in terms of all foreign-born workers, the Irish truly dominated these two fields – 87 per cent of foreign-born labourers and 89 nine per cent of foreign-born domestics came from Ireland. The overwhelming image of Paddy the hod carrier and Bridget the laundress served to solidify the stereotype of the Irish as mentally suited for only menial labour.[21] Compounding this problem was widespread discrimination. Because domestic work brought them into the homes of the native-born, Irish women more often than men were confronted with signs and advertisements such as the following from a New York newspaper in 1840:

> WANTED – An English or American woman, that understands cooking, and to assist in the work generally if wished; also a girl to do chamber work. None need apply without a recommendation from their last place. IRISH PEOPLE need not apply, nor anyone who will not arise at 6 o'clock, as the work is light and the wages are sure. Inquire 359 Broadway.[22]

Irish men, too, faced the sting of discrimination in the workplace, but for different reasons. Irish immigration, asserted one report, undercut the livelihoods of the city's 'native labouring and mechanic classes' by 'crowding them out of employment, and diminishing the rewards of industry. Needy foreigners accustomed to live upon less than our own countrymen, are enabled to produce articles cheaper and to work for lower wages.'[23] Thus, for the Famine Irish in New York, the challenge of earning a living included far more than simply securing a steady job.

The confinement of the majority of the Famine Irish to such poorly paid and sporadic work was the single-greatest contributor to another dominant aspect of the Famine experience in New York – deplorable living conditions. As bad as Five Points was when Charles Dickens visited in 1842, by 1850 it was far worse. 'It is but truth to say,' commented Archbishop Hughes, 'that their abode in the cellars and garrets of New York is not more deplorable nor more squalid than the Irish hovels from which many of them had been 'exterminated [by the British]'.[24] The governors of the public alms house reported that between 1849 and 1858 the Irish accounted for 63 per cent of admissions (18,498 persons). Statistics such as this also hardened stereotypes about the Irish, particularly because they afforded the opportunity to make stark comparisons between the Irish and their other immigrant counterparts, the Germans. In the aforementioned category of assistance, Germans accounted for a mere 4.7 per cent of admissions.[25] 'We, as a people', commented the *Christian Examiner*,

> are intolerant of ragged garments and empty paunches. We are a people who have had no experience in physical tribulation. As a consequence, the ill-clad and destitute Irishman is repulsive to our habits and our tastes. We confound ill-clothing and destitution with ignorance and vice.[26]

Not surprisingly the categories of social distress noted in the pre-Famine Irish community also grew worse. The poor health of the Irish community declined further, in part due to the sheer numbers of destitute people crowding into deplorable housing, in part also because of malnutrition and disease associated with the Famine. As the newspaper *Courier* observed in 1847:

> The ship fever, that cruel scourge of the poor emigrant, starved to death before embarking, and provided [for] in some cases

afterwards, worse than the African slave in the slave ship, has made its way notwithstanding the Quarantine Station and Hospital [on Staten Island], to this city and has made great havoc among the emigrants in the lower part of the city.

The cholera epidemic of 1849, which many attributed to Irish Famine sufferers, claimed over 4,000 lives, 44 per cent of whom were Irish. Infant mortality was high, often claiming the lives of more than one-third of children under age five. On a more broad level, for the next decade at the city's public hospital, Bellevue, 85 per cent of the foreign-born admissions were Irish. It is hard to conjure up a more tragic image than that of the countless men and women – the 'scattered debris of the Irish nation' according to Archbishop John Hughes – who survived the ravages of Famine and disease in Ireland and the privations of a long journey across the Atlantic, only to die weeks later of dysentery or tuberculosis in New York City.[27]

Crime and disorder followed poverty and disease. Of those arrested in the 1850s fifty-five per cent were born in Ireland, and lest one attribute that to anti-Irish prejudice, one needs to bear in mind that 27 per cent of the city's police force was Irish-born. Of the 2,000 women prostitutes arrested in 1858, 706 (35 per cent) had been born in Ireland. Street gangs bearing such colourful names as the Plug Uglies, Kerryonians, and Whyos emerged at this time and were predominantly of Irish background. The riots of the 1830s paled by comparison with those that occurred in 1849, 1857 and 1863, the latter being the notorious Draft Riots which claimed well over 100 lives.[28]

In response to these many trials, the Irish of New York strengthened existing institutions like the Catholic church and created new ones to fill crucial voids. Between 1845 and 1865 seventeen new parishes were established in Manhattan, providing for both the spiritual as well as the material well-being of their surging immigrant congregations. New Catholic colleges of St Francis Xavier (Jesuits, 1847) and Manhattan College (Christian Brothers, 1849) along with recently established St John's (Jesuit, 1841) began to educate young men for the professions as well as the priesthood, though the latter's increased numbers barely kept pace with the growth of the Catholic population.[29] Irish Catholic lay men and women founded in 1846 the Society of St Vincent de Paul and in 1849 the Sisters of Charity established the city's first Catholic hospital, St Vincent's. In that same year the Irish community welcomed a new newspaper, the *Irish-American*, as well as a Catholic Temperance Society and the first of many Irish County Societies (Sligo) which served both a charitable and cultural role.[30]

As the Irish grappled with the difficulties of Famine-induced immigration and settlement, New Yorkers by the mid-1850s struggled to explain how and why their city had been transformed. *Harper's Weekly* captured the sentiments of many when it editorialized on the demise of New York since the 1830s. 'What was then a decent and orderly town of moderate size, has been converted into a huge, semi-barbarous metropolis – one half as luxurious and artistic as Paris, the other half as savage as Cairo or Constantinople – not well-governed, not ill-governed, but simply not governed at all.' To no one's surprise *Harper's*, published by former Mayor and James Harper, laid the blame for these developments squarely on the shoulders of the Irish.[31]

II

Clearly, life for the Famine Irish was marked by trial and struggle. Nonetheless, a survey of the many pathologies which afflicted the Famine Irish and their efforts to overcome them serves only a limited purpose. To begin with, it obscures the fact that not all the Irish in New York in the 1840s and 1850s were destitute. In fact, successful Irish men and women could be found in virtually every aspect of New York City society. The example of merchant Alexander T. Stewart is instructive on this point. Born in Ulster, he emigrated to New York City in the 1820s and became a fabulously successful retailer specializing in fine ladies' clothing. His famed 'Marble Palace' at Broadway and Chambers Street was constructed in 1846 by John McGlynn (father of the later famous Fr McGlynn of St Stephen's Church), one of many successful Irish contractors at the time. Finally, Stewart also relied on skilled Irish seamstresses to produce his fine line of clothing. These and many other upwardly mobile Irish immigrants and Irish-Americans living in New York City offset the image of the poor Famine immigrant and provided the financial backing for many of the aforementioned charitable relief efforts.[32]

An exclusive focus on the struggle of the Famine Irish in New York also obscures the larger impact of their arrival on the city. First, it is important to consider that the other side of Irish dominance in back-breaking menial labour was its essential contribution to the rapid growth of the metropolis. At the risk of oversimplification, from a purely economic standpoint, in the American South it was the labour of enslaved Africans that made possible the Cotton Kingdom; in the north it was the sweated labour of immigrants, mostly Irish, that made possible the industrial revolution.

Second, the Irish arrived in New York at precisely the time that all white men were extended the franchise. In cities, as Amy Bridges has pointed out, this meant the birth of the political machine and so-called 'ward politics.' Although the Irish did not invent the political machine, they did become its most vital cogs, first in the Famine era as voters, later as leaders who dominated the city's political structure. So successful were the Irish in attaining political power by the 1870s, that leading politicians in New York State seriously considered depriving the poor [i.e., the Irish] of the vote.[33]

Third, the massive introduction of Catholic Irish to New York City had far-reaching implications for American Catholicism. The intensity of the anti-Catholicism experienced by the Irish in New York shaped the form of Catholicism they developed. Led by their stalwart, if confrontational, Archbishop John Hughes, New York's Irish Catholics developed an inward-focused and defensive Catholic culture and institutional network, the cornerstone of which was the parish school. While such a system of separate schools offered many tangible and psychological benefits in the short run, critics then and now argued that in the long run it inhibited the full participation of Irish-Americans in American life by fostering insecurity and localism.[34]

A fourth impact was the development, refinement and distribution nation-wide of the brutal stereotypes of the Irish. With its more than 100 newspapers and 50 magazines in the 1850s, not to mention its near corner on book publishing, New York City virtually created and then sold to the rest of America the image of the Irish as violent, criminal, drunken, venal papists. Even as late as 1928, the year Al Smith became the first Irish Catholic candidate for president, mainstream newspapers and magazines continued to publish derogatory and demeaning cartoons of Smith and his Irish supporters.[35]

Fifth, the extreme experience of the Famine Irish in New York greatly shaped their self-perception and world-view. If ever there was a prime example of Kerby Miller's thesis of a bitter, 'exile' consciousness developing in America, New York City certainly provided it. Here the Famine generation endured both economic deprivation and discrimination at the hands of people striking for their similarities to the British back home.[36]

Finally, I would argue that the Famine Irish arrival had two additional, long-range results, one in terms of historiography, the other in terms of national experience and memory. The emergence of the study of immigration history in the United States began in 1941 with the publication of Oscar Handlin's groundbreaking study of the Boston Irish. Armed with new-found statistical methods Handlin painted a grim picture of desperate immigrants, horrible living conditions, and violent discrimination.[37] His work was followed by similar studies of the Irish in Philadelphia, New York, Jersey City and other east coast metropolises, all of which dramatized the legion of obstacles that confronted the Irish and the long uphill struggle they waged to achieve economic and social success. In a word, the historic image of Five Points was so intense that it dominated for decades the historical interpretation of the Irish experience in America as a whole. Appropriately, scholarship in the last fifteen years has uncovered a geographically, economically, and socially diverse Irish-American experience. The varied stories of the Irish who passed through New York – to cities like Pittsburgh, Albany, Detroit, Cleveland, St Louis, New Orleans, Denver, Butte, and San Francisco – is one full of exceptions to the east coast, New York model. In many cases, the Irish there experienced less discrimination, less poverty, and faster upward mobility and political empowerment, and often with a less dominant political machine or Catholic Church. The Five Points experience, we now know, formed but *one of many* aspects of the overall Irish migration during the Great Famine.[38]

The experience of Famine-era Irish in New York City also opened a new and central chapter in American political culture and society. In a word, the Irish arrival prepared the United States for the successive waves of immigrants to come. The cultural, economic, religious, and political changes brought to the nation's Empire City by the Irish hegira raised the critical questions of ethnic diversity, religious tolerance, and cultural pluralism. The city's initial answers – riot, slander and calls for restriction – caused pain, but ultimately failed in the face of an emergent political creed of inclusion. By the turn of the century New York City had all but forgotten about the 'Celtic Menace.' Instead the same language of fear and derogation now focused on the Italian and the Jew. And yet forty years would pass – and 20 million immigrants arrive – before nativists achieved immigration restriction (1921). Even in curtailing immigration and extending preferences to some groups over others, they left intact the tradition and principle of continuous and diverse flow of immigration.

Tellingly, the traditions of toleration and acceptance established (however begrudgingly) in the wake of the Famine Irish arrival proved stronger than those of fear and restriction. The restrictions on immigration lasted only 40 years and were repealed in 1965 in favour of a system more equal and magnanimous (at least initially). Time will tell if these traditions will prevail yet again as the United States enters its newest phase of anti-immigration sentiment. Given the fact that so many of the legacies of the Famine in Ireland and America were tragic, the establishment and perpetuation of the principle of ethnic inclusion would be a fitting legacy for those who overcame suffering and death and arrived in New York City hoping for a second chance.

References

1 Ira Rosenwaike, *Population History of New York City* (Syracuse, 1972), p. 42.

2 See Nancy J. Curtin, *The United Irishmen* (New York, 1994); Thomas Addis Emmet, *Incidents in My Life* (New York, 1911); William Sampson, *Memoirs of William Sampson* (New York, 1807); Walter J. Walsh, 'Religion Ethnicity and History: Clues to the Cultural Construction of Law', in Ronald H. Bayor and Timothy J. Meagher (eds), *The New York Irish* (Baltimore, 1996).

3 John P. O'Connor, 'The Shamrock of New York: The First Irish-American Newspaper,' *New York Irish History*, 4, pp. 4-5; Thomas F. Meehan, 'New York's First Irish Emigrant Society', *U.S. Catholic Historical Records and Studies*, VI, part II (1912); Richard J. Purcell, 'The Irish Emigrant Society of New York', *Studies*, XXVII, no. 108 (1938), pp. 585-587; Richard C. Murphy and Lawrence J. Mannion, *History of the Friendly Sons of Saint Patrick in the City of New York, 1784-1955* (New York, 1962), pp. 20-32; John M. Farley, *The History of St Patrick's Cathedral* (New York, 1908); Kevin G. Kenny, 'Religion and Immigration: The Irish Community in New York City, 1815-1840', *The Recorder*, III, no. 8 (1989).

4 Kerby A. Miller, *Emigrants and Exiles: Ireland and the Irish Exodus to North America* (New York & Oxford, 1985), pp. 195-6; Letter of John Doyle, Irish immigrant living in New York City, to his wife in Ireland, January 25, 1818, quoted in William D. Griffin, *The Book of Irish Americans* (New York, 1990), p. 119.

5 Robert G. Albion, *The Rise of New York Port, 1815-1860*, (New York, 1939), pp. 57-8, 336-341; Robert Ernst, *Immigrant Life in New York City, 1825-1863* (New York, 1949), pp. 5-6, 187; Sampson quote from George W. Potter, *To The Golden Door: The Story of the Irish in Ireland and America* (Boston, 1960), p.219.

6 K. Miller, *Emigrants and Exiles*, pp. 193-205.

7 Roger Daniels, *Coming to America: A History of Immigration and Ethnicity in American Life* (New York, 1990), p. 129; Rosenwaike, *Population History of New York City*, p. 53.

8 Jay P. Dolan, *The Immigrant Church: New York's Irish and German Catholics, 1815-1865* (South Bend, 1975), pp. 13-14; Ernst, *Immigrant Life*, pp. 150-1.

9 Charles Rosenberg, *The Cholera Years: The United States in 1832, 1849, and 1866* (Chicago, 1962), *passim*; Paul Gilje, *The Road to Mobocracy: Popular Disorder in New York City, 1763-1834* (Chapel Hill, 1987); Joel T Headley, *The Great Riots of New York, 1712-1873* (New York, 1973, reprint: Indianapolis, 1970).

10 Charles Dickens, *American Notes* (London, 1842), pp. 88-9.

11 Samuel F. B. Morse, *The Foreign Conspiracy Against the Liberties of the United States* (New York, 1835) and *The Imminent Dangers to the Free Institutions of the United States*

Through Foreign Immigration (New York, 1835). Other anti-Catholic, anti-Irish books of that era include: Maria Monk, *The Awful Disclosures of Maria Monk* (New York, 1836); Rebecca Reed, *Six Months in A Convent* (1835); Samuel B. Smith, *The Downfall of Babylon, or the Triumph of Truth over Popery* (New York, 1833).

12 Diane Ravitch, *The Great School Wars: New York City, 1805-1973* (New York, 1974), pp.33-91; Dolan, *The Immigrant Church*, pp. 104-105.

13 Leo Hershkowitz, 'The Native American Democratic Association of New York City, 1835-1836', *New-York Historical Society Quarterly* (1962), pp.51-54; Richard Shaw, *Dagger John: The Unquiet Life and Times of Archbishop John Hughes of New York* (New York, 1977), p. 197; Michael Feldberg, *The Philadelphia Riots of 1844: A Study of Ethnic Conflict* (Westport, 1975); Ira M. Leonard, 'The Rise and Fall of the American Republican Party in New York City, 1843-1845', *New-York Historical Society Quarterly*, 50, no.2, (1966), pp. 151-192; James Hennessey, S.J., *American Catholics: A History of the Roman Catholic Community in the United States* (New York, 1981), pp. 122-126.

14 Cecil Woodham-Smith, *The Great Hunger* (London, 1962); Robert Dudley Edwards and T. Desmond Williams (eds), *The Great Famine: Studies in Irish History, 1845-1852* (Dublin, 1956).

15 Letter of John Frazer in Ireland to his brother Fitzgerald Frazer in New York City, 1847, quoted in *New York Irish History*, 9 (1995), p. 12.

16 Ernst, *Immigrant Life in New York City*, p. 122; Miller, *Emigrants and Exiles*, pp. 280-286.

17 Ernst, *Immigrant Life in New York City*, p. 188; Rosenwaike, *Population History of New York City*, p. 41 and 53.

18 Thomas L. Nichols, *Forty Years of American Life*, 2 (New York, 1968, reprint of 1864 original), p. 69.

19 Miller, *Emigrants and Exiles*, pp. 195-196.

20 *Irish American*, August 26, 1849, quoted in Ernst, *Immigrant Life in New York City*, p. 62; John Francis Maguire, *The Irish In America*, (1868), pp. 214-15; Hasia Diner, ' "The Most Irish City in the Union":The Era of the Great Migration, 1844-1877', in Ronald H. Bayor and Timothy J. Meagher (eds), *The New York Irish*, p. 91.

21 Ernst, *Immigrant Life in New York City*, p. 219.

22 Ernst, *Immigrant Life in New York City*, p. 67.

23 Association for the Improvement of the Condition of the Poor, *Ninth Annual Report* (1852), p. 22, quoted in Ernst, *Immigrant Life in New York City*, p. 103.

24 Dolan, *The Immigrant Church*, p. 37.

25 Ernst, *Immigrant Life in New York City*, p. 201.

26 *Christian Examiner*, 1848, quoted in Griffin, p. 49.

27 John Ridge, 'The Great Hunger in New York', *New York Irish History*, 9 (1995), pp. 5-12; Carl Wittke, *The Irish in America: A Political and Social Portrait* (Baton Rouge, 1956), p. 42; Ernst, *Immigrant Life in New York City*, pp. 52-54; other indications of the ill-health of the Irish abound. For example, 70 per cent of the foreign-born admissions to the city's mental hospital in the 1850s were Irish (Ernst, p. 54). The overall death rate of the Irish in 1850 was 43 per cent higher than that of their German neighbours. (Rosenwaike, p. 41.)

28 Ernst, *Immigrant Life in New York City*, pp. 58, 203; Edward K. Spann, *The New Metropolis: New York City, 1840-1857* (New York, 1981) pp. 316, 440; Herbert Asbury, *The Gangs of New York* (New York, 1928), *passim*. For full accounts of the many riots, see: Iver Bernstein, *The New York City Draft Riots: Their Significance for*

American Society and Politics in the Age of the Civil War (New York, 1990); Adrian Cook, *Armies of the Streets: The New York City Draft Riots of 1863* (Lexington, 1974); Joel T. Headley, *The Great Riots of New York, 1712-1873* (New York, 1970, reprint of 1873 edition); Richard Moody, *The Astor Place Riot* (Bloomington, 1918).

29 Despite church building efforts, the size of the average parish grew from 8,500 in 1840 to 11,000 in 1865. The ratio of priests to parishioners remained constant at one priest for every 8,500. Dolan, pp. 13, 66.

30 Dolan, *The Immigrant Church*, pp. 13, 112-13, 121-4; Bernadette McCauley, 'Taking Care of their own: Irish Catholics, Health Care and Saint Vincent's Hospital, 1850-1900', *New York Irish History*, 8 (1993-94), pp. 51-54; John Ridge, *Sligo in New York: The Irish from County Sligo 1849-1991* (New York, 1991, passim).

31 Spann, *The New Metropolis*, pp. 315.

32 Diner, "The Most Irish City in the Union", pp. 95-97.

33 Oliver E. Allen, *The Tiger: The Rise and Fall of Tammnay Hall* (New York, 1993); Amy Bridges, *A City in the Republic: Antebellum New York and the Origin of Machine Politics* (Cambridge, 1984); Steven P. Erie, *Rainbow's End: Irish- Americans and the Dilemmas of Urban Machine Politics, 1840-1985* (Berkeley, 1988).

34 Leonard Riforgiato, 'Bishop John Timon, Archbishop John Hughes, and Irish Colonization: A Clash of Episcopal Views on the Future of the Irish and the Catholic Church in America', in William Pencak, et al. (eds), *Immigration to New York* (Philadelphia, 1990), *passim*.

35 For more on the dominance of New York City in media and printing, see Edward Spann, *The New Metropolis*, pp. 406-7.

36 Miller, *Emigrants and Exiles*, pp. 338-44.

37 Oscar Handlin, *Boston's Immigrants: A Study In Acculturation* (Cambridge, Mass., 1941).

38 Donald H. Akenson, 'The Historiography of the Irish in the United States of America', in Patrick O'Sullivan (ed.), *The Irish in New Communities*, (New York, 1993).

The Great Famine and Women's Emigration from Ireland

Janet Nolan

THE GREAT FAMINE of the late 1840s accelerated long term demographic and economic changes in Irish life. While the Famine affected men and women alike, it had greater impact on women in terms of their social and economic roles in Ireland and their subsequent mass migration abroad. Nevertheless, only recently have historians linked the demographic and economic changes accelerated by the Famine to the new patterns of women's emigration from Ireland in the late nineteenth and early twentieth centuries. Until the late 1970s, for instance, just a few classic studies of Irish emigration such as W.F Adams's, *Ireland and the Irish Emigration to the New World from 1815 to the Famine* and Arnold Schrier's, *Ireland and the American Emigration, 1850-1900* existed at all and these works did not focus on the unique aspects of women's emigration in the wake of the Famine.[1] The lives of Irish women before their emigration were also understudied until Margaret MacCurtain and Donncha Ó Corráin's pioneering, *Women in Irish Society: The Historical Dimension* appeared in 1979.[2]

Beginning in the 1980s, however, the study of Irish emigration history took off. In that decade, path-breaking works such as those of David Fitzpatrick and Kerby Miller offered fresh viewpoints about Irish emigration. Books emphasizing Irish women's emigration, such as Hasia Diner's, *Erin's Daughters in America* and my own, *Ourselves Alone: Women's Emigration from Ireland, 1885-1920* also appeared in those years.[3]

In the first half of the 1990s, several more new studies of Irish life and emigration in the nineteenth and early twentieth centuries have been published, further increasing our understanding of a world once almost lost to history. Robert Scally's, *The End of Hidden Ireland* shows us the mechanisms that cleared Famine-ridden Ireland of its marginal labouring population. Ruth-Ann Harris's, *The Nearest Place That Wasn't Ireland* and Anne O'Dowd's, *Spalpeens and Tattie Hokers* trace the migration patterns of seasonal workers before the Famine. David Fitzpatrick's, *Oceans of Consolation* analyses newly discovered emigrant letters. Cormac Ó Gráda's, *Ireland: A New Economic History* explains the macro- and micro-economic forces for demographic and economic change in nineteenth-century Ireland. The impact of these changes on women has also received more study. For example, Grace Neville's, ' "She Never Then After That Forgot Him" ' uses manuscripts gathered by the Irish Folklore Commission to document women's attitudes towards their emigration in the post-Famine era. Maureen Murphy's, 'Charlotte Grace O'Brien and the Mission of Our Lady of the Rosary for the Protection of Irish Immigrant Girls' adds to our understanding of the immigrant woman's first encounter with urban America. Joanna Bourke's, *Husbandry to Housewifery* outlines the economic and cultural changes in women's lives in the wake of post-Famine economic and demographic reorganization as does Janet K. TeBrake's, 'Irish Peasant Women in Revolt: The Land League Years'. Rita Rhodes's, *Women and Family in Post-Famine Ireland* also discusses the changes in women's existences after the Famine.[4]

In the past year, even more work on women and their emigration has appeared. In the summer of 1994, Suellen Hoy and Margaret MacCurtain's, *From Dublin to New Orleans* offered an eyewitness account of the post-Famine journey of two Irish-born nuns to America. Even more recently, *The Journal of Women's History* published a special double issue on Irish women which included Suellen Hoy's discussion of the recruitment and emigration of Irish nuns to the United States in the course of the nineteenth and early twentieth centuries.[5] By the latter half of the nineteenth century, Hoy tells us, religious women, like their counterparts in the laity, travelled in large numbers to the United States largely independent of male control.

Complicating this new interest in the lives of ordinary Irish men and women in the nineteenth and early twentieth centuries, however, has been the debate over whether or not the Famine was the watershed of modern Irish history. Revisionist historians argue that the Famine was not the sole shaping force in nineteenth-century Irish life. Instead, they contend, while the crisis of the late 1840s accelerated the spread of land consolidation, pasturage, and marriage restrictions, these changes had already appeared in some areas of the country as early as the 1830s and did not reach the remote west until the 1880s, well after the Famine. The unusual contours of Irish life and emigration in the late nineteenth and early twentieth centuries were thus not the result of the Famine alone.[6] Despite the new recognition of differences in the regional timing of demographic and economic change in the half century surrounding the Famine, however, most historians agree that the Great Hunger did clear rural Ireland of most of its labouring class, either through emigration or death. In addition, the Famine marks a sea change in Irish emigration history. In the wake of six years of subsistence crisis, for the first time young single adults became the largest emigrant group.[7]

When the potato blight struck in the mid-1840s, therefore, demographic and economic change had already begun to transform rural Ireland. In the face of altered political and economic relationships with Great Britain in the first half of the nineteenth century, increasing numbers of Irish were limiting their reproduction in the face of deteriorating economic conditions. Nevertheless, while the rate of population growth had already begun to fall by the 1830s in certain regions of the country, overall numbers continued to rise. Thus, by 1845, on the eve of the Famine, eight and a half million people competed for ever-scarcer economic resources. By that year, the majority of the population in many areas were landless labourers and their families, reduced to bare subsistence on potatoes.

The Famine ended forever the precarious balance between potato subsistence and human survival in Ireland. As year after year of blight destroyed the potato crop in the late 1840s, the lives of the survivors changed permanently. Potato tillage rapidly disappeared in all but the extreme west, to be replaced by pasturage and market agriculture. Population levels plummeted and continued to fall thereafter as delayed and restricted marriage became the norm. Sustained large-scale emigration of marginal groups in the population became a fundamental fact of Irish life.

Post-Famine emigration patterns differed significantly from those of the pre-Famine period, reflecting the changes in Ireland resulting from the death of at least a million people and the emigration of another million and a half in the six years between 1845 and 1851. Before the Great Hunger, emigrants tended to be most often from the skilled artisan and small farmer classes, fleeing deteriorating economic circumstances in the face of international economic transformation. These emigrants were mostly from the north and the east, and men slightly outnumbered women among those leaving in those years. Female emigrants were usually family members accompanied by husbands or fathers. From the Famine forward, however, new emigrant patterns emerged, reflecting the permanent changes in demographic and economic life hastened by the potato blight. For the first time, large numbers of displaced agricultural labourers from the south and the south-west joined the emigrant stream. Furthermore, while families continued to form a large segment of those leaving Ireland at least in the early years of the Famine, single adults, both male and female, increasingly dominated among emigrants. Beginning in the 1850s, in some years unmarried women left Ireland in larger numbers and at earlier ages than their male counterparts. Indeed, by the late nineteenth and early twentieth centuries, the typical emigrant was an unmarried female in her late teens or early twenties, leaving the rural west and south-west, destined for the United States.

The departure of so many young, unmarried women from the west and south-west of Ireland in the wake of the Famine is unprecedented in the annals of Irish and overall European emigration. In fact, Irish emigration patterns had always been unusual in comparison to other European models of migration. For example, almost as many women as men left Ireland throughout Irish emigration history and, after the Famine, as we have seen, unmarried women travelling independently of husbands or fathers increasingly joined the emigrant stream. With the exception of Sweden, no other European country saw the mass migration of young unmarried women in numbers large enough to dominate overall emigration totals, and the Swedish phenomenon was short-lived, taking place only over a brief five-year period in the 1890s. In contrast, males were the majority of total emigration from Sweden and all other European countries in the late nineteenth and early twentieth centuries.[8]

The anomalies in Irish emigration reflect changes in women's roles in the wake of the Famine. While the Famine also altered the parameters of men's lives, especially those of the agricultural labouring class, the new world of post-Famine rural Ireland could accommodate men more easily than women, especially among the growing number of unmarried people in the population. Consequently, as Ireland transformed itself from a tillage, labour-intensive economy with a sizeable domestic industry to one in which access to land alone determined adult status, the promise of early and universal marriage ended at the same time as the demand for women's work in both agriculture and domestic manufacturing disappeared. The unmarried and unemployed woman toiling without recompense within the confines of her sister-in-law's home became increasingly common as the nineteenth century wore on. To many girls growing up on the farm after the Famine, emigration abroad seemed the only way to achieve the status of paid workers in the family economy, a status fewer and fewer women were able to attain in the altered demographic and economic world of post-Famine Ireland. In addition, emigration and subsequent employment abroad would enable displaced Irish women to marry and attain the coveted status of wife and mother in their new homes. As a result, by the end of the third quarter of the nineteenth century, the mass migration of unmarried women from rural Ireland, even the remote west and south-west, began in earnest.

The exodus of single young women from rural Ireland revealed their growing marginalization in rural life. First in the north and the east after 1830, and gradually throughout the rest of the country in the wake of the Famine, the demographic and economic patterns that had insured the importance of women in Ireland disappeared. By the third decade of the nineteenth century, domestic textile manufacturing contracted and vanished as cheaper British goods flooded Irish markets. At the same time, pasturage began to replace tillage as land owners sought to rationalize their holdings and convert to market rather than subsistence agriculture. As a result, the agricultural labourer majority of the population faced increasing unemployment and immiseration as husbands, wives, and children found fewer and fewer ways to supplement their subsistence potato patch with cash earnings to pay the rent. In fact, a wife's contribution to the family economy had often been the vital difference between subsistence and destitution. She sold butter and eggs and raised poultry for sale in local markets. She spun yarn and thread to earn wages in the widespread domestic textile industries of pre-Famine Ireland. Even before the Famine, however, especially in the newly rationalized agricultural world of the north and the east, more and more husbands and wives were displaced from their traditional economic and social position. The more prosperous fled the country, forming the first wave of the mass migration that would characterize Irish life into the present day.

When the potato blight wiped out the subsistence economy of the majority of the Irish in the terrible years after 1845, rural Ireland changed even more dramatically than it had in the years leading up to the Famine. Everywhere in the country, with the exception of the extreme west and south-west where the labouring class died of hunger and disease, boat load after boat load of refugees left the country, fleeing not only the immediate catastrophe but also the longer-range deterioration of economic opportunities.

After the Famine, as all of Ireland permanently reorganized its demographic and economic behaviour, marriage became increasingly restricted and delayed in order to control population growth. Fewer and fewer young people could marry, and those who did so married at later and later ages. The Catholic Church reinforced the culture of celibacy that the new land system required. By the late nineteenth century, Ireland had one of the highest celibacy rates of any country in Europe.[9] Furthermore, despite the attempts of the National Schools and government agencies like the commissioners of the Congested Districts Board to revive domestic industries and other traditional female crafts in the later nineteenth century, the era of early and universal marriage for women and their subsequent assumption of adult status as economic co-producers in the family economy had all but ended.

The demographic and economic transformation of Irish life in the half century surrounding the Famine affected women even more than men. While men also faced increasing restrictions on marriage and employment opportunities, the unmarried bachelor retained a public role in rural communities based on his greater ability to find employment and a social life outside the confines of the family cottage. Young men and 'old boys' could find release from their day-to-day toil in village pubs, race tracks, and livestock fairs. Thus, while they, like their sisters, were denied full access to the reins of power in rural communities, unmarried males were much more apt to have employment as well as social and recreational bonds to compensate. Young women, on the other hand, saw their employment disappear (especially since many of the remaining female jobs such as dairying were increasingly taken over by men as the nineteenth century wore on) along with their decreasing opportunities to marry.

As a result of the unevenly distributed restrictions on the lives of unmarried men and women in the wake of the Famine, more and more young women reaching maturity in the late nineteenth and early twentieth centuries lost whatever public roles their society had once provided them. As single women, they could no longer hope to achieve the status of wife and mother, the central focus of the family. In addition, they could no longer expect to find paid work and thus remain valuable members of the family economic unit. Furthermore, few compensatory outlets for their social and recreational needs were available after the Famine. By the 1890s, as Joanna Bourke has shown, growing numbers of women – married and unmarried – retreated to the domestic sphere, reflecting the growing prosperity of rural Ireland by the turn of the century as well as the diminished opportunities for women in the public world of work and play which was now almost exclusively the domain of men. Rural Irish women had a new ideal to emulate, that of the Victorian 'Angel in the House', replacing the earlier vision of women as vital economic co-producers in the family's struggle for survival. A wife was to set the moral tone for her family as she was relegated to the hearth. In addition, a wife's role as mother became increasingly important, substituting reproduction for economic production as the central purpose of her life.

Since unmarried women were most emphatically discouraged from becoming mothers in rural Ireland, the new importance of the mother and housewife as the ideal woman necessarily was denied them. Thus, the majority of young females who were unmarried and could expect to remain so throughout their lives were no longer able to achieve their traditional importance in the family as wage earners nor achieve the new ideal of mother and housewife. As a consequence, hundreds of thousands of young women without prospects at home chose to emigrate permanently. Displaced as they were, few ever returned to live in Ireland.

The young women leaving their homeland in the late nineteenth and early twentieth centuries were going to American cities, the most popular destination of all to Irish emigrants between the Famine and the First World War. Urban America offered opportunities no longer available in the altered economic and social world of post-Famine Ireland. American cities provided networks of welcoming relatives already settled in the New World who were able to provide the young woman arriving in American ports with immediate lodging, friendship, and job information. She rarely remained in the households of her American relatives for long, however. She had not come to the United States to remain a dependent in a family member's home. Instead, she most often found employment in the burgeoning service industries of urbanizing America. In fact, the overwhelming majority of Irish female immigrants (estimated to be as high as three-quarters of their total number)[10] became servants in the households of the growing middle and upper classes of urban America.

Although their employment prospects placed them near the bottom of the American economic ladder, young Irish immigrant women gained several advantages by their immigration despite low wages and a restrictive work world, at least in comparison to their prospects in rural post-Famine Ireland. First, as wage earners, they regained the economic importance enjoyed by most women before the Famine when a woman's economic contribution to the family economy had been the vital difference between subsistence and destitution. In their new homes overseas, Irish immigrant women could once again earn wages for cash remittances to their families at home. They could also marry, and wives produced babies – on the average of one every two years of married life. Infants surviving their crucial first five years provided the much-needed waged labour, old age insurance, and child care for younger siblings that the family economic enterprise depended on. As wives and mothers, immigrant women were vital to the family's survival both in their productive and reproductive capacities. In these ways, they were again economic co-producers in the family economy.

Irish women who emigrated to the United States in the late nineteenth and early twentieth centuries were successful for the most part in achieving renewed importance in the family economy. As we have seen, the young immigrant found paid employment as soon as she could after arrival. Almost immediately, she sent money back to her family in Ireland, taking her turn in the family's economic life cycle. By the late nineteenth century, Irish girls in America were sending hundreds of thousands of pounds back to Ireland every year. These remittances were used to buy livestock and make needed repairs on the still struggling farms of post-Famine Ireland. They were also used to fund the emigration of younger siblings. In fact, by the turn of the century, most first-time Irish emigrants to the United States, both male and female, had had their passages paid by older sisters already resident in America.[11] In addition, these pioneering older sisters sometimes returned temporarily to their home communities in rural Ireland to shepherd their young sisters, brothers, nieces, nephews, and cousins to ports such as Queenstown and the emigrant ship. In so doing, the returning sister was no longer an unpaid dependent within the farm community. She was now a family leader, able to help finance the farm and the emigration of both female and male relatives. She was once again an economic provider within the family and her efforts were key to the survival of her family both in Ireland and in the New World.

Furthermore, the work available to Irish women in America fostered the synthesis of the two ideals of womanhood now defining their lives. Domestic service provided both an income allowing the daughter to contribute substantially to her family's survival in Ireland as well as an education in the domestic manners of the middle and upper classes, an education that helped her when she later established her own household after marriage. Like her counterparts who remained at home, the Irish girl in America sought lessons in housewifery as much as she sought escape from the diminished opportunities afforded her in the reorganized world of late nineteenth-century Ireland. As David Fitzpatrick has noted, emigration was instrumental in the modernization of the Irish woman, both at home and abroad.[12] In fact, by the late nineteenth century, emigration was a normal part of the life cycle and America had become, in the words of Grace Neville, a 'magnet' drawing all young women to it. Manifestations of the fascination and familiarity with things American could be found in the new desire in rural areas to wear the fashionable American clothes that were often sent along with cash remittances to relatives in Ireland. A pervasive sense that there was 'no freedom in Ireland', and America was indeed an 'island of the Blessed', where liberty and democracy reigned,[13] further fueled the aspirations of young women to leave their homelands and follow their older sisters, aunts, and cousins across the Atlantic.

By emigrating, then, the Irish woman was able to achieve the hallmarks of adult life no longer available to her in post-Famine Ireland. Her wages abroad enabled her to rejoin the family economy by sending substantial cash remittances back to Ireland. She also regained her status within the family hierarchy by paying for and guiding the migration of her siblings. In addition, with time, she became a wife and mother, a status fewer and fewer women could attain in rural Ireland by the late nineteenth century. As a result, the young women who left home after the Famine regained their traditional economic importance within the family economy by finding paid work. When they eventually married, they could adopt the newer ethos of the wife and mother devoting herself to the concerns of the domestic sphere. Thus, redundant women in post-Famine Ireland recovered their demographic and economic importance after their emigration.

The American-born daughters of the women who left Ireland in the half century after the Famine illustrate the success their mothers had achieved through their emigration. For example, by the turn of the century, American urban primary education was dominated by Irish-American daughters of Irish-born mothers.[14] In addition, Irish-American women were publicly active as labour union leaders, political activists, social welfare workers, and community leaders.[15] Long before their American-born brothers entered the middle-class, Irish American women, both lay and religious, were trained professionals active in the wider world of American urban life. Indeed, if Irish social mobility in the United States is measured by the accomplishments of women, Irish-Americans enjoyed a rapid climb from a gloomy world of rural poverty into a new world of urban prosperity.

The Great Famine of the mid-nineteenth century, then, was a watershed, at least in the lives of the Irish women who left the country in great numbers in the late nineteenth and early twentieth centuries. The Famine altered the social class structure in rural Ireland by nearly eliminating the agricultural labouring class, once the most numerous group in the population. Accompanying these changes in rural class structure, the remaining population transformed its demographic and economic behaviour, leaving large numbers of young people unmarried and unemployed. Women, even more than men, were displaced by these changes and they, even more than men, emigrated abroad in search of new ways to attain an old end – becoming a valued co-producer within the family economy. As Grace Neville has written, '. . . emigration to the United States was the best and, in many cases, the only way [many post-Famine women] had to accede to adulthood (viewed as financial independence, marriage and motherhood) rather than remain in prolonged childhood in Ireland, celibate, unemployed and dependent on a male relative'.[16] After their emigration, these young women returned to older patterns of Irish female life by contributing to the family economy, marrying (usually Irish male emigrants), and bearing children.

Nevertheless, these women were not merely returning to the traditional world of pre-industrial subsistence. They and their daughters were educated, urban, international. There was no turning back after their emigration. They had broken the bonds that had prevented them from achieving a fully adult status as women within the changed world of post-Famine Ireland.

The pattern of young, unmarried women leaving rural Ireland in numbers large enough to dominate overall emigration totals continued until at least the 1960s. While the destination of the majority of these emigrants changed from the United States to Great Britain and the Commonwealth in the 1920s, record numbers of increasingly well-educated Irish women continued to leave their homeland well into the twentieth century.[17] The Great Famine, therefore, had a permanent impact on the lives of Irish women both in Ireland and abroad.

References

1   W.F. Adams, *Ireland and the Irish Emigration to the New World from 1815 to the Famine* (New Haven, 1932); A. Schrier, *Ireland and the American Emigration, 1850-1900* (New York, 1970). A classic work on Irish America also appeared in the 1970s, L. J. McCaffrey's *The Irish Diaspora in America* (Bloomington, 1976).

2   M. MacCurtain and D. Ó Corráin (eds), *Women in Irish Society: The Historical Dimension* (Westport, 1979).

3   D. Fitzpatrick, *Irish Emigration, 1801-1921* (Dublin, 1984) and ' "A Share of the Honeycomb": Education, Emigration and Irish Women', *Continuity and Change*, 1, 2 (1986), pp. 217-234; K. Miller, *Emigrants and Exiles: Ireland and the Irish Exodus to North America* (New York, 1985); H. Diner, *Erin's Daughters in America: Irish Immigrant Women in the Nineteenth Century* (Baltimore, 1983); J. Nolan, *Ourselves Alone: Women's Emigration from Ireland, 1885-1920* (Lexington, 1989).

4   Robert J. Scally, *The End of Hidden Ireland: Rebellion, Famine, and Emigration* (New York, 1995); R. Harris, *'The Nearest Place That Wasn't Ireland': Early Nineteenth-Century Irish Labor Migration* (Iowa, 1994); A. O'Dowd, *Spalpeens and Tatie Hookers: History and Folklore of the Irish Migratory Agricultural Worker in Ireland and Britain* (Dublin, 1991); D. Fitzpatrick, *Oceans of Consolation: Personal Accounts of Irish Migration to Australia* (Ithaca, 1994); C. Ó Gráda, *Ireland: A New Economic History* (Oxford: 1994); G. Neville, ' "She Never Then After That Forgot Him": Irish Women and Emigration to the United States in Irish Folklore,' in *Mid-America: An Historical Review*, 'Special Issue on the Catholic Immigrant Woman in Urban America' (ed.), J. Nolan, 74, 3 (1992), pp. 271-89; M. Murphy, 'Charlotte Grace O'Brien and the Mission of Our Lady of the Rosary for the Protection of Irish Immigrant Girls', ibid. pp. 253-270; J. Bourke, *Husbandry to Housewifery: Women, Economic Change, and Housework in Ireland, 1890-1914* (Oxford, 1993); J. K. TeBrake, 'Irish Peasant Women in Revolt: The Land League Years', *Irish Historical Studies*, XXVIII, 109 (1992), pp. 63-80; R. Rhodes, *Women and the Family in Post-Famine Ireland: Status and Opportunity in a Patriarchal Society* (New York, 1992).

5   S. Hoy and M. MacCurtain (eds), *From Dublin to New Orleans: The Journey of Nora and Alice* (Dublin, 1994); Hoy, 'The Journey Out: The Recruitment and Emigration of Irish Religious Women to the United States, 1812-1914', in the 'Special Double Issue on Irish Women', *The Journal of Women's History*, 6,4/7,1 (1995), pp. 64-98.

6   See C. Brady (ed.), *Interpreting Irish History: The Debate on Historical Revisionism* (Portland, 1994) for a full discussion of revisionism.

7   See the wide-ranging essays on the impact of the Famine on Irish life collected in C. Póirtéir (ed.), *The Great Irish Famine: The Thomas Davis Lecture Series* (Dublin, 1995) and the articles by J. Donnelly, D. N. Doyle, and D. Fitzpatrick in *The New History of Ireland*, Vol. V (Oxford, 1989).

8   For comparisons of Irish and other immigration patterns in the late nineteenth and early twentieth centuries see D. Gabaccia (ed.), *Seeking Common Ground: Multidisciplinary Studies of Immigrant Women in the United States* (Westport, 1992); W. Nugent, *Crossings: The Great Transatlantic Migrations, 1870-1914* (Bloomington, 1992); R. Takaki, *A Different Mirror: A History of Multicultural America* (Boston, 1993); V. Yans-McLaughlin (ed.), *Immigration Reconsidered: History, Sociology, and Politics* (New York, 1990).

9   These marriage patterns were not unique to post-Famine Ireland but could also be found throughout the 'Atlantic Arc'- northern Portugal, Spanish Galicia, Brittany, western Scotland, and parts of Norway – which possessed similar economic and structural features to those found in post-Famine Ireland, including the tendency for a large proportion of their populations to remain unmarried. Therefore, the increase in celibacy in post-Famine Ireland was not a peculiarly Irish cultural phenomenon. Instead, the Irish, like their counterparts elsewhere on the edges of industrializing and urbanizing Europe, behaved in a new way in the face of land reorganization and international capitalism. Those in the population who would not inherit land remained unmarried until after their emigration. See L. Kennedy, 'Europe's Reluctant Lovers?: The Irish, 1850-1990', paper presented at the American Conference for Irish Studies, Belfast, 1995.

10 C. Fanning (ed.), 'Introduction,' *Exiles of Erin: Nineteenth-Century Irish-American Fiction* (Notre Dame, 1987), p. 8.

11 M. Murphy, 'Irish Serving Girls,' in M. O'Dowd and S. Wichert (eds), *Chattel, Servant or Citizen: Women's Status in Church, State, and Society* (Belfast, 1995).

12 D. Fitzpatrick, 'The Modernisation of the Irish Female', in P. O'Flanagan, P. Ferguson, and K. Whelan (eds), *Rural Ireland, 1600-1900: Modernisation and Change* (Cork, 1987), p. 163.

13 Grace Neville, ' "Land of the Fair, Land of the Free": The Construction of the Myth of America in Irish Folklore', paper presented at American Conference for Irish Studies, Belfast, 1995.

14 Nolan, 'Irish-American Teachers and the Struggle Over American Urban Public Education, 1890-1920', *Records of the American Catholic Historical Society of Philadelphia*, 103, 3-4 (1992), pp. 13-22.

15 Ibid. 'Patrick Henry in the Classroom: Margaret Haley and the Chicago Teachers' Federation', *Eire-Ireland*, XXX, 2 (1995), pp. 104-17.

16 Neville, 'Dark Lady of the Archives: Towards an Analysis of Women and Emigration to North America in Irish Folklore, in M. O'Dowd and S. Wichert (eds), *Chattel, Servant or Citizen: Women's Status in Church, State, and Society*, (Belfast, 1995), p. 208.

17 P. Travers, 'Emigration and Gender: The Case of Ireland, 1922-60', ibid. pp. 187-99; MacCurtain, 'Late in the Field: Catholic Sisters in Twentieth-Century Ireland and the New Religious History', *Journal of Women's History*, 6,4/7,1 (1995), pp. 49-

63. For a discussion of the fate of women after independence, see M. Valiulis, 'Power, Gender, and Identity in the Irish Free State', ibid. pp. 117-36, and M. Daly, 'Women in the Irish Free State, 1922-39: The Interaction Between Economics and Ideology', ibid. pp. 99-116.

Emigrants and the Estate Office in the Mid-Nineteenth Century: a Compassionate Relationship?*

Patrick Duffy

Introduction

COMPASSION IN THE ESTATE OFFICE might not seem to be a very appropriate consideration at a time of commemoration of the Great Famine. The disasters which struck Ireland at that time have frequently been attributed to maladministration, from local to national level, or an administration which had been notably characterised by lack of compassion, even callousness – from the doctrinaire central bureaucracy down to the mechanistic application of the new poor law legislation.

Before the territorial geometry of poor law unions was introduced, and indeed even after its establishment, the estate undoubtedly formed the most important spatial and social reality for good or ill in the daily lives of most of the country population. In many cases, of course, the 'estate' was a vague enough entity in the eyes of the country people. It may have lacked local clarity or been represented in local perceptions by a middleman, and it was often characterised by incoherence, like the 'throughotherness' of crown estates like Ballykilcline.[1] But in one way or another the estate and especially the estate office represented the place where rents were paid and help might be sought in various crises. It did not matter much to the tenants whether the office or officers represented the legal landlord or simply the tenant of a distant owner. Presumably the more distant the owner – and the more intermediaries between him and the tenants – the less likelihood that help would be sought with any confidence. Rents would have to be paid sure enough however.

Therefore, when talking of 'compassion' in this context we are talking of situations where the office represented a direct landowner, and probably an estate where the owner was resident for much of the time. And probably also we are referring to estates which were large enough to warrant and maintain the semblance of an office administration which has in turn left us with some kind of collection of records. Thus we are probably talking of a fairly restricted sample and perhaps even an unrepresentative sample of the total range of estates in the country.

The object of the following essay is to see what light a well-maintained estate record can shed on the nature and management of a subsidised emigration policy in the frantic decade before the Famine. The intention also is to interrogate the wide-ranging popular attitude to emigration, especially assisted emigration, which crystallised soon after the Famine. This condemned the emigration as a conspiracy of extermination, when much evidence seems to show that, while it was a desperate measure, in a lot of cases it was welcomed by a great many potential emigrants. The assessment of 'forced-exile-by-cruel-landlords' appears mainly to have been made by those left behind in Ireland (by those who were refused assistance?) in a climate when the rapacious landlord syndrome was growing not just at grass roots level in Ireland, but also in Westminster. Kerby Miller's argument is that the rural community in Ireland created the exile motif to anaesthetise it from the pain of so much loss and to ensure continuing links with the homeland.[2] The fact that the assisted emigration in the 1840s was accompanied by house tumbling, to ensure emigrants did not return, helped to fuel the sense of outrage and conspiracy among those left. It is interesting to focus on this widespread condemnation of the estate office and landlords, for their alleged cruelty and tyranny. The landlord Shirley and his agent William Steuart Trench in south Monaghan have largely negative memories in folklore to this day. But the evidence from the 1840s suggests that they were hardly as bad as folk memory would suggest. Around Westport in County Mayo, a great many locals will still not set foot inside Lord Altamont's house and demesne – which is daily advertised as the biggest tourist attraction in the west of Ireland – though his mid-nineteenth century predecessor almost bankrupted his estate in looking after the tenants. So, popular memories perpetuate the belief that the estate bureaucracy was callous and cruel, that it was interested only in maximising rents and that it had little regard for the ordinary person.

There is also an implication that government-assisted emigration schemes, such as Peter Robinson's scheme to assist emigrants from Munster to Upper Canada in the 1820s, were well organised and caring and that the private schemes of landlords were not, though David Fitzpatrick has alluded to many well-organised landlord schemes.[3] Bob Scally suggests that the Crown tenants from Ballykilcline and other places were very fortunate in having the state look to their welfare, until they had boarded ship in Liverpool at least.[4] This poor opinion of landlord emigration has been founded on a number of well-publicised shipping disasters, such as Lord Palmerston's, which have been frequently used to illustrate the callous disregard of the landlord and his alliance with reckless coffin-shipowners. The folk memory continues in the recent publication of *Famine Diary*, purporting to document one particularly ill-fated and badly-managed migration.[5] At the height of the Famine when thousands were on the move, horror stories abounded, much like Bosnia-Herzegovina in the past couple of years.

Steuart Trench, Land Agent

William Steuart Trench in many ways epitomises the perspective of the landowner and may with care be seen as a witness to the part played by the estate office. From Queen's County (Laois), a scion of the landed class and a professional land agent for much of his life, his attitudes and philosophy may be seen to represent the priorities and interests of the landlord class. He wrote his memoirs, *Realities of Irish Life*, to perpetuate his ideas and record his contribution to solving the mid-nineteenth century crisis.[6] He was an enthusiastic proponent of assisted emigration wherever he worked as agent throughout the middle decades of the nineteenth century. For a short time he was an agent on the extensive 26,000 acre Shirley Estate in Monaghan, where he initiated a scheme of what he termed 'voluntary' emigration. He was then engaged as agent to Lord Lansdowne's estates in Kenmare where, at the end of the forties, he established an extensive scheme to assist in the emigration of the impoverished population on the Kenmare estates. In 1851, he returned to the Bath estate, neighbouring Shirley's property in south Monaghan, where he 'emigrated' another couple of thousand tenants. Trench was well in touch with contemporary trends in estate agency. Apart from its self-adulatory tone, most of his *Realities* was written in prescriptive mode for a gentry and land agency readership and his keenness on emigration in the 1840s especially must represent him as being in the *avant garde* of the profession in Ireland.

Trench's policy on emigration was fairly simple, and in face of the facts, rather logical: namely that, in the early forties, impoverished tenants on tiny holdings, in rent arrears and with little possibility of paying any rent, should be encouraged to give up their farms and be given their passage to America. This would in one move reduce future charges on the rates, consolidate farms and improve the life chances of the people themselves, though this latter point was probably not a primary consideration. Later during the Famine, he cleared Kenmare workhouse by offering all Lord Lansdowne's people there free passage. In Monaghan in the decade after Famine, he followed an eviction-driven policy based on the proposition that nobody would be evicted without being offered passage to America. Patrick Kavanagh for one, native of the Bath estate, thought this an 'excellent idea', but perhaps Kavanagh was not a typical south Monaghan countryman.[7] Folklore, however, does not regard Trench so kindly.

As Trench himself said about Kenmare, 'a cry was raised that I was exterminating the people . . .', abuse and vituperation were heaped on him.[8] In Monaghan, folklore says that his remains were attacked by rats and could not be buried until immersed in the sea at Blackrock seven miles away! In Kenmare, folklore is equally negative, but unspecific about his role. Because of the policies and practices he represented, it is interesting to look at his record for a moment. Was he so bad? Was he a despot, lacking in compassion? His memoirs failed to realise their objective and probably did not favour him for posterity. They too were execrated locally, burnt in public bonfires. The *Freeman's Journal* noted in 1869 when *Realities* was published, that 'in a New York hospital there is a ward called the Lansdowne Ward because in it died so many of those immigrants from the Lansdowne Estate in Kenmare, arriving as they did half starved, disease-ridden and penniless.'[9] His book got bad reviews led by two imperious clerics, the President of Maynooth College and the parish priest of Carrickmacross, who wrote about his agency on the Bath Estate: 'the several large farms are so many finger posts announcing that the Destroying Angel passed that way'.[10]

In his book he certainly comes across as conceited, with a condescending attitude to the peasantry that was not exceptional for one of his class in Victorian Ireland. When he wrote the book in the 1860s, he was witnessing the beginning of the end of the world and class he represented and he felt particularly besieged and embittered in his barracked-up house in Monaghan.[11] But throughout the book there is a noticeable undercurrent of compassion for the impoverished and underprivileged, tinged with a paternalism that would have been considered at the time as being characteristic of a responsible landed gentry. This is especially significant when the book is read in conjunction with an important formative report which Trench compiled on the Shirley Estate twenty years earlier in 1843.[12]

Trench's long report on the state of the Shirley property is hard hitting on the maladministration of the estate and on the treatment of the tenantry. It was clearly not intended for publication, so would reflect some deep seated personal sentiments held by Trench. He comes across as a responsible, concerned, even caring land agent. He pulled no punches, for example, in blaming the estate for a great many burdensome levies imposed on the tenants. One in particular was the system of local espionage, called 'keepers' locally, to watch all the tenants' dealings, which was apparently paid for by the tenants themselves. This system, said Trench, 'deeply wounded the feelings of the tenantry'. He also condemned the system of bog rent which he said he had never witnessed anywhere else in Ireland. He passed on to Mr Shirley a communication he had from Mr Griffith on the valuation of the Shirley Estate, pointing out that Shirley's tenants were paying 21 per cent over the general valuation. And he complained about the practice of obtaining decrees against tenants for rent and sending them to Monaghan gaol: the tenant was charged with the cost of the decree, together with his own and the Bailiff's fare to, and subsistence in Monaghan. As Trench says 'there is no man of common sense, not to speak of humanity . . . who could sanction such a system'.

Trench comes across in his report, oddly, as a sort of champion of the tenants' rights, although, in view of the later reception for his *Realities*, this might be an unfortunate choice of words. 'Even in Ireland', he claimed, 'it has never fallen my lot to witness destitution to the same degree and over such a large extent as I have seen it on this property . . . there are many tenants' houses where there are neither windows, bedsteads, tables nor chairs'. As a step towards improving conditions for those tenants who were 'better circumstanced', Trench proposed grants for improvements to house and premises, such as draining, planting, installing chimneys and proper windows. 'What I conceive they want most is kindness, encouragement, some substantial proof that the landlord is anxious for their amelioration and that they will be left to enjoy the fruits of their exertions and that everything will not be raised upon them the moment they increase its value by their industry'. He included a rather pointed calculation which showed that in the previous year, the estate had granted £16-14s-11d for tenant improvements out of a rental income of £22,954. This was Trench's proposal for the solvent tenants who could be relied on to carry on farming and paying their rent. For those who were impoverished and 'completely broken down' he proposed emigration, which he costed at £3 a head to America.

Trench's report to Shirley vindicates some of the humanitarian attitudes underlying his behaviour in *Realities*. It also provides a fitting background introduction to pre-Famine conditions on this large 26,000 acre estate in south Monaghan. Unfortunately for Trench's memory, perhaps, his proposals for improvements on the estate were not taken up, leading he claimed to his resignation of the agency. Only his emigration scheme was implemented.

The Role of the Estate Office

Under Trench, the Shirley Estate maintained an efficient office and a collection of documents relating mainly to his emigration policy throws light on the nature and implementation of the policy and how it fared with the tenants.[13]

News of the allowances for emigration spread quickly through the estate. Trench himself personally invited people in the country to participate. A great many petitions for assistance came into the office. With other petitions seeking wide ranging assistance for blankets, clothes, or money for a horse, or postponement of rent demands, these demonstrate the central place of the office as a social welfare agency in the lives of approximately 20,000 people. By any terms, the office and its officials held a most important role which they appear to have discharged with some responsibility, which appears to have contrasted with the inefficiency and croneyism characterising its operation under the previous long agency of Samuel Mitchell. In the late forties, admittedly, some of the decisions relating to old widows especially, who were craving permission to hold onto their 2 acres ('refused: she has no business with land') were very harsh and inevitably added up to a negative folk memory. But on balance in the trying times of mid-century, the records of the office show some attempts at tempering justice with mercy.

A classic example of a petition for help in the late forties epitomises the nature of the crisis faced by the estate office: Widow Hanratty, who was sheltering in one of the emergency outbuildings of Carrickmacross workhouse (which still had 1,700 inmates in the 1851 census) petitioned the landlord Evelyn Philip Shirley:

> You will recollect that you came to the poor shed that shelters Widow Hanratty at Corduff Chapel and left her refreshments and comfort for which you will have her poor blessings . . . in this life which will be short for she is famished with cold and hunger. She is confined to her bed these six years . . . has not had the comfort of a blanket and would represent this to your honour the day you visited her only she did not wish to be troublesome . . . now implores and prays that your honour will allow or cause her to get a blanket and such other necessaries as you may think will support her sinking frame for the neighbours who were kind to her heretofore are now distressed and cannot give more assistance . . .

In three months in 1843, approximately forty people were listed as having received clothes from the estate. By 1849, there were increasing references to aprons, petticoats and other items being collected from the schools on the estate. Further substantiating its social role in the district, the office was also frequently asked to arbitrate in disputes between neighbours, often over land, and indeed in domestic disputes within families. Fathers, mothers, and brothers were ordered, as the case might be, to take in an ejected family member, or to remove a troublesome sibling. Seventy years and more later, when Shirley and the office had departed the scene, such disputes usually ended up in the district courts.

Trench's policy on farm subdivision among family members was the direct opposite of his predecessor's (who seems to have generally facilitated the practice) and no doubt his refusal to allow anyone else onto a farm without his express permission[14] and his policy of paying the emigration costs of second households, including cottier households, was not too popular with some.

In February 1844, the McEnaney orphans wrote to Trench that their 'Father possessed 5 acres . . . [died and willed] that his widow should enjoy his place so long as she honestly took care of his children and remained with them unmarried but she is now doing all in her power to transgress the covenant by getting married to Peter McQuillan who has no property . . . implores your Honour in the name of Heaven to protect them by a speedy interference . . .' A peremptory note from Trench stated: 'settled, the marriage not allowed'.

There were quite a number of these petitions to intervene in marriages, to prevent or to allow them as the case might be, and it is interesting that, though invited in these cases, part of the folklore about Trench is that he stopped people getting married. A ballad called 'The marriage veto' in the 1860s contains a caustic comment on this role:

> Oh girls of Farney is it true
> That each true-hearted wench
> Before she weds must get consent
> From pious Father Trench.[15]

Emigration Petitions

Throughout the forties, appeals for assistance with emigration predominated in the record – demonstrating a keenness to get continuing help in distress, but in many cases also to avail of opportunities presenting themselves. The office very frequently refused appeals for other assistance, but instead offered help to emigrate as an alternative. Two petitions illustrate the application of this pressure on tenants. Hugh Ward in January 1844 was destitute, with only one acre of land left. He had been forced to 'leave his dwelling house, himself and his large family exposed to the inclemency of the weather without shelter either day or night . . . take his want, poverty and distress into consideration . . .' A note from Trench simply stated that he 'can do nothing but give him the means of going to America if he will give up his place'. In December 1844, Francis McCabe's story demonstrates the desperate struggle for survival for the poorest class in the countryside in the crisis years before the Famine. He lived on his aunt's farm. She died of 'complication of distemper' and he was 'put to the expense of burying her'. He had to mortgage half the farm and was unable to redeem it. During the last three years the 'death of pigs' destroyed him though 'by going to the last English harvest he got the means to clear arrears of rent but cannot pay the past half year's rent. Between himself, his wife and two children they have not one pound of day or night woollen covering and are nearly perished with the cold and know not what may happen if kind providence does not inspire your Honour to relieve them and particularly with some warm covering . . .' Again all Trench would do was offer him help to go to America.

Trench also adopted a proactive approach to encouraging people to go. In 1843, while he was riding through the estate familiarising himself with its problems before submitting his report to Shirley, he came on James McCannon who 'was living as a Cottier with Francis Murray of Derrylavan at the new mills of Mr Shirley. You were riding by the way in the month of December and you called me to the Road and asked me would I go to America and that you would pay my wife's passage and mine to America. I am prepared now according to your Honour's decision to go any time that is pleasing to you . . .'

Some of the office correspondence, as well as Trench's book, show clearly that, while it was obviously in the long term interests of the estate to 'shovel out' the paupers, the officials considered that it was also ultimately in the interests of the people themselves. In his original proposal on emigration, Trench suggested that for those with no visible means of support emigration must be considered as the only thing 'for their benefit'. It 'would put the people themselves', he said in *Realities*, 'in a far better way of earning their bread hereafter . . . it would be cheaper to him [Lord Lansdowne] and better for *them* [Trench's] to pay for their emigration at once, than to continue to support them at home'.[16] And the poor emigrants in most cases appear to have been glad of the opportunity to go: according to Trench a rush was made to get out. Davis, the London passenger agent in 1849, remarked on the safe departure for Australia of a party of Shirley's emigrants that 'I am quite sure they have been, 95 poor creatures as they are, put in a fair way of doing well for themselves'.

If the petitions among the records of the office are anything to go by, a great many of the tenants were anxious to get help to emigrate, including cottiers, schoolmasters, tradesmen, and the sons and daughters of tenantry. Peter Ward, for example, was a schoolmaster who in March 1844 sought help to go 'if your honour considers his family too numerous for your present scheme, he humbly supplicates your Honour to include the bearer [his son] in the number of your emigrants'. The family of nine sailed later that year with £15-15s assistance. Charles Mee was trained as a tailor and 'has formed a most sanguine wish for Emigration to Canada . . . humbly beseeches you to assist his passage to that Country' and Harry Mee (from another family) had a five acre farm, eleven in the family, 'unable to provide for his two eldest daughters at home or even to pay their passage to America . . . prays assistance to provide for their passage'. Passages were paid in both cases.

Many other tenants took time to make up their minds to accept offers of assistance, an understandable reaction especially if they were older with a family. This was a particular problem with the Australian emigration in 1849, when people kept changing their minds much to the annoyance of the office. The office did try to speed up the decision-making process, if one could call it that. By the late forties, when the estate undertook evictions – and was attacked for 'extermination' by *The Nation* newspaper – there was a considerable increase in the numbers seeking assistance to go. Indeed it appears that many actually knocked down their houses, so anxious were they to abide by the rules of the estate and avail of the assistance offered, and suggesting that assistance for emigration was not as readily available at the height of the crisis. Francis Magee, like a great many petitioners in the late forties was desperate to get some of his family out. He possessed a small plot of land on which he supported a wife and five children. He said that his house had been pulled down a few days ago 'and his poor wife and family have taken refuge under a few sticks and ragweeds placed against a ditch. That he is now penniless without a cabin to shelter him and humbly implores to send the two adults of his family to America . . .'. Such a modest request would ensure that the costs of the other family members might be remitted home later.

Miles Martin, in March 1847, pleaded: 'your honour sir I expect you will give me further assistance as I have done according to your wishes has my house thrown down which cost me seven pounds in building it and living since then in a tent wherein I had nearly starved with cold so I expected that both myself and family could go together but now I cannot unless your honour does consider my case . . .'. His family of five were entered on the emigration list in April having apparently paid off their arrears. Miles' indefatigable wife Margaret wrote from Liverpool on 12th April to complain about the assistance they received:

> Dear Sir, I rte you thaes few line hoping to Find your Honour in good health as God leaves us at present thank God dear Sir i am to inForm you that I thought to go to Emeraica but it is out of my power unless you relieve me with more Money or Else i must devied my poor Family and send some of them of and go to the poor house me self which is a poor ?place and I wont be Alive unless you Relieve me if you or Mr Smith does not pleus send me an answer as soon as possible or else I mus send two of them Home some are ?leanams [leanbhs?].

The passenger agent in Liverpool referred to the Martin family who could not pay enough towards their passage who were there in a 'miserable growling humour'. He eventually was able to report that he had got them on board and ready to depart by the 25th April. Liverpool was daily witnessing such misery as thousands of impoverished emigrants like the Martins spent their days wandering the town waiting for their ship.

Desperate straits called for desperate measures and there was an element of disingenuousness in some of the pleas for help. Scally has talked about the manner in which the tenantry often exploited the 'throughother' nature of the estate, how they tried to play on the office's ignorance of the real state of the farms and tenant relationships.[17] Cases made for help with emigration or other problems were sometimes elaborately overstated. Was Mary McCabe exhibiting *naïveté* or clever advocacy in her petition in February 1844? She had 'survived a heavy loss a few months ago by the death of a son and seven young pigs and that she had her rent made up in order to pay it and being admonished to buy a horse to plough her land and then sell the horse and pay the rent in full, she accordingly bought the Horse in the last fair in Ballybay which horse died in five days after in consequence of some medicine administered by the seller to make him up for sale, which losses have entirely frustrated her design . . .'.

Managing the emigration scheme

What sort of care did the office take with the organisation and management of the emigration scheme? The record shows that a considerable amount of care was taken. Since the landlord's money was involved, a strict account was kept of every penny spent, but the correspondence between the office and the various passenger agents involved in the emigration, whether in Dublin, Liverpool or London, shows a well-organised and humanitarian system in place. Much of the work involved a form of crowd control, especially after the first rush when the offers were made initially, and later as distress increased during the Famine years. A large estate such as Shirley's had to have a minimum level of administrative resources. It is clear that it would have been impossible for an estate without some sort of office administration to have undertaken such schemes.

In his *Realities of Irish Life*, Trench refers to the amount of time he spent on the Lansdowne emigration in a manner which captures the frantic pressures on the organisers of the emigration in another large estate.

> I have gone through much laborious work during my life, but I
> never went through any which pressed so hard upon my
> powers of endurance as the arrangements for the emigration at
> Kenmare. The tide of emigrants was so enormous, each
> pressing his claim and terrified lest all the money should be
> exhausted before his or her name could be entered . . . I
> frequently passed eight hours a day at this most disagreeable
> and laborious work.[18]

Depending on individual circumstances, emigrants in Monaghan or Kerry
were given a varied amount of assistance, either the bare passage money or
passage plus provisions plus landing money. The office endeavoured to
determine how much was required, based on the ability of the emigrants to pay
something towards their costs, on numbers in the party and so on. In contrast to
Scally's Ballykilcline emigrants, where the Crown office depended on poorly-
informed local officials, the Carrickmacross office appears to have had fairly
comprehensive knowledge of the estate, particularly on the extent of the cottier
population.[19] Perhaps 'compassion' is the wrong word for the management or
care of the emigrants in their journey. During 'the heat of emigration', – the
Liverpool agent's description of conditions over there in 1847 – it would have
been foolhardy in the extreme to let the emigrants head off on their own. As
Trench said of his pauper emigrants from Kenmare ('wild batches of two
hundred each'):

> There was great difficulty in keeping them from breaking loose
> from the ship, not only in Cork but in Liverpool . . . their chief
> device was to escape out of the ships almost naked, to hide all
> their good clothes which had been furnished them as an outfit,
> and to appear only in their worst rags . . . rushing through the
> streets of Cork and Liverpool in large bodies to the terror of the
> inhabitants. [20]

This behaviour was no doubt an embarrassment to the estate. In 1849, the
Liverpool agent reprimanded the Carrickmacross clerk for the condition of an
earlier group of Monaghan emigrants and hoped 'most sincerely such another
ragged pack may never appear here again'.

Trench also claimed that all the Kenmare emigrants were in 'uproarious
spirits; there was no crying or lamentation, as is usual on such occasions; all was
delight at having escaped the deadly workhouse'.[21] Whatever about the subsequent
need for a 'Lansdowne Ward' in the New York hospital, undoubtedly these
workhouse emigrants were glad to get out. This assessment of the attitudes of
emigrants, admittedly by a self-interested Trench, contrasts with Scally's reliance
on Walter Macken's image of the awesome silence of lonesome emigrants at the
quayside.[22] Other writers in the twentieth century have confirmed the silence of
emigrants at moment of departure.[23] Perhaps the pauper emigrants who were
assisted were exceptional in being delighted with the chance to escape?

In general, emigrants from the mid-nineteenth century countryside, as also
the mid-twentieth century, who had probably never been outside their parish,
would have needed careful handling to get them safely away. A 1942 recollection
of emigration in the 1870s recalled the trauma and stress for a young sixteen year
old girl on her way to America.

> At last we got into Derry and everyone made a mad rush for
> the boat thinking it would go without them [a common
> experience for first time travellers]. . . . we wouldn't be let on
> the boat until we had bought our beds and a lot of other things.
> This caused a terrible weeping and wailing among the people
> who did not seem to know these regulations. But the agents
> said they should know that already . . . I bought a bed, a tin
> mug, a tin ponny . . . we all left our names and the things were
> to be sent down to the boat . . . when I went to the boat there
> was a place fixed for me I heard and where I was to sleep. But
> to tell the truth I never found it from that day to this. The
> crowds and the pushing and shouting were awful and I still
> remember the confusion of my mind, a young green girl . . .
> there were thousands on board – could that be possible?[24]

The assisted emigrants often had an advantage over individuals going out
under their own steam, who had to overcome the problems of the journey alone,
though undoubtedly so vast was the network of migration by the 1850s that most
voluntary individual emigrants had lots of advice from former emigrants. One
such, from Clones in 1870 sent home a blow-by-blow account of the trip with a
detailed description of what to do at each turn on disembarkation at New York –
get registered, get railroad ticket, change money, go to customs, all extremely
valuable information for gauche newcomers from the country.[25]

Elliott, Shirley's Liverpool passenger agent, was meticulous in his attention to
the emigrants at the Liverpool end of the journey as they awaited passage to
America. When they arrived, if they had to wait some days for their ship they
were given a daily allowance. Many of the emigrants expressed their appreciation.
In April 1844, he reported that 'the last paid of your people got off yesterday all in
excellent humour and I must say most grateful they all appeared for the trifling
friendship and attention I tried to show them. They one and all desired I should
write to let you know how they prayed for your success as they termed it. The
ready cash they all got daily does much for them . . .' Peter Byrne, who had
received £10 worth of assistance, wrote to Trench in the same month from
Liverpool:

> I take the liberty of returning you my most sincere thanks for
> the goodness you have done to me and my brother and sister in
> assisting us to emigrate to America. I wrote to Mr Smyth to let
> your honours know my state here for which I received in
> return of it this morning thirty shillings from Mr Elliott and
> never was more awanting. We have found Mr Elliott very kind
> he has got for all his passengers on Monday a pound of bread
> each on Tuesday the same and on this day one shilling each
> now we are to get a shilling every day while we are detained
> here . . .

Brigid Corrigan, who with her husband and five children was given £16, took
ill in Liverpool and was sufficiently well cared for that Elliott managed to get her
on the boat with her family and under the care of a surgeon who happened to be
a cabin passenger: 'I have risked charging £1 on a/c of what has been done in this
case . . .'.

In general, Shirley's emigrants came well outfitted, though towards the end of
the forties, it is evident that the system was creaking with the strain of numbers,

many following ejectments at home. Following Elliott's reprimand on the condition of some emigrants in 1849, the office was careful to prevent badly outfitted passengers being sent over again. The Fox and Conlon families, who appear to have been unable to pay anything, were given extensive help and the following account details the nature of this assistance:

Pat Fox and family of Lissirill, 11 in number: Passage on the packet 19s
Dinner in Dundalk 7/8d; sea store 3/-; tin can 1/-.
Pat Conlon's family of Lissirill, 6 in number: Passage 10/6d
Dinner 4/-; sea store 1/8.

Clothes given to Pat Fox and Children:

Michael Fox	1 pair trousers
Margaret	1 shift, 1 gown, 1 flannel petticoat, 1 apron
Betty	1 shift, 1 gown, 1 flannel petticoat, 1 apron
Mary	1 gown, 1 slip
Pat jr	1 shirt, 1 coat, 1 vest
Betty and Anne,	1 apron each
Bridget	1 flannel petticoat, 1 apron
Pat sr	1 shirt, 1 trousers, 1 coat, 1 vest

Sundries supplied to Pat Fox's family:

			£.	s.	d.
Tinware:	2 x 3 gal water bottles 2/-				
	1 Boiler 8d and coffee pot 8d				
	4 panicans 8d, 1 chamber pot 7d				
	1 frypan 9d, 1 dish 8d, 8 plates 6d				
	8 stone Biscuit @3/10		1	10	8
	8 stone Oatmeal @3/4		1	6	8
	2 Barrels with locks and keys			3	6
	10lb bacon 7/6, 3lb coffee 1/8			12	6
	7lb sugar 3/6, 1/4lb tea 1/3, salt 3d			5	0
	14lb treacle & Mug 5/2,				
	1 bottle vinegar 8d			5	10
	2 small pr shoes			7	0
	1 small pr trousers			2	6
	2 small frocks			3	6
One nights lodging and food while in Liverpool				8	6
Cash on departure			2	0	0

Sundries supplied to Mary Conlon's family
3 gal tin water bottle, 1 chamber pot, 1 dish, 2 plates,
1 coffee pot, 1/4 lb. tea, 2 lb. coffee, 6 lb. sugar,
7 lb. treacle and mug, 5 lb. bacon, 1 bottle vinegar,
1 night's lodging and food in Liverpool.
Cash on departure

Total cost £3 2 8

Because south Monaghan was so close to Dundalk and the Liverpool ferries, meant that many emigrants were able to move back and forth quite readily, in contrast to regions further west. In May 1847 Elliott wrote to the office 'respecting the two young Persons who returned Home in such bad Humour when the passages ran up so high. If they come along by next Saturday's Boat I will give them their passage to New York on as fine a ship as is now in Port . . . at the terms they paid and as I offered before will pay their Steamboat fare'.

Some of the passengers tried Elliott's patience however. He was endeavouring to get as good a deal as possible for the estate, which in most cases throughout the forties meant booking ships to Canada. Many of the emigrants, however, wanted to go to the United States Henry Grimes (with his wife and four children) was one such in 1849 who refused to go to Quebec:

> nothing will do Grimes but to go to Boston where children are charged almost the same as adults . . . he handed me £2 in addition to your order but this would not be accepted for the family to Boston. I got him an offer of getting away to New Orleans this day and his friend would not permit him to go even there . . . I would not by any means stretch so far in good nature as to enable him to choose his destination – especially after losing part of his funding, Beds and Bedding etc. having gone off in the Quebec Ship intended and put on board for his family . . .

The Australian Emigration

In 1849, the estate determined to assist upwards of 200 emigrants to Australia, responding to incentives from the Colonial Emigration Office in London. The demands of this new bureaucracy in London taxed the resources of the Carrickmacross office to its limits and the correspondence illustrates the amount of effort and care which went into the emigration in response to the colonial regulations. A passenger agent had to be engaged in London whose somewhat hectoring correspondence with the little office in the 'provinces' in Monaghan is illuminating. George Morant, Trench's successor as land agent, discussed with the clerk the style of jackets to be purchased for the emigrants and the price of shoes which would be ordered from Pims in Dublin. He thought an ordinary jacket 'instead of the always absurd and unmeaning tail coat is an excellent proposition.' In terms of shoes all that was required, he said, 'is a shoe that will last the voyage and if those at 1/10 will do this then there will be no need to go to the higher price'; two pairs of strong shoes would be enough to last a woman or girl for four months. He noted that monies would have to be forwarded to London in advance and with this in mind he was looking to income on the estate which in mid-1849 was a cause of some concern. Accordingly, 'the ejectments had better be executed at once that is to say to commence on next Tuesday week if the Sheriff can attend ... Let those ... under the auspices of those rascals Swanzy and McMahon be the first dealt with and afterwards the rest in due course – levelling one dwelling house in each subdivision where there are but two upon the farm, and in no case leaving a house upon farms valued at under £4 – the same rule must apply for non-payment of rent'. By this time the rates in the union had risen in excess of 4 shillings in the pound and the policy of evictions brought about an increase in those going to America. At least 170 were assisted to America in 1849.

By August Morant was worrying about where to get soap and how much; it emerged that 2lbs. was required per person. He also concerned himself with the finer details of the trip and instructed the office to double-check the regulations to make sure nothing was omitted. 'Do you think it will do to fit the people with their clothes in Dublin or would it not be worthwhile to get them down to Carrick to be tried on? Chests will I believe be wanting. These I imagine all possess of some kind or another. We must make sure that each has two pair of shoes though it is not necessary that they should be new – if in tolerantly good repair …'.

The bales of new clothes were brought to Carrick and fitted, as far as can be determined in the local school. Boxes of cardboard which Morant considered to be 'quite as good as the ordinary trunks of the country' were eventually bought in Liffey Street in Dublin on the morning of departure. Presumably these were then filled with the supplies of the government agent and whatever spare clothing the emigrants had with them. There was a complicated correspondence with the new bureaucracy of the railway, ranging from the new Inniskeen station, to Dundalk, Drogheda and Dublin, to obtain third class carriages to Dublin. But as the only train with third class would arrive in Dublin at 10.00 p.m., this was deemed too late to bring such a large group across the city with their baggage and so they were sent by car to Drogheda and from thence by an earlier train. Board and lodging was booked in the North Wall on the night before departure where, said the ever-vigilant Morant, 'I have arranged for their safekeeping … I shall be in attendance on Saturday morning at the inspection and shall probably remain until they are actually on board.'

For the journey to Australia, most of the males were allocated 5 shirts, 5 pair stockings, 2 pair of shoes, 1 jacket, vest and trousers and had 1 'suit reserved'. Each of the females was allocated 5 shifts, 5 stockings, 2 pair of shoes, and one each of gowns and petticoats. The following account illustrates the range of provisions acquired to supply the first group of emigrants in August 1849.

	£.	s.	d.
from W G Smith Grocer, Tea/Coffee Dealer for Loaves, salt, pepper & tobacco	1	8	11
To Anne Woods for Dinner for 8 men @ 10d each		6	8
John Dawson, Woollen & Linen Draper Cmx [Carrickmacross] for 100 pairs of cotton sheets	8	15	0
Francis Reilly Carrickmacross carhire to Dundalk		3	3
Patk O'Connor, Wax, Sparmaceti & Tallow Candle manufacturer D'Olier St Dublin, 2 cwt Soap and 2 Boxes	2	13	0
Todd Burns & Co. Dublin, Linen & Woollen Drapers 6 doz. towels	1	4	0
John Richardson (Capel St Dublin ?) 48 trunks (various)	3	12	8
Mathew Jones 47 Nth Wall Boarding & Lodging for 94 emigrants	10	10	0
Bernard McKenna for conveyance of 68 adults and 26 children from Drogheda to Dublin /14 Aug [rail]	16	2	0
Millers, Basket & Travelling Trunk Manufactory, Fishamble St Dublin for 11 trunks		15	0
Dundalk & Enniskillen Railway for carriage of 2 Bales, hamper and bag		4	9
Hugh Gormley carriage of 2 Bales from Enniskillen to Carrickmacross, and a large box		3	6
Dublin and Belfast Junction Railway 94 3rd class Passengers (fares paid)			

from Dundalk to Junction per the day mail @ 12.40 p.m	7	3	0
Carolan Ward (Carrickmacross) 1 assorted caps	1	9	4

In addition there were bills for shoes, sheets, clothes and towels.

The sometimes inconsistent manner of describing the occupations of the emigrants on the forms supplied from London upset the metropolitan sense of order of Davis, the London agent: they were first listed as labourers, later on as tailors, coopers, weavers, etc. But Smith in the office retorted with some impatience that this was easy to explain in terms of the rural economy in Ireland at the time: 'these people being according to circumstances employed at these occupations in turn.' However, as there was a smaller contribution required from the estate for labourers, Davis, the wily bureaucrat, sensibly pointed out that while a 'poor man is naturally anxious to make as much of himself as he can – if he has ever struck a blow on the anvil for the village smith he dubs himself "blacksmith", which in the eyes of H.M. Commissioners is a reason for paying an extra £5'!

Following the successful embarkation of the first group, Morant determined to streamline the emigration of the second group in December. He drew up a memorandum for the office outlining his instructions for a more efficient, and more economical, operation. Emigrants were

> To be ready and assembled in Carrick the evening previous to the day of departure for Dublin. All to be dressed in suits of the new clothing. Boxes to made for each adult except in cases of 2 brothers or 2 sisters when one somewhat larger than the single boxes will suffice. These to be corded. Bonnets strong and cheap for the women. Scotch caps for the men and boys. Shoes, 2 pairs each, except where they may have one reasonably good pair of their own when one will suffice. Two lbs. of soap each. Third class to Dublin from Drogheda. Mr Lane to accompany the emigrants as before and to be provided with the necessary funds. If the emigrants are to pass a night in Dublin, Mr Lane will endeavour to provide for their maintenance at a cheaper rate than the last time. The journey to Drogheda via Ardee by vans or some such conveyance.

Conclusion

The popular image of landlord and estate which emerged in the post-Famine period is one of oppression and injustice and this image has come down in folklore to the present. Much of this was founded on eviction policies which gathered pace from the 1840s, as the population-land crisis manifested itself at the level of the estate. Emigration also became an emotive issue from this period. Miller has examined the emergence of the 'exile motif' as a societal response to the loss of millions of people from the country. Encouraging people to emigrate by means of assisted passage, therefore, was a risky undertaking for the estate in these circumstances of a rising tide of negative public opinion.

In many cases, assisted emigration was interpreted as another attempt by the landlord class to exterminate the Irish population. The association of emigration with eviction has been seen as an extension of a landlordly disregard for the wishes and welfare of his tenantry. And this belief was based on documented cases of some landlord-inspired group emigrations which ended in disaster. However, to what extent assisted emigrants – who were admittedly among the poorest class to leave in the mid-nineteenth century – were worse off than the tens of thousands of individual voluntary emigrants who were leaving at the same time is a moot point.

The evidence of the estate office in Carrickmacross suggests that in the circumstances, the estate discharged its responsibilities in a humane and considerate manner. On the large Shirley property, Steuart Trench in 1843 was reaping the harvest of decades of mismanagement. He inherited a situation where the population and farm structure was seriously imbalanced. Almost anything he could have done to solve the problems of the estate, including assisted emigration, would have been interpreted as oppressive subsequently. Indeed it might be suggested that to do nothing, as was done by many smaller or poorly-run estates with no effective administration, would probably have earned a better folk memory. But in the circumstances of the Shirley Estate in the 1840s, with a population in excess of 20,000, failure to do anything would probably have resulted in greater social and economic hardship for the people and the property.

The construction of the popular memory of Shirley's emigrants was largely the product of those left behind, who witnessed the compulsory dispossession of farms and tumbling of cabins by the estate and the emigration of their neighbours to far-away shores in the late forties. What evidence there is for the emigrants themselves indicates that they were keen to leave. As this essay has shown the officials of the estate attempted to apply management policies humanely. Generally speaking the office was as caring in its dealings with the tenants as any bureaucracy whether it was the poor law guardians, the later county councils, or indeed the social welfare agencies of the twentieth century. In the final analysis, given the circumstances of thousands of impoverished tenants on farms which had no viable economic future, and looking through the papers documenting their sorrow, misery and destitution, one must ask the question, what alternatives to emigration did the management of the estate have? One must conclude that in this decade of the 1840s, which was the worst at any time before or since, the estate officials in Carrickmacross probably did as much as could be expected of them.

References

* Extracts from the Shirley papers are published with the kind permission of Major J.E. Shirley and the Deputy Keeper of Records, P.R.O.N.I.

1 Robert Scally, *The End of Hidden Ireland. Rebellion. Famine and Emigration* (Oxford, 1995), chapters 1 and 2. (E.E. Evans, who used the term 'throughother' to describe rundale agriculture, is quoted p. 13).

2 Kerby Miller, *Emigrants and Exile: Ireland and the Irish exodus to North-America* (Oxford, 1985).

3 David Fitzpatrick, *Irish Emigration 1801-1921* (Dundalk, 1985).

4 Scally, *The End of Hidden Ireland* p. 169.

5 Gerald Keegan, *Famine Diary, Journey to a New World* (edited and presented by J.J. Mangan, Dublin, 1991).

6   William Steuart Trench, *Realities of Irish Life* (London, 1868).

7   *Realities of Irish Life* (London edition 1966), with preface by Patrick Kavanagh. (this edition referred to hereafter).

8   Trench, *Realities of Irish Life*, p. 69.

9   Quoted in L.O. Mearain, 'Estate agents in Farney – Trench and Mitchell', *Clogher Record* (1981), p. 405.

10 Quoted in *ibid*. p. 412.

11 See 'Document on Farney', *Clogher Record* (1975), p. 297.

12 'Causes of complaints stated, and certain alternatives suggested in reference to the Management of the Shirley Estate', P.R.O.N.I., D3531/S/55

13 Shirley Papers, P.R.O.N.I., D3531/P/1-3. Much of this collection has been published in P. Duffy, 'Assisted emigration from the Shirley Estate 1843-54', *Clogher Record* (1992), pp. 7-62. Unless otherwise indicated quotations in the following paragraphs are from the Shirley Papers.

14 *Shirley Papers*, D/3531/P.

15 quoted from *Dundalk Democrat*, June 1869 in *Clogher Record* (1981), p. 413. Another verse of the song says: 'O search green Erin through and through/ And tell us would you find/ Match-maker and land-agent too/ In one small farm combined.'

16 Trench, *Realities of Irish Life*, p. 65.

17 Scally, *The End of Hidden Ireland*. especially p. 71ff.

18 Trench, *Realities of Irish Life*, p. 75.

19 A comprehensive list of cottiers was compiled for 1840 to 1847, D3531/M/5/2.

20 Trench, *Realities of Irish Life*, p. 66.

21 *Ibid*. p. 67.

22 Scally, *The End of Hidden Ireland*, p. 166.

23 For example, Donal Foley, *Three Villages* (Dublin, 1977), pp. 52-5.

24 'I went to America', taken down by Anna Kelly, *The Bell* (1942), pp. 353-4.

25 P.O. Gallachair, 'Two letters from a Clones emigrant', *Clogher Record* (1962).

'Permanent Deadweight': Emigration from Ulster Workhouses during the Famine

Trevor Parkhill

T HE VALUE OF EMIGRATION as one, perhaps even the only, positive step that could be made in response to the mounting problems of lack of employment, poverty and vagrancy in Irish society in the two decades before the onset of the Famine was clearly recognised by experienced observers. The Poor Law Inquiry Commission of 1833-6, chaired by Archbishop Richard Whately, a proponent of emigration, recommended that 'arrangements for carrying on emigration shall be made between the commissioners of poor law and the colonial office, and that all poor persons whose circumstances shall require it shall be furnished with a free passage and with the means of settling themselves in an approved British colony'.[1] However, this ran so fundamentally counter to orthodox political opinion that it was effectively set aside. Instead, George Nicholls, with his vast experience of the poor law in England, was asked to re-examine the question of a poor law for Ireland. He, in turn, considered that emigration could be adopted if the cost was shared by government and local unions.[2]

> Emigration, however, not only may but I believe must be had recourse to as a present means of relief, whenever the population becomes excessive. The excess will be indicated by the pressure of able-bodied labourers on the workhouse . . . Under such circumstances, emigration must be looked to as the . . . only present remedy . . . the charge should in every case be equally borne by the government, and the union from which the emigrants proceed [and] the emigration should . . . be limited to a British colony . . .

Nearly a decade later, on the eve of the Famine, the Devon Commission of Inquiry into the occupation of land recommended that 'a well organised system of emigration may be of very great service as one among the measures which the situation of the occupiers of land in Ireland at present calls for'.[3] Following the second serious and more widespread failure of the potato crop in 1846, a further recommendation, this time from the Select Committee on Colonisation from Ireland, 'to transplant our domestic habits, our commercial enterprise, our laws, our institutions, our language, our literature and our sense of religious obligation to the more distant regions of the globe is an enterprise worthy ... if it can also be made subservient to the relief of pressing distress at home'[4] may seem inappropriate and insensitive, given the extent of the tragedy then unfolding in Ireland. Nevertheless, it served to reinforce the increasingly widely-held view of the importance of emigration as a means of combating dearth and destitution.

By then, however, it was clear, to Nicholls' regret, that there was little if any political will to introduce effective emigration schemes. 'Emigration, contrary to what was originally intended, was by the 51st Section of the [1838] Relief Act made a charge upon the electoral division. The board of guardians collectively had no powers to deal with it'.[5] In 1843 an amendment to the poor law increased the powers of the guardians to assist emigration.[6] The fact remains, however, that by 1844 only 31 paupers had been assisted to emigrate from workhouses. By 1845 this figure had increased to 76 and by 1846 to 197; a derisory total of 2 was recorded for 1847.[7] The disparity between the model of emigration as a panacea for the overcrowding of workhouses, as recommended by Nicholls and others, and the reality of a very low rate of workhouse-assisted emigration would have been all the more stark had not the guardians of workhouses in Ulster taken advantage of the possibilities allowed them by the 1838 Act and subsequent amendments to send selected inmates abroad, mainly but not exclusively to Canada.[8] These developments were prompted by a number of circumstances which encouraged Ulster workhouses to take advantage of legislative amendments to combat the problems posed by the growing workhouse population, most notably the influence of the poor law inspectors for the unions of the province, Edward Senior and C.G. Otway. Additional factors included the initiatives of guardians who were also landlords; the mounting crisis posed by the numbers of children, many unaccompanied, in Ulster workhouses; and the pattern of emigration to Canada. This migration had developed in the 30 years before the Famine and predisposed the workhouses to avail of the poor law commission's preference for assisted emigration to be directed to the British colonies.

Indeed, it is worth noting that there are instances of workhouses in Ulster arranging for the emigration of inmates, to Canada in particular, before there was any tangible evidence of potato blight. The 1843 Poor Law Amendment Act went some way towards reversing the omission of the original act and satisfied one of Nicholls' regrets, that the guardians of workhouses had no controlling power in the assistance of paupers' emigration. It stipulated that 'Two thirds of the guardians of any union, subject to the regulations of the Commissioners, may assist any poor person who has been in the workhouse for three months to emigrate to a British colony.'[9] The full cost of emigrating paupers, as it turned out, proved to be enough of a disincentive for guardians to take full advantage of this facility. Exceptions, however, were to be found in the northern district for which Edward Senior, senior poor law inspector, had responsibility. On 5 April 1845, for example, the guardians of Londonderry workhouse resolved 'that the question of emigration be taken up the first time Mr Senior (poor law inspector) may find it convenient to attend a meeting of the board of guardians'.[10] Within a week, as the minutes of 12 April 1845 meeting show, action had been taken:[11]

> A considerable number of paupers having been examined by
> the Board respecting their eligibility to emigrate to Canada
> when the following parties were selected as suitable –
>
> Patrick McLaughlin, wife and 2 children chargeable to City
> Bernard McColgan   "   "   "
> Robert McCorkell   "   "   "

Isabella Hughes and one son   "   "   "

Betty Blackburn   "   "   "

After some initial local opposition, the nine paupers were fitted out and shipped to Canada from the port of Derry. The clerk of the union at the 6 September 1845 meeting 'read a very satisfactory letter from the emigrants sent out to Canada last Spring'.[12] At the same time, a similar initiative had been tried by the guardians of Coleraine workhouse, also in Co. Londonderry. Their September 1845 meeting noted:

> a letter from the Poor Law Commissioners enclosing an extract from the weekly return of Mr Buchanan, Chief Agent for Emigration at Quebec and reporting the arrival at that port of certain emigrants from Ireland by the ship *Josephine* of Belfast among which emigrants ... were the 26 sent out from Coleraine workhouse under sanction of the Commissioner's letter of 9 May last.[13]

As well as establishing that workhouse-assisted emigration had begun in Ulster before workhouse accommodation – especially in northern workhouses – was fully taken up, a connection may be made with some of the characteristics of pre-Famine emigration from the north-eastern corner of Ireland which would have predisposed workhouses in Ulster to consider seriously the prospect of arranging pauper emigration. The north-west of the province had been trawled in the 1830s and early 1840s by the Canada Land Company for suitable prospective settlers. The port of Derry had developed links with Canadian ports, particularly St John (New Brunswick) and Quebec. Initially the interest lay in the importation of Canadian timber. Subsequently, the depression in agriculture in the post-Napoleonic War period created a ready-made emigrant market which could be accommodated in the hastily fitted-up cargo ships on their return journeys to Canada. In the 1830s, the Ordnance Survey Memoirs estimated that two out of every three transatlantic emigrants from Co. Londonderry sailed to Canada, though the majority then found their way across the border into the United States.[14] And A. C. Buchanan, the emigration agent at Quebec, mentioned in the Coleraine workhouse minutes, had since his appointment in 1828 sought to attract compatriots from his native soil, his family having been prominent in Co. Tyrone. Newspapers, particularly the *Londonderry Journal* and *Londonderry Sentinel*, carried detailed notices inviting mechanics, labourers and, in particular, families who were seen as the most effective means of developing the settlement of people in the Canadian territories to emigrate.[15]

A more specific impulse for the guardians of Ulster workhouses to arrange for inmates to take the emigrant route was the encouragement they received from the Poor Law inspectors, Edward Senior and C.G. Otway. Senior had in the northern district under his control some 17 workhouses, all in the counties of Antrim, Armagh, Down, Londonderry and Tyrone and containing, according to him, 'one-seventh of the population of Ireland'.[16] In addition to the series of consultations relating to individual pauper emigrations from 1845, it was Senior's circular letter in the spring of 1849 that reminded guardians of recent further amendments to the poor law and pointed out the benefits that lay in ridding their workhouses of inmates who could be identified as being likely long-term drains on their finances.[17] It recommended that they should send as emigrants to Canada, at the cost of the Electoral Division, anyone of the able-bodied inmates of the workhouses, especially females ... in this mode [continued Senior's memorandum] some of the permanent deadweight in the workhouse may be got rid of at a cost to the Electoral Division of about £5 or about one year's cost of maintenance ... that several of the neighbouring unions had adopted the same course.

The primary candidates were single mothers or deserted wives, and their children. Bereft of prospects – home, education and, above all, financial support – they ran the risk of remaining constant drains on the poor rates that were levied from occupiers of property to fund the workhouses. Senior's profession of the value of emigration as a humane means of reducing mounting pressure on workhouses, that was being posed by the deposit of large numbers of deserted children, was affirmed in the evidence he gave to Select Committee on the Poor Laws (Ireland) in 1849. When asked if he thought it 'desirable that any steps should be taken for relieving the workhouse population by means of emigration', he replied:

I believe it to be of the utmost importance to do so ... I should apply it to persons aged from 13 or 14 to 18 or 19, especially to girls ... I should confine it to orphans and deserted children, meaning by orphan children those who have lost the head of the family and not exclusively to those who have lost both parents.[18]

The increased numbers applying to enter the workhouses in the later 1840s and early 1850s contained a substantial and mounting proportion of single parents and orphans. In May 1848 there were 16,349 children under 15 in the Ulster workhouses, out of a total workhouse population of 33,238 – 49 per cent.[19] By July 1848 this proportion had climbed to over 52 per cent of the Ulster workhouse population.[20] By way of comparison, the percentage of children aged under 15 in Munster workhouses in July 1848 was 41 per cent, in Leinster 42.5 per cent and in Connacht 40 per cent.[21] The striking difference in ratios between Ulster and the other provinces had in fact been growing in the period 1846-8.[22]

Senior did not offer an explanation for the greater number of 'orphans' in Ulster workhouses. Although his observation that 'the tendency to a deadweight in the workhouses on the part of children is constantly increasing'[23] was indeed true, – by 1852 the total orphan population was 68,402[24] – his assertion that 'in every part of Ireland ... more than half of the inmates now consist of children ...'[25] is likely to have been based largely on his experience in Ulster. His concern at the increased tendency of parents in the district he controlled to dump offspring in the workhouses lay behind his letter to Ballymoney guardians drawing their 'serious consideration' to

a list of 134 paupers deserted by their parents or husbands, many of whom have been for years a burden on the Union. The evil moreover is an increasing one. In 34 cases [continued the minute of his letter] he had marked the residence of the parent in either the Union or its neighbourhood. He does most earnestly recommend the Guardians to spare no trouble to arrest the parties.[26]

The previous year, in March 1849, Senior had reported to the Select Committee on the Poor Law (Ireland) that

> the guardians in my district, by my advice, spare neither trouble nor expense in arresting persons who desert their families, they publish descriptions of the persons and send to different police stations and correspond with the police stations in Scotland and England; they offer rewards and very often parties are arrested from great distances in Scotland and in England.[27]

In a number of documented cases, the guardians of workhouses in the north-west of Ulster, especially Letterkenny, Inishowen, Derry and Strabane unions, not only reconstituted parents with children but also assisted the emigration of the entire family unit, with the aim of reducing the risk of them becoming the 'permanent deadweight' feared by Senior. In October 1850, the Strabane guardians

> ... authorised ... the sum of £6 ... in the emigration to America of David Devine ... whose mother and family are now about to go, their passage and expenses having been paid by their friends there, said David Devine being anxious to go with his mother and having no means whatever and, should he not go, likely to remain a burthen on the [Electoral] Division for life.[28]

The concern of Strabane guardians to provide funds for the transatlantic departure of dislocated families prompted them by May 1852 to seek the sanction of the poor law commissioners 'for the expenditure of not more than £42 to be applied for the emigration to America of Nancy Dunlop and her family amounting to 7 persons', some of whom were inmates, 'the family being likely, if they continued in the country, to remain a permanent charge on the Electoral Division'.[29] Similarly, the Letterkenny guardians approved the assisted passages of a succession of two- and single-parent families ... 'Charles Gallagher and his wife and 4 children' ... Hugh McGrath and his wife and 5 children being inmates of the workhouse during the last 2 years having applied ... to be sent to British North America' ... Catharine Gallogly and her 3 children, being inmates during the last 2 years'.[30]

By the middle of 1848, the ratio of able-bodied adults in the workhouse of Ulster was nearing three females to one male (the ratio in the other provinces was generally nearer two females to one male).[31] The evidence of the minutes of Ulster workhouses indicate that a programme to assist the emigration to North America of mothers and single female parents accompanied by their children was generally adopted and administered. This was particularly evident in Letterkenny where the guardians approved the funds required for a number of cases of assisted passage. These included 'Ann Wray and her 2 children, being inmates of the workhouse since it was opened, having applied to be sent out to her friends in British America and having no means of providing an outfit, it was resolved that the sum of £15 be allowed ... under the provisions of the 18th section of 6 & 7 Victoria Chap. 92.'[32] As in this case, the assistance often took the form of payments for outfitting or transport to the port of embarkation. There were enough instances, however, of fully-funded passages of pauper families from Letterkenny workhouse to induce James Cairns, agent for J. & J. Cooke, the

Derry shipping agent, to offer in July 1849 'to forward any number of paupers your board may think proper ... should the Guardians not wish to pay the amount of passage money when the passengers embark, the money to be paid in six months ...'.[33]

The part played by workhouse guardians in providing relief, both for the paupers and for their increasing accommodation difficulties was further enhanced, in theory at least, by the provisions of the Poor Law Extension Act of 1847 which 'extended to poor persons not in the workhouse ... the provisions of the 1843 Relief Act'.[34] It was the initially lethargic response of the guardians to this provision which caused the Colonial Land and Emigration Commissioners to lament, in their tenth general report 'it is therefore a matter of regret that in districts where labour is in excess the powers contained in the Poor Law Act for raising funds for emigration are so little resorted to.'[35] Indeed, it was not until 1849 that the more impoverished unions were permitted to borrow money with which to fund the emigration schemes which were so manifestly required. The initiative in this regard was taken by William Monsell, member for Limerick (and the future Lord Emly) in May 1849 and, subsequent to that, poor law emigration increased appreciably.[36]

In its final form, Monsell's amendment enabled guardians to apply for grants to finance emigration over and above the maximum rate. In addition to the earlier examples of individual cases, the guardians at Letterkenny, Londonderry, Coleraine and Strabane, encouraged by Messrs Otway and Senior respectively, took the opportunity thus afforded to arrange for the migration to Canada, in a block booking as it were, of substantial numbers of paupers. Over 80 paupers, who had been in Letterkenny workhouse for periods ranging from 7 months to 4 years, were shipped out from the port of Derry to Quebec in the summer of 1849.[37] In the case of Derry workhouse itself, approval was received in June 1849 from the poor law commissioners for the transporting to Canada of some 64 paupers who 'have not been less than 6 months inmates in the workhouse'.[38] In the same year, in the minutes of Coleraine guardians 'The clerk reported that the 56 emigrants from this workhouse were put on board the *Riverdale* at Belfast. On the recommendation of Mr Senior, he had paid over the money ordered by the board to Mr Grainger, the owner of the ship, to be repaid to the emigrants on their landing at Quebec'.[39] At the beginning of 1851, the Strabane guardians decided that all paupers who had been in the workhouse for two years should be considered eligible for assisted migration to Canada. A list of 58 names was compiled and the group sailed from the port of Derry to Quebec in April,1851. As had happened in the other group migrations, each emigrant was provided with a new outfit of clothes, including bed clothes, food and utensils for the journey.[40] These examples confirm the figures which indicate that the outcome of the amended legislation was a significant rise in the numbers assisted to emigrate. Nevertheless, as Christine Kinealy has pointed out, even at its peak in 1852, when a total of 4,386 workhouse-assisted passages were arranged, this amounted to only 2.5 per cent of the national total for that year of some 190,322.[41] Just as pertinently in any consideration of the role of guardians, Kinealy makes the point that the response to the opportunity to assist emigration was better taken up in workhouses – including Letterkenny, Derry, Coleraine and Strabane – where pressure was not as extreme as in areas known to have been more seriously affected.[42]

Eventually, the provisions of the 1847 Extension Act and the subsequent 1849 amendment enabled the Letterkenny guardians to follow their chairman, John Vandeleur Stewart's, expressed preference to assist passages to the United States.[43] Until then, British North America had been the stipulated destination of workhouse-assisted passages. But the precedent was not established without a struggle. The minute book records an exchange of papers between the guardians and the commissioners in the spring of 1850 relating to the refusal of the commissioners to approve the provision of Patty McDonald and her children with an outfit and clothing during their passage to the United States. The explanation offered by the Letterkenny guardians stated that

> the friends of the pauper Patty McDonald in the United States having provided free passages together with sea store for herself and 6 children stated their inability to furnish them with the necessary outfit. Under these circumstances the Guardians consider it of the highest importance to the union to take advantage of so good an opportunity of getting rid of the support of so many paupers who had been in the house for 3 years and who most certainly would have remained a charge on the rates ... The board therefore hope that the Commissioners [will take] into consideration that the Guardians acted in ignorance of the course being forbidden by law.[44]

Undaunted, two years later the Letterkenny guardians

> resolved that application be made to the Poor Law Commissioners for permission to send out Margaret M'Elhinny and family to the United States of America, Mr Samuel Marshall one of the landlords of the division having guaranteed to pay £10, being one half of the expenses ... and the other half be charged to the Electoral Division of Gartan to which Margaret M'Elhinny and family are chargeable.[45]

There can be no coincidence that assistance with this landlord-sponsored passage was the sort of help J.V. Stewart had in mind when he gave evidence to the Select Committee on Poor Laws (Ireland) in 1849. On the question of how impoverished areas might be helped, he expressed the view that 'those are the districts to which, with the aid of the proprietor, loans and grants to aid emigration might be made'.[46]

In view of this practical and businesslike approach to assisted emigration as a means of addressing the problem of paupers who threatened to be long-stay liabilities, it comes as no surprise to find that 29 female orphans from Strabane workhouse and 30 from Letterkenny accompanied the other 4,102 young females who were sent to Australia 1848-50.[47] This was a scheme designed initially to help solve the Australian colony's labour shortage and the imbalance of the sexes at a time when there was a commensurate imbalance of sexes among the under-15 age group which dominated the workhouse population. Briefly put, there were too many females in the workhouse and too few females among the colonists. It was conceived initially by Earl Grey, the British Secretary of State for the Colonies in Lord John Russell's Whig government. At his suggestion and with his support the Colonial Land and Emigration Commissioners inquired in 1847 and 1848 about using Irish workhouses as a source of female migrants. They subsequently communicated with the poor law commissioners and urged them to circularise the guardians of each poor law union explaining how the experiment might be conducted.

However, colonial criticism of this female orphan scheme, provoked by the scandal over the orphans who arrived on board the aptly-named *Earl Grey*, rose to such a crescendo, that the experiment was brought to a hasty conclusion in 1850, after only two years. Before then, however, the orphan immigration depot in Adelaide had been likened to a 'government brothel' and Earl Grey and the Lord Lieutenant of Ireland had been labelled 'dupes of an artful female Jesuit' who sought 'to Romanize the Australian colonies'.[48] An inquiry was instituted in Australia and copious evidence sought from Belfast since it was the 64 'Belfast girls', as they came to be known, on board the *Earl Grey*, against whom allegations of improper conduct were brought, principally by Henry Grattan Douglass, the ship's surgeon superintendent.[49]

> The greatest part of the Belfast girls are notoriously bad in every sense of the word ... Mary McConnell, Georgiana Mulholland, Mary Black and Margt Cassidy were well known in Belfast as public girls ... all ... were for the most part addicted to stealing, and to using the most obscene and gross language, language that no person decently brought up could use.

The conciliatory counsel of the Poor Law Commissioners, submitted in evidence to the New South Wales Legislative Council, that 'the true explanation of that which was reprehensible in the conduct of the emigrants from Belfast must be sought in the peculiar circumstances of that town', especially as the girls had been exposed 'at an early age to the contamination of evil example and ... the use of improper language', was not enough to revive public or government confidence in the scheme.[50]

The workhouses serving Ulster unions sent some 900 of the overall quota of 4,150 orphans, representing 23 per cent which, if anything, signified that, in numerical terms at least, Ulster was slightly under-represented.[51] By far the best represented Ulster workhouse was Enniskillen, with 107. Indeed, apart from the houses at Dublin and Skibbereen, this was the largest single dispatch of orphans in Ireland. Cavan with 60, Armagh with 57, Lisnaskea with 44 and Derry with 40, Cookstown with 33 and Donegal and Dungannon with 31 each, lend weight to the impression that the orphan problem concerned guardians of workhouses in the south and west of the province sufficiently to take any advantage they could of unloading young people with no dependants. As far as a long-term judgement on the benefits which the enforced migration brought to the orphans themselves, Trevor McClaughlin's research has shown that, on the whole, the Colonial Land and Emigration Commissioners' conclusion 'it is impossible to overrate the boon which this emigration confers upon a class entitled to public sympathy but not enjoying in this country any prospects'[52] is not full-blown hyperbole. In general, the evidence does indeed suggest that the majority of girls fared better in Australia than would have been their lot had they remained, workhouse-bound, in Ireland. Individual cases in the admission registers, which record the condition the orphans were in when they applied to enter the workhouse, go some way towards confirming McClaughlin's redemptive judgement that 'the Irish female orphans had an honourable history in Australia as pioneer women ... and as women of strength, courage and endurance ... Although much maligned, the female orphans literally became mothers to the Australian character'.[53] For example, the admission registers of Armagh record, among others, Cathy Tamoney, 'aged 19, Roman Catholic, thinly clothed, hungry' who entered the workhouse on 13 December 1845 and left it on 16 March 1846, only to re-enter it the next day, St Patrick's Day 1846, and Susan Wilson aged 13, Established Church, 'thinly clothed, destitute, bastard', entered the workhouse on 21 December 1847, both remaining there until sent to Australia in May 1848.[54]

By and large, however, it was not simply parentless children who made up the increasing numbers of 'orphans'. Rather, it was single parents, usually young mothers, accompanied by children, who were included in the official classification of orphans drawn up by the poor law commissioners. The minutes of Ulster workhouses also record a number of examples of guardians agreeing in principle to provide further financial assistance for orphans and single-parent families for whom money has been received from the second parent, or other relatives, now in America. Application was accordingly made by the Strabane guardians to the poor law commissioners for

> ... the sanction of ... the outlay of £5 in sending 2 paupers, Susan McArthur aged 8 and Isabella McArthur aged 6 to America, their father having sent home sufficient funds from that country to enable the remaining part of the family to go out. By expending this sum the Electoral Division of Ballymagorry will get rid of a large family, the whole of whom are likely to become inmates of this house should they remain in this house, their mother having died in the workhouse in August last.[55]

At the same meeting, 1 April 1851, it was 'ordered that Mary Jane McDermott be discharged into the care of the Rev. William Browne to whom her mother, who is in America, has sent funds to take her out of the country.'[56] In the years to the mid-1850s, the Strabane guardians considered a steady stream of requests to augment the funds families had found for themselves, either in Ireland or, more commonly, in America. Among others, they approved 'the expenditure of £3 in aid of the emigration to America of Matthew Elliott aged 10 years, Wm Elliott, 8 and James Elliott, 6, resident in Strabane whose passages have been paid for by their father.'[57] In 1853 the Strabane guardians may have taken quiet satisfaction in receiving an 'application from Charles Lynch, an inmate seeking support to enable him and his wife and children to emigrate to Quebec where his son and 2 daughters are, having been sent out by the board of guardians in April 1851 ... The children in Quebec having sent money to assist the family in emigrating.'[58] The guardians of Larne workhouse applied 'to sanction the expense of the emigration of William Johnson, a labourer aged 45 and his wife and 4 children, the youngest 7 years old, to a British colony under the 14th clause of the Extension Act ... the sum of £10 having been supplied by relations in America'.[59] There are enough similarities in these cases to suggest that assisted emigration from the workhouses in much of Ulster also displayed characteristics of the chain migration process that had gradually developed in the 30 years prior to the Famine and which became more and more apparent during it. Family members tended not to emigrate all at the same time. It was, instead, often the case that one member of a family went out first, in pioneer style, and sent back money, by one means or another, to enable the rest of the family to join him.

The influence of the Colonial Land and Emigration Commission in encouraging emigration to relieve the surfeit of paupers may be seen in the workhouse records for the later 1840s and early 1850s. There are instances of the poor law commissioners being requested by guardians to assist passages for single-parent families in workhouses to join convicts in Australia, their fares already guaranteed by the colonial land and emigration commissioners. Under the free settler scheme, convicts who had served their sentence could apply to bring out their families, the commissioners paying the passage. Letterkenny guardians, for example, considered the case of

> Elizabeth Birney, inmate of the workhouse and wife of a convict in Van Dieman's Land having got a free passage for herself and 7 children … from the Colonial Land & Emigration Commissioners to Van Dieman's Land but having no means of proceeding to Dublin as directed or of providing an outfit, that the sum of 21 pounds be allowed by the Guardians … to enable Elizabeth Birney to procure an outfit for her and her children.[60]

Lisburn guardians were advised in 1848 by the poor law commissioners in the case of the wife and children of convict John Dawson in Van Dieman's Land, who were in their care, 'that this indulgence is only granted on the recommendation of the Governor of the colony'.[61] Four years later, however, in 1852, Strabane guardians recorded a 'letter from the Colonial Land and Emigration Office … replying to a letter from Eliza McKeever, an inmate of the workhouse, requesting a free passage for herself and family to Van Dieman's Land to her husband who is a convict and stating that the passage would be granted provided half of the cost of the passage be paid'.[62]

Scattered throughout the records of Ulster workhouses for the later 1840s and early 1850s are 'one-off' requests being considered and granted. Lisnaskea guardians 'received a letter from the Governor of Grange Gorman convict prison stating that Ann Judge, a convict in the prison, had received permission to bring her 2 children, Mary Ann aged 6 and John aged 5, with her into transportation … Consequently, the guardians considered it better to send the children with their mother and save the union of any further expense'.[63] Ballymoney guardians approved the expenditure on behalf of John McKillop who 'would require a suit of clothes – he is going to America and has been so long in the workhouse that he has outgrown what he had on when he came in'.[64]

There is scope in this descriptive account of workhouse-assisted emigration to provide ammunition for the 'too little, too late' view of the official response to Famine relief and also to support claims that, however inadequate they proved to be, the guardians did as well as the crippling circumstances permitted. Pauper emigration from the workhouses tailed off in the mid-1850s, just as soon as it seemed to be gaining momentum.[65] And, although there are isolated examples in the records of Ulster workhouses thereafter,[66] the principal initial failings – government reluctance to adopt pauper emigration, and lack of financial means at the guardians' disposal – which had dogged the idea from the outset, consigned it to a predictable fate.[67] As far as the workhouses of Ulster are concerned, the response to the opportunities presented by the eventual amendments to the legislation was most evident in the unions of the north of the province – Letterkenny, Londonderry, Strabane and Coleraine in particular. This should not be taken as an acknowledgement of overcrowding: each of the workhouses mentioned, and a good number of others, recorded 'no pressure' or 'no great pressure' on their accommodation as late as mid-winter 1847.[68] The numbers of orphans sent to Australia from Ulster workhouses in the Earl Grey scheme indicate something of the unduly large number of parentless children accumulating in Ulster workhouses as the Famine progressed. It was, perhaps, the concerted response of guardians in the north-west to the poor law inspectors' encouragement to send their 'permanent deadweight' to Canada, a development which took advantage of the amending legislation and also built on the emigrant route established in that area in the two pre-Famine decades, which characterised the activity of Ulster workhouses as they struggled to cope with the mounting scale of tragedy.

References

1   *Third Report of Commissioners for Inquiring into the Condition of the Poorer Classes in Ireland*, B.P.P. 1836[43]XXX, p. 27.

2   Report of George Nicholls Esq ... on Poor Laws, Ireland B.P.P. 1837[69]LI, p. 32.

3   *Report from Her Majesty's Commissioners of Inquiry into the State of the Law and Practice in Respect to the Occupation of Land in Ireland*, B.P.P. 1845[605]XIX, p. 28.

4   *Report of the Select Committee of the House of Lords on Colonisation from Ireland*, B.P.P.1847[737]VI, p. xvi.

5   Sir George Nicholls, *A History of the Irish Poor Law* (1856, Reprint 1957), p. 275.

6   *Act for the Further Amendment of the Law for the Relief of the Poor in Ireland*, 6th & 7th Vict. Cap.92, Sect. 18. 'Two thirds of the guardians of any union ... may assist any poor person who has been in the workhouse for 3 months to emigrate to a British Colony ...'.

7   *Report of Select Committee ... on Colonisation from Ireland*, p. xi.

8   Gerard O'Brien, 'The New Poor Law in Pre-Famine Ireland', *Irish Economic and Social History*, XII (1985), pp. 33-49 outlines the pre-1845 emigration of paupers adopted by the guardians of Cork Union.

9   *An Act for the Further Amendment of the Law for the Relief of the Poor*, op.cit.

10   P.R.O.N.I., BG21/A/2, p. 183.

11   P.R.O.N.I., BG21/A/2, p. 186.

12   P.R.O.N.I., BG21/A/2, p. 224.

13   P.R.O.N.I., BG10/A/4, 13 Sept. 1845.

14 These figures were confirmed by the *First Report of Commissioners for Inquiring into the Condition of the Poorer Classes in Ireland* which reported in 1836. The Appendix gave the breakdown of emigrants' destinations who left from the Port of Londonderry as:

	St John (New Brunswick)	QUEBEC	USA	TOTAL
1832	2396	2607	2640	7643
1833	1789	1523	2730	6042
1834	1432	1082	1402	3916

First Report of Commissioners for Inquiring into the Condition of the Poorer Classes in Ireland, B.P.P. 1836[35]XXX, Appendix C, part I, p.76.

15 Trevor Parkhill, 'Between Revolution and Famine: Patterns of Emigration from Ulster to North America 1776-1845' in John Gray & Wesley McCann (eds), *An Uncommon Bookman: Essays in Memory of J.R.R. Adams* (Belfast, 1996), pp. 59-73.

16 *Third Report from the Select Committee on Poor Laws (Ireland)* B.P.P. 1849[137]XV, Pt 1, q. 21369, p. 179.

17 P.R.O.N.I., BG5/A/6, p. 31.

18 *Third Report from the Select Committee on Poor Laws (Ireland)* q. 2331-4, p. 191.

19 *Papers Relating to the Relief of Distress: Paupers in Workhouses* B.P.P. 1847-8[999]LIV, pp. 220-1.

20 *Papers Relating to the Relief of Distress.*

21 *Papers Relating to the Relief of Distress.*

22 There is no equivalent disparity in those aged under 15 evident in the 1841 Census for the 4 provinces, either in the percentage of males and females together, or simply females. The percentage of the population aged under 15 in Ulster was 41.39, third in line behind Leinster (38.04%) and Munster (40.02%) and ahead of Connacht (42.76%).*Vide Report of the Census Commissioners, Ireland*, B.P.P. 1843[504]XXIV, pp. lxxiv-lxxv.

23 *Third Report the Select Committee on Poor Laws (Ireland)* B.P.P. 1849[137]XV, Pt 1, q. 2336.

24 *Hansard (Commons)* 3, CVIII, 811-3; see also Joseph Robins, *The Lost Children: A Study of Charity Children in Ireland 1700-1900* (Dublin, 1980), p. 239.

25 *Third Report from the Select Committee on Poor Laws (Ireland)* q. 2336, p. 113.

26 P.R.O.N.I., BG5/A/6, 12 Jan. 1850, p. 331.

27 *Third Report from the Select Committee on Poor Laws (Ireland)*, q. 2449, pp 123-4.

28 P.R.O.N.I., BG27/A/2, 15 Oct. 1850.

29 P.R.O.N.I., BG27/A/2, 18 May 1852.

30 P.R.O.N.I., BG100/A/2, 13 July 1849.

31 *Papers Relating to the Relief of Distress and the State of the Unions in Ireland: Paupers in Workhouses* B.P.P. 1847-8[999]LIV, pp. 220-1.

32 P.R.O.N.I., BG100/A/2 f.90, 18 May 1849.

33 P.R.O.N.I., BG100/A/2 f.104, 6 July 1849.

34 *An Act to Make Further Provision for the Relief of the Destitute Poor in Ireland* ('The Extension Act'),10th and 11th Vict., Cap. 31, Sections 13-15.

35 *Tenth General Report of the Colonial Land & Emigration Commissioners* B.P.P 1850[1204]XIII, p. 5.

36 Oliver MacDonagh, 'The Poor Law, Emigration and the Irish Question,1830-55', *Christus Rex*, No. 12 1958, pp. 26-37. MacDonagh's estimate of an average annual figure of 5,000 by the 1850s has subsequently been revised downwards by Christine Kennedy, *Vide* f. 41.

37 P.R.O.N.I., BG100/A/2. See also Brian Trainor, 'Emigration from Irish Workhouses during the Famine *c.*1845-50', *Directory of Irish Family History* research No. 17, 1994, pp.75-88,which contains a detailed list of the emigrants including name, age, marital status, length of time in workhouse etc. I, and many researchers before me, am grateful to Brian Trainor for the extensive provision he has made of such material and which is now accessible in P.R.O.N.I.

38 P.R.O.N.I., BG21/A/5, 30 June 1844.

39 P.R.O.N.I., BG10/A/7, pp. 60-8. See also list of emigrants in Brian Trainor, op.cit.

40 P.R.O.N.I., BG27/A2, 14 Jan., 4 Feb., 18 March 1851.

41 C. Kinealy, *This Great Calamity* (Dublin, 1994), p. 310.

42 Kinealy, *This Great Calamity* p. 312, cites the example of Strabane guardians who 'devoted much of their time in 1850 and 1851 to devising schemes for pauper emigration, even though the worst of the Famine was over in the union by 1849'.

43 *Seventh Report from the Select Committee on Poor Laws (Ireland)* B.P.P. 1849 [237]XV Pt 1, p. 30. J.V. Stewart, chairman of Letterkenny guardians testified on 20 April 1849: 'At present Boards of Guardians cannot aid emigration of paupers to the United States ... [there is] a strong argument for the extension of the system ... as emigration to the Unites States is less expensive than to Canada'. In point of fact, emigration to the Canadian ports of Quebec and St John, New Brunswick from the port of Derry had been consistently cheaper since the late 1820s.

44 P.R.O.N.I., BG100/A/2 f.191; BG 100/A3, f.14.

45 P.R.O.N.I., BG100/A/3, 10 Aug.1852.

46 *Seventh Report from the Select Committee on Poor Laws (Ireland)* B.P.P 1849[209]XV, Pt 1, q.5355, p. 459.

47 Trevor McClaughlin, *Barefoot and Pregnant? Irish Famine Orphans in Australia* (Melbourne, 1991), p. 160.

48 McClaughlin, *Barefoot and Pregnant?*, p. 1.

49 National Archives Ireland, CSORP 1849 0.9048, Minutes of Evidence Taken Before the Orphans Immigration Committee, 12 Oct.1848.

50 Letter from Arthur. Moore, Chief Clerk, Poor Law Commssioners,14 July 1849, which appears in *Votes and Proceedings of the Legislative Council of New South Wales*, vol. I, 1850, pp. 397-436, as quoted in Trevor McClaughlin, *Barefoot and Pregnant?*, pp. 67-73.

51 Trevor Parkhill, 'Permanent Deadweight: Ulster Female Pauper Emigration to Australia,1848-50', *Ulster Local Studies* 10, No.1 (1988), Journal of the Federation for Ulster Local Studies.

52 *Ninth General Report of the Colonial Land and Emigration Commissioners* B.P.P. 1849[1082]XXII, p. 13.

53 Trevor McClaughlin, *Barefoot and Pregnant?*, pp. 22-3.

54 P.R.O.N.I., BG2/G/1.

55 P.R.O.N.I., BG27/A/2, 1 April 1851.

56 P.R.O.N.I., BG27/A/2, 1 April 1851.

57 P.R.O.N.I., BG27/A/2, 8 Oct.1851.

58 P.R.O.N.I., BG27/A/2, 21 June 1853.

59 P.R.O.N.I., BG 17/A/3, p. 54, 1 April 1848.

60 P.R.O.N.I., BG100/A/2, f. 85, 27 April 1849.

61 P.R.O.N.I., BG19/A/5, p. 505.

62 P.R.O.N.I., BG27/A/2, 13 July 1852.

63 P.R.O.N.I., BG20/A/4, p. 234, 6 July 1850.

64 P.R.O.N.I., BG5/A/6, p. 88, 2 June 1849.

65 George Nicholls, *A History of the Irish Poor Law*, p. 403, footnote m noted that 'the amount expended from the poor-rates in 1855, to assist the emigration of 830 poor persons from different unions, was £6,859. In the previous year the amount had been £22,651...'.

66 P.R.O.N.I., BG17/GJ/1, 21 Oct. 1915 includes papers relating to the emigration of Samuel Martin and Bridget Wiggan from Larne workhouse.

67 A useful perspective to the pauper emigration schemes is evident in Christine Kinealy's summary that 'Landlord-assisted emigration ... accounted for no more than 5 per cent of all emigration from Ireland which, although small, was higher than either state-assisted or Poor Law emigration ...'. C. Kinealy, *This Great Calamity*, p. 314.

68 *Correspondence relating to the State of the Union Workhouses in Ireland* B.P.P. 1847[863]LV, p. 147.

'The Great Hunger?' Irish Famine: Changing Patterns of Crisis

Patrick Fitzgerald

UNDOUBTEDLY ONE OF THE BENEFICIAL 'spin-offs' from the recent upsurge in public interest in the Great Irish Famine had been the capacity to focus attention upon contemporary deprivation. Worthy as it is to use an understanding of the Great Famine to help alleviate suffering today, it is important from an historical perspective to look back beyond the 1840s as well as forward from them. While that decade did not mark the end of want in Ireland, neither did it mark the beginning. In looking at Ireland's experience of famine and subsistence crises in the longer term the obvious starting point is the production of a table which identifies periods of particular distress.

I

There have been notable efforts in the past to log Ireland's crisis heritage. In a sense the foundations were laid by John Rutty who in the 1770s sought to trace the path of meteorological variation in Ireland.[1] The first comprehensive table of Irish famines appeared, however, in the wake of the Great Famine. Then Sir William Wilde, as part of the 1851 census, drew up a tabular presentation charting from the pre-Christian period to 1850 all Irish pestilences, cosmical phenomena, epizootics and famines.[2] Not only a 'classic of great scholarship, erudition and industry' Wilde's efforts constitute as Sir Peter Froggatt has noted 'the standard reference work in the subject'.[3] The next notable tabulation appeared almost a century later when Redcliffe Salaman laid out the course of potato crop failures in Ireland in his 1949 classic on the history and social influence of the tuber.[4] Of more recent vintage is the table constructed by Professor Leslie Clarkson which appeared in a collection of essays entitled *Famine: The Irish Experience 900-1900* and which seeks to identify famines and subsistence crises between 1290 and 1900 and to differentiate between them.[5]

In my own table, constructed to chart the course of episodic crises between 1600 and 1845, I have not positively distinguished between famines and subsistence crises (see Appendix 1). Rather I have selected a number of indices which reflect the presence of distress and give some indication of its severity. Of these indices, it will be the impact upon patterns of migration, particularly to Britain which will be focusing upon in this paper. Before proceeding to look at migration, there are a number of preliminary points relating to the table and of a more general nature which should be addressed.

The first observation is a broad point relating to the nature of poverty and how we define it in pre-industrial Europe. Joel Mokyr in his survey of the pre-

Famine economy suggests excess mortality resulting from food shortages as an alternative to income per capita for evaluating poverty, not least because the latter takes only limited account of income inequality.[6] If one accepts Mokyr's thesis, even with reservations, it becomes clear that Ireland's poverty throughout the period between 1600 and 1850 was a persistent and serious structural problem. Periodically Ireland suffered significant excess mortality induced by subsistence crises over two centuries after this phenomenon had disappeared in England and a century and a half after it had disappeared from all but the peripheral fringe of Scotland.[7] Both in geographical and social terms Ireland, within a British Isles context, retained a much larger sector potentially threatened by deprivation leading to death.

Whilst it may be sensible to link our perception of Irish poverty more closely to susceptibility to subsistence mortality one should be wary of presenting the impression that poverty was a purely cyclical phenomenon. Want was undoubtedly accentuated during crisis years but the root causes of poverty at an individual level were often sustained and related to structural problems connected with for example, access to land, access to an effective welfare mechanism or simply one's stage in the lifecycle. In short, whilst poverty intensified and broadened in crisis years it rarely evaporated in between.

One important feature which emerges from the table of subsistence crises is the degree of regional diversity in relation to the impact of particular crises. Indeed, nowhere is this variability more marked than with respect to the Great Famine. We are now well aware of the fact that by the nineteenth century a stark polarity existed between regions in the east such as the relatively developed Lagan Valley or the prosperous grain belt of Wexford and Kilkenny and on the other hand, broad stretches of the western seaboard where clachan and rundale predominated and huge numbers lived in dire poverty. Yet as recent work on Waterford has demonstrated there could be sharp and numerous variations in the impact of famine even at townland level.[8] Whilst our detailed knowledge of the spatial impact of crises in the early modern period is more limited it would be unwise to assume that the distribution of distress then was significantly more even. As Professor William Smyth has observed, seventeenth-century Ireland, in terms of population density and economic development was characterised by 'violent contrasts and subtle gradations'.[9] Not only could crises be regionally specific within Ireland, but Ireland itself often stood apart from the wider experience of its near neighbours. For example, fairly intense shortage and distress were experienced during 1708-9 throughout much of Western Europe, but unlike the major famine of 1739-41, had limited impact in Ireland. Perhaps even more mysterious was the disparity apparent with late seventeenth-century Scotland. In 1674 both countries were troubled by harvest failure, yet the very severe famine which afflicted Scotland during the later 1690s seems to have entirely missed Ireland even in the north east.[10] It may be, in fact, that as we discover more about the nature of subsistence crises in early modern Ireland we will find that national crisis really represents more accurately the aggregate of local crises, not least because of the limited development of supra regional economies prior to the mid-eighteenth century.

A further dimension thrown into perspective by the table is the relationship which existed between periodic distress and the incidence of crime and popular protest. It is clear that Ireland's populace, particularly its urban populace, could react to food shortages and price rises by recourse to direct action. The evidence relating to food riots in this period would suggest that the behaviour of the crowd was based upon a similar perception of a moral economy detected in contemporary England.[11] Action was essentially conservative in nature and addressed specific and limited goals, such force as was used is best understood as a physical extension to a mutually understood dialogue between rulers and ruled. A review of evidence from the period of the Great Famine might suggest that such a popular response was most marked in the towns and the more commercially advanced regions.[12] Here, the workings and manipulations of the market were best understood, the juxtaposition of relative comfort and dire poverty most pronounced and the continual flow of exported foodstuffs most obvious and disconcerting at a popular level.

II

Migration stimulated by subsistence crises took a number of distinct forms. The first of these to be considered is internal migration. This undoubtedly increased during crisis years although the paucity of records pose a substantial obstacle to our understanding of the exact scale, character and pattern of such movement. As David Dickson has rightly observed 'the classic indication of seventeenth and early eighteenth-century crisis was a massive rise in vagrancy, with whole families taking to the roads to beg.'[13] Vagrancy of course was a crime, defined in Ireland by an act of 1542.[14] It is important to stress the arbitrary character of local enforcement, one parish vestry's dangerous vagabond could be another's worthy pauper. Unfortunately the few records of criminal procedure in this period tell us little of the movement of individuals. Other archives however drawn from both central and local government, serve to reveal the particular reactive measures taken in response to an upsurge in the numbers of wandering poor. The distribution of badges or licences to the resident, deserving poor, the appointment of officers to expel the wandering beggar, efforts to establish houses to correction or regulate the free flow of consumables in the market-place were all common responses during periods of dearth.[15] When it came to suppressing vagrancy however, the absence, before 1838, of any effective national poor law tended only to expose the limitations of such uncoordinated action.

What can be clearly observed in the seventeenth century is the appearance in Ireland of a trend characteristic of contemporary European society. That is significant rural-urban migration, particularly during or in the immediate wake of subsistence crises.[16] In these economic circumstances two types of such migration have been identified, although the difference between them may, in reality, have been as much apparent as real. Betterment migrants on the one hand, tended to be drawn towards towns in the wake of crises in order to take advantage of employment opportunities vacated by those who had either perished or moved elsewhere. Raymond Gillespie has tentatively suggested that such migration may be detected in Dublin during the crisis of 1621-4.[17] A second form of 'pure' subsistence migration, in which push factors predominated, was clearly identifiable during the more serious crisis in the late 1620s and early 1630s. Then the same city was literally inundated with migrants which Dubliners cited as 'foreign' poor.[18] Foreign in the contemporary, parochial sense, meaning non-citizens rather than non-nationals.

By the mid-1630s the impact of this influx was fully apparent. City worthies complained about the numbers of strange beggars and the extent to which they had erected shanty style cabins upon the commons and along the highways in the city's suburbs.[19] The opening of two houses of correction at the same time and the appointment of a provost martial, supported by ten armed men to suppress illegal begging, adds to the picture of crisis management.[20] Municipal records drawn from other Irish towns suggest that the impoverished suburban settlement was not unique to seventeenth-century Dublin. During the course of subsistence crises in the eighteenth and early nineteenth centuries the scale of spasmodic movement from the countryside to the towns increased.[21]

From this perspective it is striking how little detailed knowledge we have about rural-urban migration and settlement in the major port cities during the Great Famine.[22] Given our current state of knowledge, it may be considered rash to automatically accept the conclusion that internal mobility of Ireland's population was universally constricted between 1845 and 1851. Cousens, in his examination of the geographical origins of Famine emigrants concluded that 'the tendency to rush for succour to the towns was on the whole short-lived and insignificant' and that 'migration within Ireland during the Famine was remarkably restricted'.[23] Besides representing a necessary prerequisite to his broader conclusions on emigration, it should be pointed out that Cousens based his conclusion on the census returns of 1841 and 1851, both of which failed to enumerate many who were not permanently resident. Work by Nicholas and Shergold on Irish inter-county mobility before 1840, based on a source independent from the census, show that Cousens' conclusions concerning pre-Famine internal migration require revision. The pre-Famine Irish moved more frequently and over longer distances than he had allowed.[24] With respect to the Famine years Cousens tended to contrast mass emigration with restricted internal migration, yet whilst the numbers leaving Ireland overshadowed those on the move within it, the two processes were intrinsically linked. Not only did people obviously have to travel to ports to leave Ireland, a proportion, as Robert Scally has recently illustrated, were liable to slip away before taking ship.[25] Reports from Derry, Belfast, Drogheda, Dublin and Cork all detail the influx of the impoverished rural poor.[26] The majority undoubtedly moved on in the holds of emigrant ships but by no means all. It is worth reflecting upon the fact that the population of County Dublin actually increased between 1841 and 1851 despite the large numbers who perished from cholera and other diseases, many of those drawn into the towns in the later 1840s were simply no longer around to be enumerated.

Without labouring the point it is worth responding to another of Cousens' claims, that is, it was easier to receive aid through official channels by retaining one's original residence rather than wandering the country.[27] Whilst this bold statement is substantially true, it takes insufficient account of the very considerable numbers who remained beyond the scope of the poor law or could not obtain adequate provision by recourse to it. As late as 1850, for example, in the union of Dungarvan, County Waterford, by no means the worst affected area in the country, we find the posting of a police guard and the fixing of broken glass to the exterior wall of the workhouse in order to keep out 'a mighty assembly of vagrants' seeking entry.[28] It is perhaps not insignificant that one of the popular names attached to the raging epidemic fever of the late 1840s was 'road fever'.

III

In the seventeenth century subsistence migration across the Irish Sea to Britain was in many ways a natural extension to internal movement. Ulster and Munster were only 8 and 26 hours respectively away from Scotland and the south-west of England. Even at this early stage London exercised a considerable pulling power upon migrants from throughout the Celtic fringe. An upsurge in the numbers of poor Irish migrants in London was usually detectable in the wake of subsistence crisis in Ireland. In 1605, for example, following war, harvest failure and plague in Ireland, the privy council was informed by the Lieutenant of the Tower of London, that in the eastern suburbs of the city there existed 'a cluster of base tenements termed Knockfergus, peopled with Irish of very base sort who live only by begging'.[29] Further complaints about the criminality of these immigrants and of the high rates of bastardy serve only to heighten the parallels with commentary about those Irish rookeries which evolved in the capital over 200 years later.

Such subsistence migration reached a peak in the late 1620s and early 1630s as Ireland suffered a series of harvest failures leading to famine conditions. Gauging precisely the scale of this migration is difficult as no official record of entry or exit was kept on either side of the Irish Sea in this period. It is clear, however, that the movement was significant. In 1629 alone Bristol corporation was obliged to commission seven ships in order to transport over 1,200 Irish home. During 1629 and 1630 Somerset quarter-sessions raised the then considerable sum of £250 towards the cost of shipping Irish vagrants from Minehead. At the same time justices in Pembrokeshire in south-west Wales had to part with £75 to repatriate over 300 Irish.[30] If one bares in mind that Ireland's population at this point was little more than an eighth of what it was in the 1840s it is clear that the scale of such removals in relative terms bare comparison with the flood of removals from Liverpool and Glasgow in 1847-8.

On the basis of a profile of Irish migrants recorded during these years the following broad conclusions may be advanced. Firstly, that those leaving Ireland around 1630 and indeed again in the early 1650s were not ethnically homogeneous. The pattern of surnames, supplemented by other evidence, points to the presence of both settler and native stock amongst the migrants. The harvest crisis of 1627-32 came as a profound jolt following the decades of relative growth and prosperity since the end of the Nine Years War in 1603. Greater account needs to be taken of the 'backwash effect' exercised upon British settlement in Ireland before the major exodus brought on by the rising of 1641.

Secondly, the most striking feature about the occupational profile of those departing was the very limited extent to which they were directly employed in agriculture. Rather, the majority of migrants may be characterised as servants and artisans. In common with emigrants of the nineteenth century most were young adults and females were well represented making up 38% of the total. They tended to travel in groups, often made up of extended families, with young children commonly encountered.

Thirdly, in examining the geographical origins of migrants the distribution of source material surveyed should be noticed. The data is drawn from records relating primarily to southern and particularly south-western England. In light of this fact one might anticipate the sample to be skewed towards those drawn from the south of Ireland. This is, indeed, the pattern which emerges. However, a broader scan of the records of municipal and central government combined with the work of those interested in vagrancy in England more broadly serves to confirm this basic pattern.[31] Where the distribution is probably most unrepresentative is in its failure to reflect movement between Ulster and Scotland. We know from the records of the Scottish Privy Council that there was an influx of vagrants from Ireland in 1629 and 1630 but the absence of local records comparable to those in England make it impossible to chart where in Ireland these vagrants originated.[32]

If one looks in more detail at the origins of vagrants who hailed from counties Cork and Waterford it becomes clear, on an admittedly small sample, that individuals were drawn from the port towns and from along the major river valleys of the Suir, Bandon, Blackwater and Lee. These were precisely the areas where British settlement had been carried on most intensively, representing the most fertile, economically developed and populous regions in the province. The river valleys of Munster in this period represented advanced channels for in migration and source regions of out migration. It would appear that those native Irish who fled to England in crisis years were neither excluded or remote from the forces of the market but rather enmeshed in the new commercial network.[33] As recent work on the origins of the 1641 rising have demonstrated, considerable numbers of the native Irish were financially indebted to members of the settler community.[34]

IV

Looking forward a century to the famine of 1740-1 and the subsistence crisis of 1756-7, elements of continuity and change may be identified in the pattern of migration to England.

Evidence relating to the age of Irish vagrants arrested in England in these years again suggests the preponderance of young adults. Children were still commonly encountered, whilst women continued to make up a considerable proportion of vagrants arrested, constituting 42 per cent of a sample of 123 Irish vagrants who received passes in Buckinghamshire during these years.[35] Unfortunately less information is available about the occupational background of subjects arrested in this period.

However, a wider review of evidence suggests that migration in crisis years now overlaid a more consistent stream of migrants moving in search of employment. Given what we know about the excessive size of the Irish landowner's household staff, it may be conjectured that a proportion were seeking places in domestic service. Yet the Irish are found in London at this stage, working in the textile trades, the building trade, tinsmithing, coal heaving, dock work and the whole gamut of unskilled manual occupations.[36]

Evidence relating to Irish vagrants who passed through Wiltshire during the 1730s and 1740s reveals another interesting feature which may serve to some degree to explain the high profile of female migrants. In Wiltshire we find several Irish women, some with children explaining to local justices that they had come to England in order to search for husbands who had been English or Scottish soldiers serving in Ireland. Given that some 5-10,000 British soldiers were stationed in over fifty garrison towns, mainly in the south of Ireland, it is likely that such accounts were not untypical.[37]

The geographical pattern of migration shows distinct signs of evolution over the course of one hundred years. The evidence of Irish vagrants passing through Wiltshire confirms the continued significance of the routeway between the Severn estuary and London. The Irish presence in the west country is confirmed by the records of Bristol Corporation and hinted at by the regular occurrence of Irish names in the city's mid-eighteenth century gaol delivery fiets.[38] However, in the crises of both the early 1740s and mid-1750s the routeway from the north-west of England to London evidently saw a volume of Irish migrants much greater than had been the case a century before. By 1750 provision had to be made for the erection of a house of correction at Great Neston near Chester in order to house large numbers of vagrants awaiting shipment from Parkgate back to Ireland.[39] A decade before, the Lancashire grand jury had struck rates for the payment of masters of vessels shipping vagrants to both Dublin and Cork through Liverpool.[40] The strongest evidence for the emergence of this north-west, south-east channel derives from an archive held at Aylesbury in Buckinghamshire detailing the passage of over 120 Irish vagrants on the main road from London to Chester during the 1740s and 1750s.[41] Thus we can detect in these decades the outline of the primary paths of Irish migration into England identified firmly for the 1820s by Redford in his work on labour migration in England.[42]

An examination of these Buckinghamshire vagrant passes during the years 1740-1 and 1756-7 reveals that those who migrated to England were drawn from a wider area in Ireland than those who departed during the late 1620s and early 1630s. Many migrants were drawn from Leinster and south Ulster, whilst Dublin accounted for the largest single concentration. Curiously no migrants from the early 1740s were drawn from Munster, where famine conditions were most severe. Yet when one looks at the pattern for 1756-7 one finds the major Munster port cities of Cork and Limerick well represented, perhaps confirming that conditions then were most severe in the ports.[43]

The difficult years of the early 1770s saw a massive surge in numbers emigrating to North America, primarily from Ulster but by no means exclusively so. Whilst these were unambiguously years of real distress in Ireland, contemporary comment on the crisis may have been heightened by the contrast which was cast with the preceding decade, marked as it was by fairly rapid economic expansion. If the emigrants of the early 1770s demonstrated differences from those who departed in the late 1720s, early 1740s or mid-1750s it was in their level of skills and perhaps less tangibly, in their individual motivation to seek out fresh opportunities in the New World.[44]

Whilst thousands sailed west, others looked east to England. In Cheshire the records relating to the passing of Irish vagrants have been comprehensively preserved for only the year of 1773. Yet in this one year over 500 Irish were processed, most having been arrested in the Midlands, East Anglia or the south-east.[45] The general profile of these migrants does not appear markedly different from that of mid-century. Groups travelling with children were common, whilst the gender balance was again quite even, 59 per cent male, 41 per cent female. The absence of any marked seasonality in the distribution would suggest that this migration was not primarily related to harvest labour.[46]

The geographical distribution of where these vagrants had been drawn from in Ireland also relates closely to the pattern established by subsistence migrants a generation before. The core feeder region remained Leinster and south Ulster with County Cork again well represented. Dublin continued to account for a quarter of all migrants. From this it may be discerned that the rapid growth of Dublin was manifesting itself upon patterns of Irish migration to England. Throughout early modern Europe urbanisation tended to increase levels of mobility, a similar trend is likely to have been at work in Ireland. In a sense those drawn to Dublin from the Irish countryside had already severed important communal and familial bonds. This psychologically eased the migrants path, whilst the numerous small vessels trading between Dublin and Chester made the flight, in difficult years, a practical and affordable proposition. For those with experience of Dublin, the second largest city in the British Isles, London may have exercised a particular draw. Persuasive evidence exists of a growing Irish presence amongst the lower orders in London during the course of the eighteenth century.[47] In a recent study of those hanged at Tyburn, in the city, between 1703 and 1772 Peter Linebaugh established that no less than 14 per cent were of Irish birth.[48] Whilst we have no accurate guide to the size of the total London Irish community at this point there can be little doubt that this figure was exceptionally high. Apart from anything else this serves to illustrate that the high profile of the Irish in nineteenth-century English criminal statistics, although sometimes exaggerated, had long roots. Equally interesting is the disproportionate number of Irish hanged, who had experience of life outside Ireland, often as soldiers serving in continental armies. In essence the message which emerges is that many of the Irish drawn to London in the eighteenth century bore little resemblance to the popular if grotesque caricature of the Irish migrant which emerged during the nineteenth century, that is, as a naive, illiterate, uncouth, almost sub-human specimen fresh from the bogs of Ireland.[49]

Before moving on to look at migration to Britain during the Great Famine, a brief stop in the mid-1820s. Cormac ÓGráda, on analysis of quarterly returns of 3,000 Irish vagrants passing from Colnebrook to Maidenhead for deportation during the years 1824 and 1825, which incidently, coincided with the crisis years of 1825 and 1826, found that most were drawn from Munster, with almost three quarters coming from County Cork alone.[50] Although Cork was severely effected by the potato failure and textile depression of these years, the very skewed distribution may again relate to the location. Maidenhead, to the west of London, lay on the main road from the capital to Bristol. An impressionistic survey suggests that Irish vagrancy was still characterised by mixed groups travelling with young children. In this respect one may be detecting a divergence between those moving to England and those emigrating to North America. The latter, not least because of cost, tended to cross the Atlantic alone, hoping that in the future other members of the family might follow.

V

The position in regard to the study of Irish migration to Britain during the Great Famine is somewhat anomalous. At no time in the past had the gross volume of migration come close to equalling the scale of the movement experienced during the late 1840s and yet, paradoxically, detailed records of the process and particularly information on the origins of migrants are comparatively rare. Such was the prolific scale of the influx into Britain in these years that even the notoriously officious Victorian statistics compiler wilted. During the years of the Famine many of the urban poor law unions which saw the largest numbers of Irish, resorted to wholesale removal, often of dubious legality. In 1847, for example, Liverpool ordered the removal of 15,008 Irish paupers, whilst the surrounding county of Lancashire accounted for more than half of the 52,000 removal orders applied for throughout England and Wales between 1845 and 1849.[51] Besides the north-west of England, Glasgow and the south west of Scotland and the south coast of Wales were particularly active in removing Irish paupers.

To some degree the scale of the exodus to Britain in these years reflected the extent to which Irish emigration to North America had in the preceding decades been channelled through the ports of Liverpool and to a lesser degree, Greenock in Scotland.[52] Thus, of those who crossed the Irish Sea during the Famine, the majority subsequently re-emigrated to the New World. Whilst economic recession in Britain compounded the urge to cross the Atlantic for those who could afford it, perhaps a quarter of a million came to and remained in Britain in the six years following 1845. Not all of those who followed this path were without means or skills but with a passage between the two islands available for as little as two or three shillings, Britain, as David Fitzpatrick has observed, was always liable to constitute the 'low cost and low return option' for Irish emigrants.[53]

As the tide of Irish pauperism descended upon Britain following the repeated crop failures, it excited a wave of reactionary opinion fuelled by the fear and frustration of those who increasingly encountered the wretched wandering Irish poor at close quarters. The London *Times* in April 1847 captured the prevailing mood whilst evoking the language of foreign invasion, in stating that:

> The sudden apparition of 20 French war steamers, followed by as many ships of the line, may be less evil, less fatal, less destructive, less confounding than the daily importation of thousands who cannot be driven from the shore or resisted at their landing.[54]

A scan of local and national newspaper reports indicates the frequency with which the Irish arrivals were described as shoals, not only did they emerge from the Irish sea in seemingly endless huddled masses but clearly were able to slip through such broad-meshed nets as were erected to impede them. The sudden pressures exerted by wave after wave of Irish paupers was felt nowhere more intensely than Liverpool and amongst those who sought to respond to the crisis one should certainly draw attention to the many individual examples of unrestrained effort, compassion and selflessness. Yet, in the teeth of deep domestic depression and soaring poor rates it was almost inevitable that the official municipal response would be more defensive and less charitable in character. From 1846 the board of poor law guardians in Liverpool mounted a determined campaign to chivvy the board of trade into placing effective restraint upon the flourishing trade in ferrying those fleeing from Famine across the Irish sea. Whilst it is indisputable that conditions on board vessels plying this route were horrific, it is difficult to avoid the conclusion that the language of humanitarian concern in which appeals to the board were couched was largely dressing.[55]

The real goals were to ensure that the numbers of migrant vessels could carry would be limited and should ideally be priced out of the range of most Irish paupers. In exasperation the Liverpool poor law guardians in 1849 met with their equivalents from Glasgow and other Scottish boards in order to bring more concerted pressure on the government.[56] Such efforts to encourage effective, legally backed regulation upon the Irish Sea traffic met with limited success. Despite piecemeal efforts to enforce existing regulations, gaping holes persisted. The essential problem dated back to the 1620s, when rogue masters with relatively small craft could disembark undiscerning passengers at a host of small coves and inlets the length of Britain's western coastline.[57]

Whilst Liverpool acted as a magnet for those driven from the south and the west of Ireland, Glasgow and Strathclyde tended to see more migrants drawn from the north of Ireland, particularly from the southern and western counties of Ulster, where the impact of the Famine was felt more acutely. There must have been numerous cases like that of an unnamed individual from County Cavan who was noted by the parochial board of Blantyre as having gained lodgings at a local farmhouse in April 1847. It emerged upon further enquiry that he had come over from Ireland in the summer of 1846 and got work upon the railway, but then injured himself in the course of his work. Still in poor health himself, his wife had died three weeks previously and three of his children had gone off to beg. The action of the parish in this case is not recorded but it would appear that removal was being considered as the man's two remaining children, aged 9 and 7 were quizzed as to the parish in Cavan in which they had been resident.[58] Such was the virtual hysteria which accompanied the removal procedure during these years that the laws relating to legitimate settlement for Irish migrants in both Scotland and England were regularly flouted. There are examples of persons long resident in parishes who were illegally forcibly removed to Ireland when they sought poor relief.[59] The bitterness of disputes which erupted between the authorities in Belfast and Glasgow or Dublin and Liverpool was only surpassed by the inhumanity exercised upon the individuals trapped by bureaucratic mayhem. Reminiscent of the unseemly disputes which erupted between Irish parishes in the eighteenth century over the responsibility for abandoned foundlings, certain victims of the Famine were but pawns caught in a game of chess played across the Irish Sea. In 1848, for example, one Sean Cairns, who applied for relief in Glasgow was removed back to Belfast where he was swiftly put back on board a vessel bound for the Clyde by the city's irate guardians.[60]

In order to understand why some of these gross injustices occurred it is necessary to appreciate the thinking which underlay the recourse of poor law officers to the removal of Irish paupers. Such was the overwhelming scale of the influx during the 1840s that it was quickly appreciated by local officials on the ground that not all of those who applied for relief could be repatriated: the resources and administrative machinery were simply inadequate. Removal thus came to serve in large part as a deterrent to those who might seek relief, consequently restricting the rapid inflation of poor rates. The sporadic nature of removals and the recurrent removal of those who had a valid legal claim to relief served to keep the Irish migrant guessing, for those who had little knowledge of the law and were ill inclined to challenge disputed settlement, the tendency was to withdraw from poor lists or avoid registering. A fact all too well appreciated by those collecting and distributing the resources of relief.[61]

In this context the actions of those immigrants who deliberately committed crimes to secure a prison place are understandable. They at least secured shelter and food, more than was on offer on England's roads or back in Ireland.[62] The manipulative strategy adopted by certain boards of guardians was especially cruel for Irish immigrants. Exclusion from official relief often precluded settlement. Thus the Irish were often forced to fall back upon a wandering existence based on casual begging or opportunistic petty crime, reinforcing the English stereotype of the incorrigibly idle, scrounging Celtic cousin. Whilst the early Victorian penchant for theories of genetic conditioning sharpened the long established perception of native Irish idleness, there were fears that like a contagion this scrounging ethos would contaminate the resident lower orders. This concern was vented most eloquently by a Glasgow petition of March 1847 which spoke of 'the most pernicious example to the lower classes of this city' offered by the Irish who depend upon parish sources for support rather than their own industry.[63]

Of course, refugees from famine did pose a real threat of contagion through diseases which could be contracted by Englishmen regardless of class. The fear engendered was by no means new, in 1630 the personal physician of Charles I singled out the filth of Irish vagrants as a prime source of plague.[64] Recent work of Jona Schellekens has tested the theory that typhus epidemics in England corresponded with periods of famine in Ireland, because Irish migrants travelled to England in search of work and food, and hence spread infection and increased mortality. His conclusion is that 'mortality decline in England in the eighteenth century was exogenous to socioeconomic and demographic processes in the country', and indeed 'English health was constantly under threat from Irish famines'.[65] The perception of the Irish has changed little in 350 years.

References

1   J. Rutty, *A Chronological History of the Weather and Seasons, and of the Prevailing Diseases in Dublin* (London, 1770).

2   Census of Ireland, 1851: Reports on Tables of Death, British Parliamentary Papers (hereafter BPP), 1856 [2087-1] XXIX , pp. 41-235, 257-333.

3   P. Froggatt, 'Sir William Wilde and the 1851 Census of Ireland', *Medical History*, 9 (1965), p. 306.

4   R. N. Salaman, *The History and Social Influence of the Potato* (Cambridge, 1949), pp. 603-7.

5   E. M. Crawford (ed.), *Famine: The Irish Experience 900-1900: Subsistence Crises and Famine in Ireland* (Edinburgh, 1989), p. 226.

6   J. Mokyr, *Why Ireland Starved: A Quantitative and Analytical History of the Irish Economy, 1800-1850* (London, 1983), p. 15.

7   A. B. Appleby, *Famine in Tudor and Stuart England* (Liverpool, 1978); E. A. Wrigley and R. S. Schofield, *The Population History of England 1541-1871: A Reconstruction* (Cambridge; 1981); M. Flinn (ed.), *Scottish Population History* (Cambridge, 1977); I. D. Whyte, *Scotland Before the Industrial Revolution: An Economic and Social History, c.1050 – c.1750* (London, 1995), pp. 121-127.

8   D. Cowman and D. Brady (eds), *The Famine in Waterford 1845-1850* (Dublin, 1995).

9   W. J. Smyth, 'Society and Settlement in Seventeenth-Century Ireland: The Evidence of the "1659 Census" ', in W. J. Smyth and Kevin Whelan (eds.), *Common Ground: Essays on the Historical Geography of Ireland* (Cork, 1988), p. 60.

10   J. S. Bromley (ed.) *The New Cambridge Modern History, vi. The Rise of Great Britain and Russia 1688-1725* (Cambridge, 1971), p. 881; S. J. Connolly, *Religion, Law and Power: The Making of Protestant Ireland, 1660-1760* (Oxford, 1992), p. 48 T. C. Smout, *A History of the Scottish People, 1560–1830* (London, 1969), p. 144.

11   S. J. Connolly, *Religion, Law and Power*, pp. 219-20.

12   The whole subject of crime and popular protest during the Great Famine cries out for deeper study but some insight may be found in the following. W. Fraher, 'The Dungarvan disturbances of 1846 and sequels' in Cowman and Brady (eds). *The Famine in Waterford 1845-50*, pp. 137-152; Kinealy, *This Great Calamity: The Irish Famine 1845-52* (Dublin, 1994), pp. 68-9; C. Ó Gráda, *Ireland: A New Economic History 1780-1939* (Oxford, 1994), pp. 199-204; S. H. Palmer, *Police and Protest in England and Ireland 1780-1850* (Cambridge, 1988), pp. 471-81; S. Curley, 'Transportation in Clare before and after the Famine' in B. Reece (ed.), *Irish Convicts: The Origins of Convicts Transported to Australia* (Dublin, 1989), pp. 81-113; J Williams, *Ordered to the Island, Irish convicts and Van Diemans Land* (Sydney, 1994); C. Poirteir, *Famine Echoes* (Dublin, 1995), pp. 68-84.

13   D. Dickson, 'The Gap in Famines: A Useful Myth?' in Crawford (ed.), *Famine: The Irish Experience 900-1900*, p. 108.

14   33 Henry VIII, s. 1, c. 15.

15   P Fitzgerald 'Poverty and Vagrancy in Early Modern Ireland' (unpublished PhD thesis, Queen's University Belfast, 1994).

16   J. De Vries, *European Urbanisation 1500-1800* (London, 1974).

17   R. Gillespie, 'The Harvest Crisis of 1621-4 and The Irish Economy' in Crawford (ed.), *Famine: The Irish Experience 900-1900*, p. 89.

18   J. T. Gilbert (ed.), *The Calendar of the Ancient Records of Dublin* (Dublin, 1889), 3, pp. 220-1, pp. 303–4; Representative Church Body, Dublin, P 328/5/1 f/133.

19   Gilbert, *Calendar of Dublin*, 3, pp. 298-9.

20   British Library, Harleian MS 2138 28/11/1634; Gilbert, *Calendar of Dublin*, 3, pp. 220-21, 223; Pearse Street Public Library, Dublin, Gilbert Collection, MS 169, f. 200; *Calendar of State Papers Ireland 1625-32*, p. 611; National Library of Ireland, MS 23, 424, p. 55.

21   P. Fitzgerald 'Poverty and Vagrancy in Early Modern Ireland', pp. 119-21.

22   J. Prunty, *Dublin Slums 1800-1925: A Study in Urban Geography* (Dublin, 1995); J. Bardon, *Belfast: An Illustrated History* (Belfast, 1982), p. 97; Kinealy, *This Great Calamity*, pp. 171-3.

23   S. M. Cousens, 'The Regional Pattern of Emigration during the Great Famine 1846-51' in *Transactions and papers of the Institute of British Geographers*, No 28 (1960), pp. 119-34.

24   S. Nicholas and P. R. Shergold, 'Irish Intercounty Mobility before 1840', in *Irish Economic and Social History*, XVII, 1990, pp. 22-43.

25   R. J. Scally, *The End of Hidden Ireland: Rebellion. Famine and Emigration* (Oxford, 1995), p. 176.

26   *Londonderry Standard*, 11 December 1846; *Belfast News-Letter*, 24 December 1846; A. J. Malcolm, *The Sanitary State of Belfast* (Greer, 1852); State Paper Office, Dublin, R.P. 1847/Z 5037; C. Ó Gráda, *The Great Irish Famine* (Basingstoke, 1989), pp. 58-9;

J. O'Rourke, *The Great Irish Famine* (Dublin 1874, 1989), pp. 178-9; H. Litton, *The Irish Famine: An Illustrated History* (Dublin, 1994), pp. 90-2.

27   S. M. Cousens, 'The Regional Pattern of Emigration'.

28   W. Fraher 'The Dungarven Disturbances of 1846, and sequels' in Cowman and Brady (eds), *The Famine in Waterford 1845-1850*, p. 149.

29   Salisbury. *Calendar of the Manuscripts of the … Marquess of Salisbury* vol. XVII, Historical Manuscripts Commission (hereafter H.M.C.), London, pp. 448-9.

30   Bristol Record Office, Common Council Proceedings, 1629, f 27; J. Latimer (ed.), *Annals of-Bristol in the Seventeenth Century* (Bristol, 1902), p. 102; E H Bates (ed.), *Somerset quarter sessions records*. Charles I (Somerset Record Society, 1909, xxvi), pp 104, 131; P.R.O., SP 6/144/62.

31   P. Fitzgerald, 'Like Crickets to the Crevice of a Brew-house', Poor Irish migrants in England, 1560-1640 in P O'Sullivan (ed.), *The Irish World Wide: History Heritage - Identity. Volume one: Patterns of Migration* (Leicester, 1992), pp. 13-35.

32   *Register of the Privy-Council of Scotland*, 1629 – 30, III, second series, p. 354.

33   P. Fitzgerald, 'Like Crickets to the Crevice of a Brew-house', pp. 13-35; N. P. Canny 'The 1641 Depositions as a source for the writing of Social History: County Cork as a Case Study' in P. O'Flanagan and C. G. Buttimer (eds), *Cork: History and Society* (Dublin, 1993), pp. 249-309.

34   B. Mac Cuarta (ed.), *Ulster 1641: Aspects of the Rising* (Belfast, 1993) pp. 110-14, 135; M. Perceval-Maxwell, *The Outbreak of the Irish Rebellion of 1641* (Dublin, 1994), p. 231.

35   Buckinghamshire Record Office, Q/FR/11, Q/FR/95, Q/FR144, Q/FR/165, 2/FR/226, Q/FR/232. Q/FR/242, Q/FR/243, Q/FR253, Q/RSv/3-6.

36   P. Fitzgerald, 'Poverty and Vagrancy in Early Modern Ireland', pp. 425-441.

37   Wiltshire Record Office, A1/330/1-2.

38   E. G. Butcher (ed.), Bristol Corporation of the Poor 1696-1834 (Bristol, 1932), pp. 81-2, 99-100, 110; G. la Moire (ed.), *Bristol Gaol Delivery Fiets 1741-99* (Bristol, 1989).

39   Cheshire Record Office, QJF 178-9. On the subject more generally see G.W. Place, 'The Repatriation of Irish Vagrants from Cheshire 1750-1815', *Journal of the Chester Archaeological Society*, 68 (1986), pp. 125-41. G. W. Place, *The Rise and Fall of Parkgate Passenger Port for-Ireland, 1686-1815* (Manchester, 1994), pp. 172-92.

40   Kenyon Mss., H.M.C. Rpt 14, App 4 (1894), pp. 470-1.

41   Buckinghamshire Record Office, Q/FR11, Q/FR95, Q/FR144, Q/FR165, Q/FR226, Q/FR232, Q/FR242, Q/FR243, Q/FR253, Q/RSv/3-6.

42   A. Redford, *Labour Migration in England 1800-50* (London, 1926).

43   Buckinghamshire Record Office, Q/FR11.Q/FR95, Q/FR144, Q/FR165, Q/FR226, Q/FR232, Q/FR242, Q/FR243, Q/FR253, Q/RSv/3-6.

44   R. J. Dickson, *Ulster Emigration to Colonial America 1718-1775* (Belfast, 1966), pp. 76-81; L. M. Cullen, 'The Irish Diaspora of the Seventeenth and Eighteenth Centuries' in N. P. Canny (ed.), *Europeans on the Move: Studies in European Migration 1500-1800* (Oxford, 1994), pp. 113-149.

45   Cheshire Record Office, QAV2.

46   On the seasonal harvest migration which became substantial during the early decades of the nineteenth century, see B. M. Kerr, 'Irish Seasonal Migration to Great Britain 1800-1838', *Irish Historical Studies*, 3, No 12 (1943), pp. 365-80; A.

O'Dowd, *Spalpeens and Tattie Hokers: History-and Folklore of the Irish Migratory-Agricultural Worker in Ireland and Britain* (Dublin, 1991); R. M. Harris, *The Nearest Place that Wasn't Ireland: Early Nineteenth Century Irish Labour Migration* (Iowa, 1994).

47   J. Lucas (ed.), *Peter Kelm's account of his visit to England* (London, 1892) pp. 82-3; N. Rogers, 'Popular disaffection in London during the '45', *London-Journal*, i, No 1 (1975), pp. 5-27; G. Rude, 'Mother Gin and the London Riots of 1736', *Guildhall Miscellany*, i, pt. 10 (1059), pp. 53-62.

48   P. Linebaugh, *The London Hanged: -Crime and Civil Society in the eighteenth century* (London, 1991), p. 228.

49   Linebaugh, *London Hanged*, pp. 292-301; On the Victorian caricature see L. P. Curtis Jnr., *Apes and Angels: The Irishman in Victorian Caricature* (Newton Abbot, 1971) and D. G. Paz, 'Anti-Catholicism, Irish Stereotyping and Anti-Celtic Racism in mid-Victorian Working Class Periodicals', in *Albion*, X111 (Winter, 1986), pp. 601-16.

50   Cormac Ó Gráda, Ireland: *A New Economic History 1780-1939* (Oxford, 1994), p. 77.

51   *Report of the Select Committee on Poor Removal*, BPP 1854, X11, p. 369.

52   W.E. Vaughan (ed.), *A New History of Ireland,* v (Oxford, 1989), pp. 625-7; W. F. Adams, *Ireland and Irish Emigration to the New World from 1815 to the Famine* (Baltimore, 1980), pp. 154-7.

53   Vaughan, *New History*, v, p. 627.

54   *The Times*, 16th April 1847.

55   F. Neal, 'Liverpool, the Famine Irish and the Steamship Companies', in *Immigrants and Minorities*, 5, no 1 (March 1985), pp. 28-61.

56   C. Kinealy Irish Immigration into Scotland in the Nineteenth and Twentieth Centuries' in *European Immigration into Scotland: Proceedings of the 4th Annual Conference of the Scottish Association of Family History Societies* (Glasgow, 1992), p. 11.

57   The best documented case of such an illegal shipment in the early seventeenth century is that of the 'Peter' of Dungarven which landed Irish refugees near Bristol in May 1630. Somerset Record Office, Q/SR, 62, ff. 38-42.

58   Strathclyde Regional Archives, C01/22/21, pp. 29-30.

59   M. E. Rose, 'Settlement, Removal and the New Poor Law' in D. Fraser (ed.), The *New Poor Law in the Nineteenth Century* (London, 1976), pp. 25-45; D. Ashworth, 'Settlement and Removal in Urban Areas: Bradford 1834-71' in M. E. Rose (ed.), *The Poor and the City: the English Poor Law in-its Urban Context* (Leicester, 1985), pp. 57-88.

60   Strathclyde Regional Archives, D HEW 1/1/1, pp 417, 429.

61   D. Ashworth, 'Settlement and Removal in Urban Areas', pp. 82-3.

62   F. Neal. 'A Criminal Profile of the Liverpool Irish', *Transactions of the Historical Society of Lancashire and Cheshire*, 140 (1990), pp. 161-99; Lancashire Record Office, Q6R 2/42, p. 19; *Liverpool Mercury* 15th May 1849.

63   Strathclyde Regional Archives, D HEW 1/1/1, pp. 84-5.

64   P.R.O., S P 16/533/39.

65   Jona Schellekens, 'Irish Famines and English Mortality in the Eighteenth Century', *Journal of Interdisciplinary History*, XXVII (1996), pp. 41-2.

Subsistence Crises 1600-1845

Crises Years	Cause	Accompanying disease and Demographic Impact	Impact on Market/Prices	Civil Disorder/ Increase in Crime	Geographical Scope	Increase in vagrancy and external subsistence migration
1600-1604	Harvest failure. Impact of war.	Very limited sources, probably quite severe as 'plague' became widespread.	Municipal sources suggest six to seven fold increase in grain prices at height (on 1590's benchmark).	Limited evidence if one excludes depredation of armies.	National.	Some evidence of both.
1621-1624	Poor harvests and Cattle disease.	Slight evidence from limited sources.	Shortage of grain led to price increases but not to levels of 1602.	Limited evidence.	National but possibly more severe in towns and east.	Some evidence of both.
1627-1632	Failed and deficient harvests.	Spotted fever, smallpox and catarrh all reported. Limited sources, probably worse than 1621-4 but less severe than 1600-4.	Limited evidence. Heavy increase in grain prices suggested by need to import corn from England for first time in 20 years.	Evidence of increased cattle theft and sensitivity to needs of the poor in urban markets.	National. Possibly more severe in west than 1621-4.	Firm evidence of both.
1642-1643	Impact of war. Deficient harvest.	Accompanying epidemic disease ensured substantial excess mortality.	Limited evidence.	Widespread spoilation of crops by the military.	Most severe in combat zones.	Some evidence of both.

Crises Years	Cause	Accompanying disease and Demographic Impact	Impact on Market/Prices	Civil Disorder/ Increase in Crime	Geographical Scope	Increase in vagrancy and external subsistence migration
1648	Impact of war.	Probably of similar severity to above.	Limited evidence.	Widespread spoilation of crops by the military.	Most severe in combat zones.	Some evidence of both.
1651–1653	Widespread plague in 1651 exacerbated by harvest failures and famine in 1652.	Plague undoubtedly killed more than famine or war. The crises may have accounted for a quarter of a million deaths.	Corn prices more than quadrupled by 1653.	Limited evidence.	National but most severe in the towns.	Evidence of both.
1674	Harvest failure.	500 dead from hunger reported in Diocese of Armagh. National impact limited in comparison to 1651-3.	Limited evidence.	Limited evidence.	Unclear but appears to have been more severe in Ulster.	Some evidence of increase in vagrancy.
1689–1691	Impact of war. Livestock depletion.	Light by comparison with earlier periods of conflict.	Beef, butter and pork exports prohibited 1691.	Limited evidence.	Most severe in combat zones.	Limited evidence. Some increase in vagrancy probable.
1708–1709	Deficient harvest.	Light impact.	Embargo on the export of grain in 1709.	Limited evidence.	Most severe in Munster.	Limited evidence.

Crises Years	Cause	Accompanying disease and Demographic Impact	Impact on Market/Prices	Civil Disorder/ Increase in Crime	Geographical Scope	Increase in vagrancy and external subsistence migration
1720-1722	Economic depression and a poor harvest was the culmination to a series of difficult years.	Smallpox was prevalent around this time. Some evidence of a serious upsurge in excess mortality in Dublin.	One shilling loaf of household bread reduced to minimum weight in summer of 1720.	Some evidence of popular protest.	Possibly more severe in Dublin.	Some evidence of increase in vagrancy.
1725-1729	Prolonged failed and deficient harvests from 1725 leading to widespread reduction in 'winter subsistence' potato crop.	Evidence from Ulster and Dublin suggests that epidemic disease between 1727 and 1730 was sufficient to check or even set into reverse the population growth of preceding decades.	The price of oats, barley, and wheat all rose significantly between 1727 and 1729. In 1728 the weight of the household loaf was reduced to almost half its pre- and post- crisis weight. In December 1728 the export of grain was prohibited in Dublin. Coal prices also almost doubled in 1728.	Food riots erupted in several Munster towns in order to prevent the export of foodstuffs. Civil disorder was also evident in Dublin.	Dublin and Ulster appear to have been worst hit whilst Munster appears to have escaped the worst effects of famine.	Firm evidence of both. In addition we find the first clear evidence that economic crisis in Ireland was fuelling emigration to North America.
1734-1736	Deficient harvest and some signs of depression in the linen industry.	Light impact.	Wheat prices rose by about a third from what they had been in the early 1730s.	Limited evidence.	Unclear.	Some evidence of increased movement to England and North America.

Crises Years	Cause	Accompanying disease and Demographic Impact	Impact on Market/Prices	Civil Disorder/ Increase in Crime	Geographical Scope	Increase in vagrancy and external subsistence migration
1740-1741	A sequence of a wet summer, a severe winter frost and a summer drought caused severe damage to the grain harvest and potato crop.	Whilst actual starvation probably killed more than at any time since the early 1650s, epidemic diseases such as typhus and dysentery did most damage. Somewhere between 250-400,000 perished, relatively an even higher death rate than the Great Famine.	In Dublin wheat prices more than doubled. Oats in both Dublin and Ulster rose in price to similar levels. Potatoes, though not commercially marketed to the same extent, appear to have increased in price even more sharply.	Food riots were reported in Dublin, Cork, Sligo and Carrick-on-Suir.	Almost the mirror image of 1725-9. The impact was felt nationally but certainly more severe in the southern half of the country.	Firm evidence of both. Emigration also increased but the relatively short duration of the crisis may have held back a flood.
1744-1746	Deficient harvest and livestock disease.	Light impact.	The wholesale importation of grain from England where the harvest was good ensured price control and adequate supply.	Limited evidence.	Most severe in the north and west of Ireland.	Little evidence of either but some surge in emigration to North America.

Crises Years	Cause	Accompanying disease and Demographic Impact	Impact on Market/Prices	Civil Disorder/ Increase in Crime	Geographical Scope	Increase in vagrancy and external subsistence migration
1755-1757	Failure of grain harvest and potato crop.	Some evidence of excess mortality.	Whilst grain was again imported, a poor harvest in England made this more difficult. In 1756 grain prices in Dublin were as high at any point since 1741.	Food riots occurred again most seriously in Belfast, prompting the imposition of the first effective poor rate.	National but perhaps most intense distress in port towns.	Evidence suggests an increase in the number of vagrants.
1764-1767	Failed potato crop and poor grain harvest.	Some evidence of excess mortality.	The price of wheat in Dublin reached 1740-1 levels for first time. Acute distress checked to some degree by corn importation and the prohibition of grain export and use for distillation.	Food riot in Kilkenny in 1766. Some evidence to suggest growing awareness of link between poverty and crime.	National.	Evidence of an increase in vagrancy and emigration to North America.
1769-1770	Main factor may have been failure of the potato crop.	Light impact.	Potato and oatmeal prices were well above average in Kilkenny and grain was in short supply in Dublin.	Limited evidence.	May be anticipated to be worse in areas of high potato dependence.	Limited evidence.

Crises Years	Cause	Accompanying disease and Demographic Impact	Impact on Market/Prices	Civil Disorder/ Increase in Crime	Geographical Scope	Increase in vagrancy and external subsistence migration
1771-1773	Deficient grain harvests, combined with a severe slump in the linen trade.	The primary demographic impact stemmed from emigration rather than mortality.	The shortage of grain in Dublin caused prices to rise above previous peaks.	Civil disorder was most severe and widespread in east Ulster where it was closely linked to rent increases.	National but most severe in Ulster.	Evidence suggests some increase in vagrancy, subsistence migration to England and most significantly emigration to North America
1777-1778	Distress was largely linked to a further slump in linen trade.	Light impact.	Food prices seem to have remained fairly stable but with unemployment increased and credit tight purchase was difficult.	In Drogheda there were riots to control the supply of food.	National but worst in textile districts and in towns.	With emigration stemmed due to the American War, vagrancy and subsistence migration increased.
1782-1784	Failed and deficient harvests with depression in linen trade. Destruction of 1783 potato crop.	Undoubtedly some excess mortality but muted in towns by surprisingly effective poor relief.	At the peak of the crisis in the early summer of 1783 the household loaf was almost half its weight of early 1780. Potato prices showed signs of inflation.	Food riots were reported throughout the country. In Munster where the harvest had not been so severely effected rioters sought to prevent export.	National but lighter impact in Munster.	The unprecedented upsurge in demand upon the House of Industry in Dublin suggests a significant rise in vagrancy. After 1782 emigration was also heavy.

Crises Years	Cause	Accompanying disease and Demographic Impact	Impact on Market/Prices	Civil Disorder/ Increase in Crime	Geographical Scope	Increase in vagrancy and external subsistence migration
1795-1796	Poor harvest and failure of potato crop.	Evidence suggests some increase in excess mortality.	In Dublin the cost of a barrel of wheat broke the £2 barrier for the first time. An increase of 25% on 1790 price.	Food riots and looting of corn meal and flour reported in Dublin.	National.	Sectarian conflict in south Ulster put large numbers on the road in the north and west. Emigration also brisk.
1799-1801	Poor harvest and failure of potato crop.	Hunger induced disease may have killed 50,000.	Dublin wheat prices doubled in two years, breaking the barrier of £3 per barrel. Oats and potato prices also rose sharply.	A positively interventionist approach by government seems to have contained disorder.	National.	Limited evidence.
1816-1818	Failure of harvest and potato crop on top of economic recession.	Again estimated 50,000 + excess deaths, largely from typhus. The mass demobilisation of Irish soldiers undoubtedly made the situation worse.	Another peak in wheat prices in Dublin.	In 1817 jails throughout the country were reported to be fuller than at any time in the previous 20 years. Transportation for non-political offences also increased.	National but possibly worse in north and west.	Firm evidence of increase in vagrancy. It would also appear that a larger percentage of those emigrating in these years could be classified as poor.

Crises Years	Cause	Accompanying disease and Demographic Impact	Impact on Market/Prices	Civil Disorder/ Increase in Crime	Geographical Scope	Increase in vagrancy and external subsistence migration
1822–1823	Potato failure and economic recession.	Excess mortality was kept to a minimum by a combination of private and official relief.	Prices for foods other than the potato remained stable but the reduction in incomes limited purchasing power.	The onset of the worst distress served to quell agrarian crime but 'ordinary' crime may have increased.	Worst effects felt in areas of potato dependence in south and west.	Limited evidence of any stimulus to migration.
1825–1826	Poor potato crop and slump in textile trade.	Excess mortality was again fairly limited except in Dublin where up to 5,000 may have succumbed to fever.	Again the main problem was income reduction rather than price inflation.	Agrarian crime showed no sign of an upsurge whilst effective relief in Dublin checked civil disturbance there. Some evidence of increase in theft.	Similar to 1822–3 but also severe in towns with textile sector.	Firm evidence of increased migration to Britain. Emigration also appears to have increased.
1830–1832	Poor potato crop.	The absence to typhus and impact of relief restricted excess mortality to remoter pockets in the west. But cholera in 1832 killed close to 50,000.	Food prices in general remained low in these years. Those worst affected relied upon the potato as the sole subsistence crop.	Limited evidence.	Most severe in the west, particularly Mayo.	A new peak in Irish emigration to North America.

In the years between 1832 and 1845 there was no famine and it is difficult to distinguish subsistence crises on a national scale. Some deficiency in the potato crop was noted in 1833, 1834, 1835, 1836, 1839, 1840 and 1842 but the impact was generally localised and often reflected an extension to the duration of seasonal dearth prior to late harvesting.

Black '47 : Liverpool and the Irish Famine*

Frank Neal

WE ARE FORTUNATE that the first British census to record place of birth was that of 1841.[1] (see Table 2) This coincided with a growing number of investigations into the social conditions in British towns, all of which painted, with remarkable consistency, a picture of large scale squalor and serious threats to the health of Britain's population. Lack of clean water, sanitation and adequate housing meant that cholera and 'fever' were endemic. The cholera outbreaks in 1832 and 1837-38 shook the middle classes, triggering off more investigations into sanitation and related issues.[2] The wretchedness of much working class life was not only the result of sanitation and housing deficiencies, it also reflected poverty based on low incomes and intermittent employment.[3] Even before the Famine crisis, the Irish immigrants into Britain were predominantly poor, unskilled and uneducated. As such they were forced into those sectors of the labour markets where there were no barriers to entry, by definition, the unskilled labouring sector. The 1841 census revealed that of the 16 political wards in the borough of Liverpool, Vauxhall, Exchange, St Paul's, Scotland and Great George were areas of large scale Irish settlement.[4] They were also characterised by the worst social conditions. In Vauxhall 57 per cent of the population lived in cellars, of the other Irish wards, the figures were St Paul's 40 per cent, Scotland 39 per cent, Exchange 30 per cent and Great George 30 per cent. Writing at this time, Dr Duncan expressed the opinion:

> ... but when it is considered that there are not less than 50,000 of the lower Irish resident in Liverpool, it will be understood that some portion of it, at least, must be the result of their own indifference. Even when a plentiful supply of water is at hand, the inhabitants of the filthy courts inhabited by the Irish too often neglect to avail themselves of its services, and when the removal of a nuisance is in their power, they seem to think it hardly worth the trouble which it would occasion them ... But it is to be remembered that many of the evils which I have pointed out are, perhaps, the inevitable results of poverty; and I believe the fever, to a certain extent, is an inseparable accompaniment of extreme poverty affecting large masses of the community. Among the causes of fever in Liverpool I might have enumerated the large proportion of poor Irish among the working population. It is they who inhabit the filthiest and worst-ventilated courts and cellars, who congregate the most numerously in dirty lodging-houses, who are least cleanly in their habits, and the most apathetic about everything that befalls them. It is among the Irish that fever especially commits its ravages; and it is they who object most strongly to be removed to

the hospital from their miserable abodes … No one interested in the welfare of his poorer brethren can contemplate the prospect without a feeling of melancholy foreboding; and I am persuaded that so long as the native inhabitants are exposed to the inroads of numerous hordes of uneducated Irish, spreading physical and moral contamination around them, it will be in vain to expect that any sanitary code can cause fever to disappear from Liverpool.[5]

Black '47 was to confirm Duncan's worst fears.

I

The disastrous return of the potato blight in 1846 and the inadequate response of the British authorities in terms of relief, triggered off a flight of destitute people seeking escape from the horrific conditions in the Famine counties. Liverpool, Glasgow, Cardiff, Swansea and Newport were swamped with Famine refugees, Liverpool is the only port for which reasonable data exist concerning pauper immigration. Edward Rushton, Liverpool's stipendiary magistrate, noticed the numbers of Irish immigrants arriving in unusually large numbers in October 1846. During 1847 this immigration assumed crisis proportions.[6] Table 1 illustrates the scale of Irish immigration into, and through Liverpool, over the whole crisis period.

Table 1:
The Estimated numbers of Irish landing at the Port of Liverpool, 1847–1853

Year	Deck passengers who were emigrants and jobbers	Deck passengers who were evidently Paupers	Total	Paupers as a percentage of total
1847	180,231	116,000	296,231	39
1848	158,582	94,190	252,772	37
1849	160,457	80,468	240,925	33
1850	173,236	77,765	251,001	31
1851	215,369	68,134	283,503	24
1852	153,909	78,422	232,331	34
1853	162,299	71,353	233,652	31

Sources: For the years 1847, 1850-3, *Report of the Select Committee on Poor Removal* (1854) p. 358, Appendix 8, pp. 593-4. For the years 1848 and 1849, the data are from the weekly press reportings of the landings of Irish at Liverpool. *Sixth Report of The Select Committee on Settlement and Poor Removal* (1847). Minutes of Evidence, E. Rushton (Stipendiary Magistrate of Liverpool) q. 4370-1. Rushton ordered the police to count all the Irish landing at Liverpool, each day, from 13 January 1847. *Select Committee on Poor Removal* (1854), Evidence of A. Campbell includes copy of a letter from E. Rushton to the Home Secretary, dated 21 April, 1849. This contains the figure of 296,231 for 1847.

Of the 296,231 people landing at Liverpool from Ireland during 1847, 116,000 were described by Dr Duncan as 'half naked and starving'. However, the Irish *en route* to America also made demands on local accommodation and often claimed relief. The impact of this level of Irish Famine immigration on the population of the borough and other main areas of Irish settlement, is shown in Table 2.

Over the intercensal period 1841-51, the Irish born population of the borough of Liverpool increased by 34,174 or 69 per cent and the spatial distribution of the Irish in Liverpool indicates that the majority of Famine immigrants went to the established Irish areas.[7]

Table 2:
Irish-Born Residents of Liverpool, Glasgow, Manchester, Salford and London 1841–91

Town	1841	1851	1861	1871	1891
Liverpool (Borough)					
Population	286,656	375,955	443,938	493,405	517,980
No. Irish-born	49,639	83,813	83,949	76,761	66,071
Irish as % of pop.	17.3	22.3	18.9	15.5	12.6
Glasgow (Burgh)					
Population	274,533	329,097	–	477,156	565,840
No. Irish-born	44,345	56,801	–	68,330	60,182
Irish as % of pop.	16.1	18.1	–	14.3	10.6
Manchester and Salford					
Population	306,991	401,321	460,428	379,374	703,507
No. Irish-born	33,490	52,504	52,076	34,066	32,270
Irish as % of pop.	11.06	13.1	11.3	9.0	4.6
London					
Population	1,873,676	2,362,236	2,803,989	3,254,260	4,211,743
No. Irish-born	73,133	108,548	106,879	91,171	66,465
Irish as % of pop.	3.9	4.6	3.8	2.8	1.6

Sources: Census Reports 1841, 1851, 1861, 1871 and 1891.

II

A large number of the Irish arriving in Liverpool in 1847 were not simply poor, they were destitute and as such the poor law authorities in Liverpool had a statutory obligation to provide relief, in terms of food, clothing and medical assistance. In the Liverpool parish at this time, the poor law guardians were known as the select vestry, members of which were elected annually by ratepayers. The money for poor relief was raised by a poor rate levied on the tenants of property. Under the law existing before the onset of the Famine crisis, the only people with a legal right to poor relief were those who had acquired the legal status of 'settled' in the parish. This was acquired by a number of rather arcane principles, the main one being that of being born in the parish. Under this

Elizabethan system, the Irish born had no legal right to long term poor relief in English parishes.[8] In August 1846, after the first appearance of the potato blight, the law was changed to allow all persons who could prove five years continuous residency in a parish, the right to relief. People claiming relief who did not have the status of settlement or five years residency, could be *removed* to the parish in which they *did* have settlement. The significance of this for the long stay Irish in England was that the Five Year Residency Act gave them protection from the threat of removal back to Ireland. The Famine Irish had no such rights to relief and no protection against removal. The situation in Liverpool from October 1846 onwards was therefore that the select vestry had a legal obligation not to allow the arrivals to die of want but had *no legal obligation* to provide long term relief.

The relief available to the poor in general was provided in one of two ways. A person could be admitted to the workhouse on Brownlow Hill (now the site of the Roman Catholic Cathedral) or, on application to the parish office in Fenwick Street, receive money and tickets for food and clothing. The two forms of relief, indoor and outdoor, were not available to the able bodied in Ireland. Under the Irish poor law, all *pre-Famine* recipients of relief, principally the old, sick and young, had to enter the workhouse, with its harsh regime. The numbers arriving at Liverpool at the end of 1846, however, were so great that there simply was not enough accommodation in the Liverpool workhouse to deal with the destitution pouring ashore. Also, the Irish did not like entering the workhouse and so the provision of outdoor relief became the main way in which the Famine Irish in Liverpool were assisted. It is also, important to note that the Famine immigration crisis of 1847 coincided with a downturn in the British economy and unusually large numbers of English, Welsh and Scots were also seeking poor relief. A system which could cope with 'normal' poverty in Liverpool broke down under the pressure of claims for relief by the Irish. The scale of the problem facing the Liverpool authorities became clear by the end of December 1846. During the week ended 19 December 1846, the numbers of Irish paupers relieved was 13,471. This compared with 888 relieved in the corresponding week of the previous year.[9] From 19 December 1846 the situation rapidly worsened. An alarmed local press was watching events closely and the reports carried convinced middle-class Liverpool that, quite apart from any concern over the wretchedness of the arrivals, there was a major financial crisis looming for ratepayers. The *Liverpool Mercury* of 15 January 1847 carried a leader headed 'Frightful Distress in Liverpool'.

> Those who see the state of our streets from early morn to midnight, and especially those who visit the parish offices, need no further evidence of the condition of Liverpool at the moment … the fact is that in the cold and gloom of a severe winter, thousands of hungry and half naked wretches are wandering about, not knowing how to obtain a sufficiency of the commonest food, nor shelter, from the piercing cold. The numbers of starving Irish, men, and children daily landing on our quays is appalling, and the parish of Liverpool has at present, the painful and most costly task to encounter, of keeping them alive, if possible. Never was the simple truth so plainly discernible as at this moment, that the pauperism of a nation ought to be provided for by national means. The barbarism of local taxation … stands forth now in all its deformity …

This leader features what was to become a growing complaint, that one particular town, Liverpool, was supporting the crushing degree of poverty arising from a national calamity.

III

The developing crisis has three specific but related features. First, there was the simple logistics of dealing with unprecedented numbers claiming relief and the consequent need to raise the necessary finance. Second, there was the problem of dealing with an outbreak of typhus in the town on an epidemic scale and finally, the political response to the Famine immigration. Under normal circumstances, those seeking outdoor relief would have attended the parish offices in Fenwick Street. A relieving officer would investigate the validity of the claim and if this was established, relief would be given in the form of food tickets, clothing or notes for medical assistance. Usually four relieving officers were sufficient to deal with such cases. By January 1847, this system could not cope. Fenwick Street was constantly crowded with Irish seeking relief and the relieving officers gave up trying to establish the legitimacy of individual claims, usually undertaken by visiting the claimant's dwelling. The assistant poor law commissioner for the north-west was Albert Austin and he shared the concerns of the select vestry. The records of the relieving officers soon outlined the size of the difficulties piling up.

The numbers in Table 3 do not enable us to identify the *individuals* receiving relief over any period of a week because some claimed on successive days. However, on 23 January 1847, 22,574 individual Irish received soup tickets and Albert Austin became concerned over the numbers of children in the total. For example, the ratio of children to women on 23 January was 3.1 to 1. This simply did not add up with the numbers of Irish women and children coming ashore from the Irish steamers. For example, from 13 January to 31 January inclusive, the total number of men, women and children *landing* was 8,657, 5,061 and 2,968 respectively, a total of 16,686. The ratio of children to women was therefore 0.59:1. This discrepancy between the numbers of children arriving and the number being claimed as dependents led Austin to believe that fraud was taking place, the Liverpool Irish were borrowing children to boost their relief. Austin suggested that the town be divided up into twelve relief districts, each with its own office, and two relieving officers. All claimants were to be visited wherever they lived and different coloured food tickets issued in each district. The select vestry accepted his recommendations and also set up a sub-committee, The 'Irish Relief Committee' to supervise the provision of relief for the Famine Irish.[10]

The new system came into existence on 2 February and the effect on the number of Irish claiming relief was dramatic. On 1 February, 3,496 men, 3,592 women and 15,260 children were given relief in the form of bread and soup. On 2 February, the numbers were 895 men, 1,283 women and 2,818 children, a total of 4,996 and a drop of 78 per cent in total Irish claimants. Despite the elimination of much of the fraud, the numbers claiming relief continued to rise. During April the average total number of Irish relieved per day was about 10,000, reflecting the increasing influx of Famine refugees and concern over the cost to ratepayers mounted.[11]

Table 3:
The Numbers Irish Persons relieved with Bread and Soup
on Selected Days in January 1847, in the Parish of Liverpool

Date	Men	Women	Children	Total
January 4	546	661	2,449	3,656
January 5	655	866	2,486	4,007
January 6	751	1,119	3,216	5,086
January 7	815	1,125	3,135	5,075
January 8	816	1,196	3,784	5,796
January 9	1,727	1,965	6,199	9,891
January 11	1,862	1,885	6,539	10,286
January 12	1,919	2,105	7,111	11,135
January 13	1,843	2,039	7,010	10,892
January 14	2,027	2,069	7,872	11,968
January 15	2,125	2,197	9,352	13,674
January 16	1,840	2,059	8,750	12,649
January 18	2,758	2,932	12,363	18,053
January 19	3,282	3,348	12,552	19,182
January 20	3,820	3,525	11,795	19,140

SOURCE: Appendix to *Thirteenth Annual Report of the Poor Law Commissioners*, B.P.P. 1847[873]xxviii, pp 115-6.

The survival strategy of the Famine refugees included not only the use of parochial relief but also availing themselves of a considerable volume of private charity. One of the principal charities was the Liverpool District Provident Society. During 1847, 57 per cent of all those relieved were Irish.[12]

IV

Though parochial aid and private charity were essential for the survival of many Famine immigrants, the question of accommodation was equally crucial, particularly in the cold weather. For people arriving with few or no economic resources the options were limited. One possibility was moving in with friends and relatives. This clearly happened and exacerbated the already appalling overcrowding in Liverpool's slums, the worst conditions being found in the cellars. At the beginning of 1847, there were over 14,000 cellars in Liverpool. Most of these had been condemned as unfit for human habitation and under local legislation, the process of clearing these pestholes had begun just as the Famine crisis erupted. During 1847, thousands of Irish Famine refugees illegally occupied empty cellars.[13]

The press abounded with reports of the conditions under which the immigrants were existing. On 13 March, the *Liverpool Journal* carried an account of a meeting of the select vestry at which it was reported that:

> Amongst a certain number of individuals in a cellar in Bent Street, it was reported that four persons were lying down in one bed, with fever, that twenty four grown-up young men

and their sisters were sleeping in a filthy state in the room, and that fourteen persons were sleeping in another filthy place. Thirty-six persons were found huddled together in a room elsewhere and eight had died of fever in one home.

Such scenes were repeated all over the town. Many of these reports carried overtones of moral disapproval of men and women sleeping in the same rooms and beds. The reporters in many cases seemed shell shocked at the scenes of absolute destitution spreading through the town which had, before the Famine, already achieved the reputation of being the unhealthiest town in Britain.[14] An additional source of worry to the select vestry and other concerned individuals was the stream of cases of Irish immigrants dying from 'want of the necessaries of life'. In fact, about twenty-three such cases occurred during 1847. Set against the total number of Irish immigrants it may be considered small but the reports of coroners' inquests made grim reading for middle class Liverpool.[15] A case that particularly horrified the public was that of Luke Brothers. The eight-year old boy died on Saturday 8 May, in a cellar in Banastre Street, the heart of Irish Liverpool. The Brothers family had arrived from Ireland, father, mother and five children and moved into a cellar. Almost continually after arriving, they had been ill. When able, the children had gone out to beg, but the family remained in a desperate condition. Henry Christmas, surgeon, carried the post mortem on Luke and reported that 'I could not find the slightest trace of food in the stomach'. He was strongly of the opinion the child had died of starvation. He also said that in the same cellar, lying on the mud floor, were five other people down with typhus and that there were four other typhus cases in the house. The coroner was so upset by the case that he made the jury visit the cellar and also reported the conditions he found to the mayor.[16]

The concern of ratepayers over the cost of providing relief and the cases of starvation were eclipsed by the fear of dying from typhus, which was universally known as 'Irish fever'. In fact the term 'fever' at this time covered a number of illnesses including typhus, relapsing fever and typhoid. The Famine influx occurred at a stage in medical science when the transmission mechanism for typhus was not understood. In fact it was carried by body lice and so overcrowding was central to the spread of the typhus epidemic that occurred throughout Britain during 1847.[17] In Liverpool, the spread, measured in numbers and location, was tracked by Dr Duncan throughout the year. In January, 44 fever deaths were recorded. By July, the total was 828 and it was estimated that 8,000 were being treated. The greatest number of victims were in the recognisably Irish districts of Vauxhall, Scotland, Exchange and Great George. The death rate in Vauxhall was 1 in 17 of the population; 1 in 21 in Exchange and 1 in 22 in Great George. This compares dramatically with one in 228 in middle class Rodney Ward.

The rest of the country was watching events in Liverpool closely. *The Times* in particular kept its readers informed of the progress of the typhus epidemic. On Monday, 5 April, it told its readers:

... The dead are taken by relatives to the workhouse cemetery at all hours of the day, sometimes at night, in coffins sometimes nailed, sometimes not, and if the gates happened to be closed, they are left outside or put over the wall. Some of the medical men, frightened by the number of patients are resigning their situations though their numbers have been doubled and an additional number must be applied ...

This report was fairly accurate in its highlighting of the nature of the problem facing the authorities. The select vestry had a responsibility to provide medical aid for the poor. This could be done by subscribing to the town's two medical dispensaries and giving the sick poor notes for medicine. It also had a small hospital in the workhouse grounds in Brownlow Hill. This had eighty fever beds, adequate under normal circumstances, but in the crisis following the immigration of such large numbers of destitute and sick Irish, the provision was woefully too little. The select vestry members were almost overwhelmed by the scale of the problem. The first decision was to increase the number of beds in the workhouse by using the chapel and the committee room. This was followed, in March, by a resolution to erect fever sheds in the grounds of the workhouse. This resulted in a protest from the nearby residents of Abercromby and Rodney wards, fearful for their own safety. These fears were brushed aside and the sheds were provided.[18] By June 1847, there were 900 fever patients in the workhouse.[19] In addition to the expanded hospital facilities at the workhouse, sheds were rented in the North docks in Great Howard Street, and these provided another 3-400 beds.[20] Despite all these efforts, large numbers of fever and dysentery victims were having to be treated in their cellars and rooms.

A particular cause of concern arose from the belief that the steamers arriving from Ireland were bringing more fever sufferers to Liverpool.[21] If this was true, then it would negate all the efforts made in Liverpool to stop the spread of disease. After much pressure on Whitehall, the select vestry received permission to use the vessels, the *Akbar* and the *Newcastle* as lazarettos moored on the Mersey. The policy adopted was that all Irish steamers arriving in the Mersey with fever victims on board had to fly a yellow flag. They would be boarded, doctors would then have the infected persons transferred to the *Akbar*. The *Newcastle* was used as an additional hospital for Liverpool patients.[22] The provision of extra hospital beds was not the only problem facing the Liverpool authorities. Extra nurses and doctors had to be hired and such was the fear of death from typhus it meant the pay offered had to be correspondingly increased above the usual rates.

The scale of the problem is indicated by the fact that over a twelve year period, 1835-46, the average annual number of paupers buried in the parochial cemetery in Cambridge Street was 1,367. During April 1847 alone, 654 paupers were buried in the same cemetery and over the year the total number was 7,520.[23] By September 1847, the Liverpool authorities felt the crisis was over. However, the true cost in human terms had been enormous. In the parish, 7,475 had died of fever, diarrhoea and dysentery, the majority Irish. Duncan estimated that nearly 60,000 contracted fever and 40,000 dysentery and diarrhoea. Fever alone, he calculated left 1,400 women widows and 4,000 orphans. The casualties among those especially at risk were high.[24] Catholic priests picked up lice when they visited the cellars to give the last rites and during the year ten died. One Unitarian minister also died of fever contracted in performing his duties among the poor, as did ten doctors and over twenty relieving officers and nurses. Duncan was convinced that the epidemic had been brought by the Famine Irish and wrote in his report, concerning the deaths of officials who died of typhus:

... and others whose duties brought them into contact with the
Irish paupers, and many hundreds of the English residents in
comfortable circumstances, most of whom might have still
been alive had Liverpool not been converted for a time into a
'city of the plague' by the immigrant Irish who inundated the
lower districts ...[25]

V

Given the sheer scale of Irish immigration into and through Liverpool, and
the consequent financial and social costs involved in providing relief, it is not
surprising the citizens of Liverpool felt aggrieved. There was a general acceptance
that simple Christianity as well as the law, demanded that the suffering Irish
should be assisted.[26] However, early in 1847, when there was no foreseeable end
to the influx, there was a strong feeling that a particular town should not have to
bear the whole of the cost of what was a national tragedy. In December 1846, the
select vestry had already petitioned the Home Secretary, asking that Irish
immigration should be halted.[27] This was clearly a hopeless ploy; there was no law
which would halt the influx and restrictions of movement since both were against
the spirit of the age and impracticable. This request was followed by the plea for
central government to repay the select vestry for the cost of Irish relief in the
town. Again, this was refused.[28] A particular cause of concern was the belief that
the steamship companies were carrying immigrants to Liverpool at too low prices
and that vessels were carrying too many deck passengers for safety. The select
vestry sent representatives to surrounding Lancashire towns seeking help in
petitioning the government for a tightening of legislation regarding passenger
traffic. Ultimately, in 1849, this pressure bore some results but was too late for
the 1847 crisis.[29] A sustained political campaign for an amendment to the Irish
poor law was strongly supported by Liverpool, Glasgow and other areas of Irish
settlement. This campaign was based on the view that if outdoor relief for the
able-bodied persons was available in Ireland, then such large numbers of Irish
would stop coming. Allied to the campaign was the demand that the law of
removal be simplified so that those Irish claiming long term relief in British
towns, and who did not have residency rights, could be more easily sent back to
Ireland where outdoor relief should be provided. Both these legislative changes
occurred in June 1847 and the Liverpool authorities began clearing the cellars of
Irish and removing them to Ireland.[30] These policies were doomed in their
objective of stopping or significantly slowing down pauper immigration. The
factors pushing people out of Ireland were as strong as ever: poverty, harsh
workhouse conditions and inadequate relief. Simultaneously, the pull factors
were strong: a more liberal English poor law and better job opportunities. During
1847, Liverpool removed 15,000 to Ireland, but many of these would have
returned. It was simply impossible to police such a policy.[31] Where the threat of
removal *did* succeed was in reducing claims for outdoor relief in order to avoid
removal.

Does the evidence support the contention that Liverpool suffered a crippling
financial burden during the Famine crisis? The poor law guardians or select
vestry, had a legal responsibility to provide indoor and outdoor relief, and medical
aid, to those entitled to such. The money required was raised from a poor rate

levied on property owners or tenants. This meant that in principle, the amount raised in any one financial year equalled the rateable value of property in the parish, times the rate per pound levied. In practice, many ratepayers were excused on the grounds of poverty. In the financial year ending 25 March 1847, the total rateable value of property in Liverpool was £1,021,898. A poor rate of two shillings and one penny should have raised £106,447 but in fact only 72 per cent was raised on 40,000 houses. The reasons for this shortfall was partly due to inefficient rate collection but principally because many ratepayers in homes assessed below £12 rent per year were excused on grounds of poverty. Rushton estimated that tenants in 32,000 out of 40,000 homes were excused the payment of rates.[32] This background needs to be remembered when examining the available statistics. The table below refers to expenditure on indoor and outdoor relief in Liverpool over the whole period of the Famine crisis.

Table 4:
Total Annual Expenditure on Poor Relief in the Liverpool
Poor Law Union 1845–54

Year Ending	Irish £	Non-Irish £	Total £	Irish as % of Total
25 March 1845	3,140	26,980	30,120	10.4
25 March 1846	2,916	28,367	31,283	9.3
25 March 1847	12,613	32,250	44,863	28.1
25 March 1848	25,926	39,364	65,290	40.0
25 March 1849	12,674	40,340	53,014	24.0
25 March 1850	14,049	39,068	53,117	26.4
25 March 1851	12,528	37,272	49,800	25.2
25 March 1852	13,479	38,699	52,178	25.8
25 March 1853	12,251	33,355	45,606	26.9
25 March 1854	14,433	36,602	51,035	28.3
Total	**124,009**	**352,297**	**476,306**	**26.0**

Notes: These statistics do not cover costs of medical officers, salaries or other establishment charges. They refer essentially to food, clothing and other necessities of life distributed both indoor and outdoor.
Source: Extracted from *Select Committee on Poor Removal* B.P.P. 1854(396)XVII, Appendix 8, p. 592.

The impact of the rising level of Irish pauper immigration is seen in the increase in expenditure from £2,916 to £12,613 in the financial year ending March 1847. However, it would be wrong to conclude that all of this increase was the result of the Famine. The passing of the Five Years Residency Act in August 1846 meant that many Irish who were long stay residents in Liverpool but who had not claimed relief for fear of removal now became a charge on the parish. The increased cost was estimated by Rushton to be £7,037.[33] This meant that the increase in poor relief expenditure over the financial year 1846/7 attributable to the *Famine refugees* was £5,576, still a considerable amount. The real impact of the Famine on expenditure by providing immediate relief was the spending during the financial year 1847/8. Again, allowance must be made for the increased expenditure arising from the Five Year Residency Act so that from £25,926 we must deduct *at least* £7,037, leaving £18,889. This was an unprecedented increase in poor law spending.

Equally striking, is the falling off in direct expenditure on relief, from £25,926 to £12,674 over the financial year 1848/9. Can we conclude the Famine crisis was over? The simple answer is no. The falling off does not reflect a diminution in pauper immigration nor a picking up of the economy. The passing of the Irish Poor Law Amendment Act and the Poor Law Amendment Act in June 1847, resulted in the Liverpool authorities taking a tough line regarding removals to Ireland. This was because the Poor Law Amendment Act made the legal procedure involved in ordering a removal much simpler and from June 1847, many Irish stopped applying for relief out of fear of removal. Thus, the expenditure of £12,613, minus the cost of long stay Irish paupers, £7,037 leaves an expenditure of £5,576 on recently arrived Irish. Allowing for the expenditure on long term Irish from August 1846 onwards we can estimate the rates burden arising from the Famine Irish as shown in Table 5.

Table 5:
Estimates of the Burden on the Parish of Liverpool Arising from the Provision of Indoor and Outdoor Relief for the Famine Irish

Year Ending	Expenditure on recently arrived Irish £	Total Rateable Value of Property assessed	Rate per Pound in pence
25 March 1847	5,576	1,021,898	1.3
25 March 1848	18,889	1,187,095	3.8
25 March 1849	5,637	1,212,805	1.1
25 March 1850	7,012	1,202,512	1.4

Source: B.P.P. (HC) *Annual Reports of the Poor Law Commissioners and Poor Law Board*; B.P.P. (HC) *Select Committee on Settlement and Poor Removal* (1847); B.P.P. (HC) Poor Law (1852) 'A Return on the Annual Value of Property Assessed to the Poor Rate'.

The rate of 3.8 pence in the pound for the year ending 25 March, 1848 reflects the Famine influx. However, as already noted, 8,000 of the total of 40,000 tenants and owners paid the rates so that for these the rate actually paid was higher. In the absence of a more detailed breakdown of rateable values the precise burden cannot be estimated.[34] It is safe to assume that the majority in this category were healthy persons living in Abercromby, Rodney and Lime Street wards. It is equally safe to assume that these same persons were the employers of unskilled labour whose wages were kept down by the immigration of Famine Irish. The rate per pound that can be attributed to the Famine during the financial year 1848/9 was 1.1 pence. In that year, 99 per cent of rates were actually raised due to the implementation of a more efficient system of collection and vigorous examination of those excused payment. This meant that the burden was reduced on the wealthier ratepayers. For a labourer renting a home at £10 a year, the 1848/49 rate attributed to the Irish Famine would have been 11 pence over the year, hardly a crippling burden. However, the full cost would have been greater because, at the moment, it is not possible to accurately estimate the cost of medical relief during the year ending 25 March 1848, particularly the heavy cost of the typhus outbreak and removals to Ireland.[35]

The short term consequences of the Famine crisis of 1847 were numerous. An initial result was horrific overcrowding of Liverpool's bad housing stock and the consequent virulence of the typhus outbreak. Throughout the nineteenth century there were periods when mortality rates equalled or exceeded those of the Famine period 1846-51.[36] Also, there was a permanent increase in expenditure by the parish in Irish pauperism though the evidence does not support the view often expressed that it was a crippling economic burden. One feature of Liverpool life exacerbated by the Famine inflow was a heightened sectarian tension. It is no coincidence that the 1851 Twelfth of July processions in Liverpool were the biggest ever held up to that time and in the subsequent rioting, three died. Long term effects were a large pool of unskilled labour which benefited employers, a deeply divided working class because of the politicisation of religious conflicts and a constraint on the growth of the labour movement because of Roman Catholicism, a Protestant working-class Toryism and Irish nationalism. Conflict on the streets between Catholics and Protestants continued peaking in the 1909 riots.[37] The poverty of the Irish resulted in an over-representation in the borough's criminal statistics. In 1864, 58 per cent of all committals to the borough gaol were Catholic. In 1876, the percentage had risen to 70 per cent.[38] The large Irish presence influenced both the accent of working class Liverpool and its culture through to the present day.

References

⋆   The author would like to express his gratitude to HMV plc., for financial support in a research project on Irish communities in nineteenth-century Britain.

1   The 1841 census was the first to record country of birth so that before this year there are no official statistics regarding the numbers of Irish-born persons in Britain. However a number of estimates were made by Catholic priests, using baptism records. In the case of both Liverpool and Manchester see G. Cornewall Lewis, *Report on the State of the Irish Poor in Great Britain*, B.P.P. 1836[40]XXXIV, pp. i-xlviii; *Poor Inquiry (Ireland)*, Appendix G, p. 9 (Liverpool), p. 43 (Manchester).

2   There are a number of books which deal with a voluminous body of anecdotal and statistical evidence. In particular see J. Burnett, *A Social History of Housing 1815-1970* (Newton Abbott, 1978); J. Roach, *Social Reform in England 1780-1880* (London, 1978); F. B. Smith, *The People's Health 1830-1910* (London, 1990); I. C. Taylor, 'Black Spot on the Mersey' (unpublished Ph.D., Liverpool University, 1975); A. S. Wohl, *Endangered Lives: Public Health in Victorian Britain* (London, 1983). This last named is particularly recommended.

3   J. H. Treble, *Urban Poverty in Britain 1830-1914* (London, 1979).

4   J. D. Papworth, 'The Irish in Liverpool, 1835-71: Family Structure and Residential Mobility' (unpublished Ph.D., Liverpool University), 1982, chapter 3, Table 8.

5   *Local Reports on the Sanitary Condition of the Labouring Populations (Sanitary Inquiry (England))* B.P.P. 1842[H.L.]XXVII. Local Report, No. 19, Dr. Duncan, 'On the Sanitary Conditions of Liverpool', pp. 291-4.

6   *Sixth Report of the Select Committee on Settlement and Poor Removal* B.P.P. 1847[409]XI, Minutes of Evidence, E. Rushton, qq. 4370-1 (referred to hereafter as 'Removal

(1847)'. *Accounts and Papers*, B.P.P. 1847[764]L, Memorial to the Home Secretary From the Select Vestry of the Parish of Liverpool, dated 24 December 1846, pp. 435-7. This expresses concern over the number of Irish paupers landing at Liverpool. Concern also reported in *Liverpool Mail*, 26 December 1846, *Liverpool Courier*, 13 January 1847.

7   Papworth, 'The Irish in Liverpool, 1835-71', chapter 3, Table 8.

8   For studies of this system see, M. E. Rose, *The Relief of Poverty 1834-1914* (London, 1972); M. E. Rose (ed.), *The Poor and the City: The English Poor Law in its Urban Context 1834-1914* (Leicester, 1988), P. Wood, *Poverty and The Workhouse* (Stroud, 1991).

9   *Liverpool Mercury*, 15 January 1847.

10 *Appendix to the Thirteenth Annual Report of the Poor Law Commissioners*, B.P.P. 1847[816]XXVIII, 1. Appendix A, no 8; Report of Albert Austin on 'The Relief of the Irish Poor in Liverpool'. This contains a very full description of the problems facing the Liverpool authorities up to 30 April 1847.

11 *Appendix to the Thirteenth Annual Report of the Poor Law Commissioners*, p. 116.

12 *Select Committee on Poor Removal* (B.P.P. 1854(396)XVII), Appendix no. 8, 'Returns of the Mendicity Department of the Liverpool District Provident Society from the Commencement of the Society's Operations, distinguishing the Birthplaces of the Recipients for each year, 1830 to 1853', p. 593.

13 *Report of the Inspector of Nuisances. Minutes of Health Committee* held on 31 May 1847, Liverpool Record Office, 352 MIN/HEA 11, Health Committee Minutes 1 January 1847 – August 1847 and Liverpool Medical Officer of Health Reports 1847-50, H 352. 4 HEA, p. 5.

14 *First Report of the Commissioners of Enquiry into the State of Large Towns and Populous Districts*, B.P.P. 1844[572]XVII, Appendix, Dr. W. H. Duncan, 'On The Causes of the High Rate of Mortality in The Borough of Liverpool', p. 13.

15 For examples of such reports regarding Liverpool see *Manchester Guardian*, 27 January 1847; *Halifax Guardian*, 9 January 1847; *Gore's General Advertiser*, 21 January 1847; *Liverpool Mercury*, 22 January 1847; *Liverpool Chronicle*, 6 February 1847.

16 *Liverpool Mercury*, 11 May 1847; *Liverpool Albion*, 10 May 1847.

17 The issues involved in dealing with typhus and cholera epidemics during the period under discussion are the subject of a growing number of studies. See C. Hamlin, 'Predisposing Causes and Public Health in Early Nineteenth-Century Medical Thought', *The Society For the Social History of Medicine* (1992), pp. 41-70. Bill Luckin, 'Evaluating The Sanitary Revolution: Typhus and Typhoid in London, 1851-1900', in R. Woods and J. Woodward (eds), *Urban Disease and Mortality in Nineteenth-Century England* (London, 1984), pp. 102-119. A. Hardy, 'Urban Famine Or Urban Crisis? Typhus in the Victorian City', *Medical History*, 32 (1985), pp. 401-25.

18 *Liverpool Courier*, 14 April 1847. This edition carries a report of the Select Vestry meeting held on 13 April, at which a report was given of complaints made to the councillor for the Abercromby ward. See also *Liverpool Courier*, 28 April 1847. Meeting of 200 ward members to complain about fever sheds in workhouse grounds.

19 *Liverpool Standard*, 15 June 1847. Meeting of the Select Vestry held on 8 June, 1847.

20 Health Committee Minutes, 17 May, 1847. Report from Dr. Duncan.

21 For a detailed treatment of competition on the cross-channel routes and the conditions under which the Famine Irish were transported to Liverpool, see F. Neal 'Liverpool, the Irish Steamship Companies and the Famine Irish', *Immigrants and Minorities*, V, 1 (1986), pp. 28-61.

22 *The Times*, 8 May, 1847. Sir George Grey told the House of Commons that the select vestry could use these ships as lazarettos. *Manchester Guardian*, 16 June, 1847. *Liverpool Standard*, 15 June, 1847. Mr Walker and his wife, from the southern dispensary in Liverpool were appointed Superintendent and Matron of the *Akbar* at a salary of forty shillings per week.

23 *The Times*, 8 May, 1847. This contains a copy of the petition from the select vestry to the House of Commons in which statistics of burials are given. The total number of burials are recorded in the Register of Burials at the Parish Cemetery of St Mary's, Cambridge Street, Liverpool (Liverpool Record Office, CEM/283/MRY/11-13).

24 Liverpool Medical Officer of Health Reports 1847-50, pp. 18-19.

25 Ibid, p. 18.

26 *Liverpool Mercury*, 29 January, 1847. Copy of letter. Augustus Campbell to the Secretary of State for the Home Department, dated 28 January, 1847.

27 *Liverpool Mail*, 26 December, 1846.

28 *Liverpool Courier*, 13 January, 1847. Meeting of the select vestry on 12 January, 1847. Letter read from Secretary to Sir George Grey, pointing out there was nothing the government could do.

29 F. Neal, 'Liverpool, the Irish Steamship Companies and the Famine Irish'.

30 *Liverpool Chronicle*, 19 June, 1847. *Manchester Guardian*, 30 June & 7 July 1847. *Liverpool Albion*, 26 July, 1847.

31 Secretary to select vestry to Poor Law Commissioners, 31 October, 1851. Complaint that the removal system being used by the Irish to obtain free trips home. P.R.O. (L.), MH12/5969/10883/51.

32 *Select Committee on Settlement and Removal* (1847). Minutes of Evidence. E. Rushton, qq. 428-9; Mr Lowndes, q. 4578.

33 E. Rushton, op.cit. qq. 4339-55.

34 A detailed breakdown of the property rated at above £10 per year would enable the financial contribution to the poor rate to be accurately allocated to the various categories rather than simply averaging. However, no such breakdown has been found.

35 The author is at present completing a book, *Black '47: Britain and the Famine Irish* (Macmillan, forthcoming 1997). In this, a more detailed cost analysis of the cost of the 1847 Famine influx is being undertaken for Liverpool, Manchester and Glasgow.

36 A. T. McCabe, 'The Standard of Living on Merseyside 1850-75' in S. P. Bell (ed.), *Victorian Lancashire* (Newton Abbott, 1974), Table 1, p. 129.

37 For a full account of the sectarian conflict in Liverpool, see F. Neal, *Sectarian Violence: The Liverpool Experience 1815-1914* (Manchester, 1988).

38 F. Neal, 'A Criminal Profile of the Liverpool Irish', in *Transactions of the Historic Society of Lancashire and Cheshire*, 140 (1990), Table VII, p. 173.

Migrant Maladies: Unseen Lethal Baggage

E. Margaret Crawford

THE FIRST MEDICAL OFFICER of Health in Great Britain, appointed to the city of Liverpool, William Henry Duncan, wrote in his inaugural report:

> The 1st of January 1847, found … pauper immigration steadily increasing, and it continued in such a rapidly progressive ratio, that by the end of June not less than 300,000 Irish had landed in Liverpool. … hordes of sickly and half starved Irish continued to pour into the town, and that fever continued to spread, *pari passu* … the cases becom[ing] so numerous as completely to baffle the attempts of the parish authorities to provide the requisite hospital accommodation.[1]

Not all immigrants into Liverpool finished their journey there or the surrounding region; they used the port merely as a staging post *en route* to North America.[2] Nevertheless, there remained a large number of starving and sick destitutes escaping from the ravages of Famine in Ireland who travelled no further than England, Scotland or Wales. Not only did they bring their poverty, but also lethal, unseen baggage in the form of disease. Many were sick on leaving Ireland, others became ill on the journey, and more fell ill shortly after landing.

In the years immediately before the Famine disquiet was expressed by Duncan and others about the insanitary conditions of the housing in the large city conurbations in Great Britain. In particular, districts inhabited by Irish immigrants were identified as especially unsavoury,[3] their squalid lodging houses and cellars habitations perceived as pools of infection. Thus even before the Great Famine the Irish were castigated as harbingers of disease.

Compared with other British towns and cities, Liverpool had high levels of disease and the highest death rate in the country: 36 per 1,000 in 1846[4] compared with a national rate of 22 per 1,000. As a port, Liverpool had a large number of casual labourers. Work was sporadic, and wages intermittent, with the consequence that the labour force was badly housed and poorly fed. Dirt, disease and malnutrition flourished. Furthermore, Liverpool was no stranger to imported disease, since it was a major port *en route* to exotic locations. To protect the city 'lazarettos' or quarantine ships were moored in the Mersey Estuary, to which ailing seamen with unknown or suspected dangerous diseases were disembarked.[5]

At the beginning of 1847 concern was voiced in Parliament about the mass influx of Irish immigrants escaping the Famine into Liverpool.[6] Two issues were at stake: the cost to the rate payers who financed the poor law upon which the destitute depended; and the spread of disease. According to Duncan the fever was confined to those districts housing the Irish, the English inhabitants being healthy.[7] In May 1847 a petition from the select vestry of Liverpool was read by Sir Benjamin Hall to the House of Commons expressing their anxiety:

> That some of the immigrants come over in a state of actual infectious disease, and a large number of so predisposed to it that they fall sick shortly after their arrival, and so propagate disease and death among an otherwise healthy population. That the consequences are most disastrous and alarming to the people – dysentery, diarrhoea, small-pox and typhus abound.[8]

The Home Secretary, Sir George Grey, told the House in reply that the crisis was not new; it had been brought to his attention on numerous occasions by the municipal and parochial authorities. He declared that between the 15 January 1847, when accurate figures were first kept, and May of the same year 180,000 Irish had disembarked at the port of Liverpool.[9] Of these, between 40,000 or 50,000 emigrated, leaving between 60,000 and 80,000 remaining in England and Wales.[10]

In response to mounting pressure from the Liverpool authorities to stem the spread of infection, the government issued instructions to the custom-house authorities directing them to designate two former quarantine ships, as 'lazaretto' or hospital ships.[11] The ships employed for this task were the *Akbar* and the *Newcastle*. The *Akbar* was not ready for immediate use, but when fitted out would accommodate 300 patients. The initial plan was to reserve the *Akbar* for Irish immigrants arriving at the port in a diseased state. The *Newcastle* was to be used for fever patients from the town.[12] Two medical officers, Dr Cameron and Mr McCallan, were appointed to board ships in the Mersey estuary as they arrived from Ireland. Mr Harvey was the surgeon on the lazarettos. These arrangements were recorded in early May 1847. From a public health aspect they were not too soon, for in one week in that month 1,035 Irish arrived on Monday, 677 on Tuesday, 825 Wednesday, 1,105 Thursday, 1,010 Friday, 667 Saturday and 2,445 on Sunday – in all a total of 7,764 Irish immigrants.[13]

In addition, two further measures were implemented. The city health authorities provided public wash-houses and a dry heat disinfecting station where clothing could be treated.[14] Nevertheless, by the end of 1847 Duncan estimated that almost 60,000 people had contracted fever and a further 40,000 suffered diarrhoea and dysentery. From these diseases alone 8,500 died. The death rate from all causes was 1 in 14 of the town's population, the equivalent of 71 per 1,000.[15] This figure was twice the 'normal' rate. During the quarter July to September 1847 fever deaths were recorded from the following sub-districts of Liverpool:[16]

St Martin's	291
Dale Street	250
St Thomas	301 total deaths on lazarettos
Mount Pleasant	324
Islington	105
Great Howard Street	No figures

Many Irish migrants proceeded to Manchester, only to fall ill there. However, the reasons for the prevalence of disease in Manchester were complex. The grain harvest of 1845-6 was poor and the basic industries were depressed, unemployment high and food prices inflated and so the pangs of hunger were widespread. The registrar of Deansgate, Manchester summed up the conditions thus: 'famine made her dwelling in their homes, and her attendant horror, typhus, relentlessly swept his victims to the grave.'[17] The 'hungry forties' became etched in the memory of the British labouring class even without the help of the Irish.

Lancashire was not the only county to receive immigrants from across the Irish Sea. Virtually all ports on the western coast from Scotland southwards were used to disembark the Irish. Many migrants from the south and south-east of Ireland alighted at South Welsh ports bringing with them fever. Dr Tuthill Massey on reading reports of 'the Irish fever', wrote to the *Dublin Quarterly Journal of Medical Science* on 'Fever in South Wales'. He identified the carriers of disease as labourers from Cork, Cloyne, Kinsale, and Skibbereen sailing across the Irish Sea to Swansea and Cardiff, then travelling on to the colliery villages in the region looking for work. Their physical condition on arrival was wretched, having endured already months of deprivation. Many were sick on arrival or became sick shortly afterwards with fever. A temporary fever hospital had to be opened to accommodate the large numbers of patients. Massey described it as no better than a barn, and not worthy of the name hospital. The conditions there were appalling even to the hardened doctor who recalled:

> The darkness terrified me as I stepped over the beds of those creatures as they lay side by side, moaning and groaning, and those who were able calling for "Water! water! oh! the thirst!" A candle was required to examine the anxious face, the flushed cheek, and the parched tongue, of those who lay in the angles of the building.[18]

During the period May to November 1847 Dr Massey attended 'upwards of 6,000 Irish'.[19] While most cases seen by Massey were of typhus, a few cases of relapse [relapsing fever] were treated, and these he attributed to 'incaution in diet'.[20]

Doctors elsewhere, particularly where the Irish population was inflated' because of the Famine, noted an increase in the incidence of fever, in some places reaching epidemic proportions. Dr Hughes of London had:

> little doubt that the fever, as an epidemic, or perhaps rather an endemic affection, has been imported from Ireland ... The importation of the poor Irish into Liverpool ..., and their extension to Leeds and other places, appears undoubtedly to have been followed by the occurrence and wide diffusion of fever in those places. I cannot but believe that similar consequences have followed similar causes in London also.[21]

Hughes listed several reasons for blaming the Irish. Fever had been rare in his hospital before migrants from Ireland arrived in London. Since their arrival, however, fever admissions were larger 'than [had] been for the last eighteen or twenty years, and I am Authorised to say, even for the last fifty years'.[22] Secondly, the early cases occurred almost exclusively among the Irish. Hughes noted that out of 38 fever patients in the hospital at one time, 36 were Irish. Of his own case load 24 were Irish and 14 English. Thirdly, many patients treated at the hospital had only just arrived from Ireland. Finally, the fever prevailed among the 'very lowest orders ... and always emanated from districts – courts and alleys – densely populated with Irish.'[23] Hughes concluded that 'the existing fever, as an epidemic or endemic affection was imported from Ireland, and that from the lower class of Irish, it had been gradually communicated to the English residents of this district.'[24] He continued:

> I cannot but believe that it had extended widely among the Irish, not so much from the want of food ... as from the habit of crowding together in the densely populated houses of courts and allays, and particularly from the extremely dirty and careless habits of many of the sufferers. Famine had, I believe, had less influence in its production or dissemination than filth.[25]

Similar reports appeared in the medical journals from Scotland. In Glasgow the fever epidemic raged with great ferocity. Admissions to the Glasgow Royal Infirmary during the four year period 1846-9 show the severity of the epidemic. (See Table 1.)

Table 1:
Admissions to the Glasgow Royal Infirmary

Year	Relapsing Fever	Typhus
1846	777	500
1847	2,333	2,399
1848	513	980
1849	168	342

Source: 1847 figures in J.C. Steele, 'View of the Sickness and Mortality in the Royal Infirmary of Glasgow during the year 1847: illustrated by Tables of the different Diseases', *Edinburgh Medical and Surgical Journal*, 70 (1848); C. Creighton, *History of Epidemics in Britain*, p. 208.

Of the 9,290 cases in Glasgow, 57 per cent were found to be Irish, of whom one-third had resided in Glasgow for less than one year. Burials in Glasgow greatly increased in 1847. During the non-crisis years they averaged 8,452, but in 1847 interments more than doubled to 18,071. In Dundee burials rose by about 75 per cent.[26] In Edinburgh the fever epidemic was less severe. Nevertheless, during a four month period between June and September 1847 the city parochial board sent to the infirmary 887 patients of whom 485 died. Of these 70 per cent were fever cases.[27] Nine-tenths of the patients were Irish who had flocked to the charity workhouse. The Royal Infirmary was unable to cope with the mass influx, and so large sheds capable of housing 80 to 100 beds were erected.

Typhus erupted in Ireland during the last three months of 1846. It then appeared in Glasgow at the end of 1846, in Liverpool during January of 1847, in London and Edinburgh by March and Manchester during April.[28] The disease reached its zenith in the summer of 1847, and did not wane until the end of 1848. The source of fever was unanimously identified with Irish migrants. Doctors such as Paterson of Edinburgh, observed that, 'almost every case admitted into the Infirmary at the beginning of the epidemic was from Ireland'.[29] One Scottish doctor, Steele, demonstrated his point with statistics, shown in Table 2.

Table 2:
Cases of Fever in Royal Infirmary, Glasgow in 1847

	Irish	Scottish	English	Others
Royal Infirmary	3,106	2,094	15	9
City Hospital	1,326	896	38	
Barony Hospital	884	890	25	7
Total	5,316	3,880	78	16

Source: J. C. Steele, 'View of the Sickness and Mortality in the Royal Infirmary of Glasgow during the Year 1847', Edinburgh Medical & Surgical Journal, 70 (1848), p. 169.

The diseases that Irish migrants brought with them to Britain fell into two broad categories, infectious and non-infectious. The main infections were typhus, relapsing fever, typhoid, diarrhoea and dysentery. Three diseases, typhus, relapsing fever and the vitamin deficiency disease, scurvy were particularly well documented in the medical literature, and so it is upon these ailments that this chapter will concentrate.

Sir William P. MacArthur's scholarly work on disease during the Great Irish Famine has not been surpassed.[30] The following account relies heavily on this pioneering essay. Typhus and relapsing fever are infections transmitted from person to person by infected body lice. Typhus, rickettsia prowazedi, affects the small blood vessels, which are extensively damaged by the organism. The brain and skin vessels are particularly vulnerable to attack, which explains the frequently described symptoms of delirium and stupor, and the characteristic spotted rash. The onset of typhus is manifest by shivering, headache and aching pains. Later symptoms of bloodshot eyes, muscular twitching and stupid mental state give the impression of drunkenness. The rash appears about the fifth day and the other symptoms intensify, often culminating by the fourteenth day in a crisis. At this point victims either succumb or recover.

Relapsing fever is caused by a thread-like spiral organism called a spirochaete. Infection takes place usually through the skin. The name of the disease stems from the numerous relapses which take place during the course of the illness, the interval between each episode being about seven days. The onset is sudden, often accompanied by a severe rigor and gastric symptoms of sickness and vomiting – hence the name 'gastric fever'. In addition, bleeding from the nose is a frequent complication. Another popular name for this disease was 'yellow fever' because some patients became jaundiced, giving the body a deep orange-brown appearance.

Of the two fevers, relapsing fever was less lethal. During the Famine years the death rate from typhus was generally three or four times higher than that from relapsing fever. Unlike typhus, relapsing fever was not endemic and so some doctors did not recognise it. When relapsing fever took hold in a community, 'the pre-existing typhus was often outdistanced by [relapsing fever] for it ... was disseminated much more rapidly than typhus'.[31]

The phrase 'famine fever' was applied both to typhus and relapsing fever, although more often to the latter than the former. In England the epidemic was almost entirely typhus; in Scotland both relapsing and typhus fevers were treated, though most cases were typhus. Several features of the fevers of the 1840s differed from earlier episodes. The outbreaks were more severe than the epidemic of 1837 though of shorter duration. Some doctors did not distinguish between typhus and relapsing fever, viewing them as clinical variants of the same infection. This conclusion was accepted because they witnessed characteristics of both diseases in the same patient. Also doctors treating individuals from the same household, found some exhibiting symptoms of typhus while others were clearly suffering from relapsing fever. We now know that the two diseases were co-existing.

Numerous sources refer to the high mortality among the medical profession, clergy, administrative staff such as relieving officers, police, hospital staff and others who caught 'fever' in the course of their duties. Dr Massey described twenty-four patients under his care, including the hospital chaplain, the surgeon, the master and his son, the matron, numerous nurses, the porter, the union gardener, a Roman Catholic priest and others whom Massey claimed all, 'got the fever from the Irish'.[32] The Roman Catholic journal *The Tablet* reflected the prevailing concern by the long descriptive obituaries to deceased priests. On 26 June 1847 an obituary recorded the death of the Reverend J. Carroll, priest in the Welsh district of Merthyr Tydvil. His demise was caused by fever, which he had contracted while ministering to the Irish community.[33] Deaths among the Roman Catholic clergy were sufficiently numerous to warrant reference to it in the Registrar-General's Report of 1847 as well as in *The Tablet*.[34] The registrar of Great Howard Street, in Liverpool in 1847 wrote:

> Eight Roman Catholic priests and one clergyman of the Church of England have fallen victim to their indefatigable attention to the poor of their church. Indeed, their exemplary conduct in visiting and relieving the sick had been the theme of praise with all.[35]

The concern of the Catholic church about their clergy's health was so acute that their journal reproduced a text entitled, 'Translation of Dr Decock's Directions for the Treatment of Typhus'.[36]

Mortality among doctors was high.[37] Two leading Irish doctors, William Stokes and James William Cusack, carried out a survey of deaths among 'physicians, surgeons, diplomats of a university or chartered corporate body, apothecaries, and also pupils entrusted with the care of people particularly during the late epidemic'.[38] Many English doctors treating typhus patients, like their Irish colleagues, and the clergy, paid the ultimate price too for their labours. *The Lancet*, reported numerous deaths of physicians and surgeons, who 'caught the fever in the discharge of their duty, and sank under the dreadful malady.'[39]

There are several noteworthy points about fever as it affected the 'better classes'. Firstly, the disease was usually confined to the infected individual of the household, and did not spread to other members. Secondly, relapsing fever was rare; typhus was the more common. The mode of transmission provides the explanation. Typhus can be transmitted by infected faecal dust gaining entry through inhalation, conjunctiva of the eye or broken skin. To contract relapsing fever, direct contact with the louse is necessary. Finally, mortality among the better classes was higher compared with the poor. Unlike the poor, the wealthy had no immunity built up from previous episodes. In addition, many philanthrophic workers were from the older age groups and their hearts failed to withstand the strain typhus placed on them. Thus for many, philanthrophic service signed their death warrants.

Precise statistics for typhus and relapsing fever are not available. The Registrar General provided mortality figures for typhus but they include both typhus and typhoid. These diseases were not distinguished until 1869.[40] However, as an indicator of the magnitude and distribution of the fever epidemic the following Registrar General's figures are revealing:

Table 3:
Deaths Rate per 100,000 from Typhus in England and Wales

Registration Divisions	1847	1848	1849
London	135	152	105
South Eastern	115	121	113
South Midland	164	151	124
Eastern	113	97	100
South Midland	92	91	95
West Midland	159	120	96
North Midland	137	102	87
North Western	364	136	101
York	162	106	88
Northern	135	98	69
Wales	165	103	114

Source: *Annual Reports of the Registrar General 1847-9.*

The north-western division in which Liverpool and Manchester were located recorded the highest mortality, Wales, West Midlands and the South Midlands following, though at a considerably lower rate. Murchison, in his classic work on fever published in 1862, has estimated that the total number of fever cases in England for 1847 was probably upwards of 300,000. In Liverpool alone it was estimated that around 10,000 people died of typhus.[41] Data for Scotland are not available.

Another disease associated with the Irish during the Great Famine was scurvy. It made an appearance in Britain during 1847 too. Unlike fever, scurvy is not infectious, but is caused by a dietary deficiency, the lack of vitamin C. While the disease had been identified as early as the 1760s, and a remedy discovered, a full understanding of the cause was still far off. Land scurvy was a rare ailment in Ireland in the early nineteenth century. It was first observed late in 1845, and accounts of scorbutic symptoms appeared in Irish medical journals early in 1846. In Britain symptoms were reported later, though unlike Ireland, there was no doubt about diagnosis.[42]

The distribution of the disease was widespread. Doctors from Scotland,[43] and England, in locations as far apart as Edinburgh and Exeter identified cases of scurvy. Many physicians realised that those heavily dependent on the potato were vulnerable when supplies were scarce. As in Ireland, blight (*phytophthora infestans*) damaged the British potato crop in 1846. Trade in general was depressed and the price of provisions was high. While hunger was not on the Irish scale, nevertheless, an indication of the suffering can be gauged by the record of diseases afflicting the destitute. Prophetically the Registrar General's report for 1846 anticipated the appearance of scurvy:

> It is certain that scurvy, which was formerly common, has almost disappeared since the potato entered largely into the food of the population. If, now that the potato has grown scarce, this disease, characterised among other symptoms by swollen bleeding gums, again become prevalent, its simple prophylactics should be had recourse to.[44]

A footnote in the report added, 'this anticipation of the appearance of scurvy was unfortunately realised.'[45]

Many medical reports of the 1840s described the salient features of scurvy. Initially scorbutic patients complained of tiredness, breathlessness, and mental depression. Later cutaneous haemorrhages, from bleeding under the surface of the skin, produced purple blotches (purpuric spots) which usually appeared first on the limbs, and then on other parts of the body. Joints became swollen and painful because of haemorrhaging. The gums were red, soft, spongy, swollen and easily bled. Eventually teeth loosened and fell out. Scurvy unrestrained was a killer disease, death being the result of haemorrhages into the heart muscle or brain.

Numerous articles in the medical journals discussed the incidence of scurvy, its causes, its symptoms and remedies. Drs Ritchie and Christison treated over 250 patients suffering from scurvy in Glasgow and Edinburgh hospitals. Dr Lonsdale physician to the Cumberland Infirmary attended between 90 and 100 patients. Drs Turnbull of Liverpool, Laycock of York and Shapter of Exeter all were presented with scorbutic symptoms in their hospitals.[46] Two groups were identified as particularly susceptible: Irish migrants and males. Not only were the Irish affected, but also tradespeople, labouring families and rural populations.[47] The link between these groups was their normal consumption of large quantities of potatoes. On the question of sex imbalance, it could be argued that more males migrated from Ireland than females. However, evidence from Ireland indicates that even under the same conditions males were more vulnerable to scurvy.[48] Steele, in his paper on the 'Pathological Statistics of Glasgow Infirmary for 1847', presented figures of scorbutic patients treated during that year, shown in Table 4.

Table 4:
Scorbutic Patients treated in the Glasgow Infirmary

Age Group	Total	Dismissed		Died	
		Males	Females	Males	Females
1 to 14	–	–	–	–	–
14 to 20	5	5	–	–	–
20 to 30	37	25	12	–	–
30 to 40	25	21	4	–	–
40 to 50	22	19	3	–	–
50 to 60	9	9	–	–	–
60 upwards	4	3	–	1	–

Source: Steele 'Pathological Statistics of Glasgow Infirmary for 1847', *Edinburgh Medical and Surgical Journal*, 70 (1848), p. 155.

For an explanation of the sex imbalance we have to look at modern nutritional research. There is considerable evidence to show that there are lower concentrations of vitamin C in men than women, even when dietary intakes are matched, suggesting that there is a difference in the metabolism of vitamin C between men and women.[49] Why this disparity exists is unclear.

With the exception of Dr Christison of Edinburgh, who blamed scurvy on the lack of milk in the diet,[50] doctors ascribed the disease to the lack of vegetables and in particular the potato.[51] The right connection had indeed been made. For although vitamin C is an unstable substance, being soluble in water and destroyed by storage and heat, and furthermore, the potato is only a moderate source of vitamin C, nevertheless this vegetable was the main dietary source of many.[52] Moreover, the large quantities consumed provided sufficient levels to forestall scorbutic symptoms. In the case of Irish immigrants, their high consumption of potatoes before the Famine supplied them with far in excess of the daily requirement of vitamin C (30-60 mg), and placed the Irish labourers' diet in the mega-dose league. The fact that scurvy also appeared among the British poor is an indicator of how important the potato was in their diet. Levitt and Smout's work on the Scottish working class in 1843 shows that the potato was a prominent item in the daily diet particularly in the Western Highlands.[53]

Other factors also contributed to the appearance of scurvy. First, unlike some vitamins, vitamin C cannot be manufactured endogenously. Consequently dietary supplies are the sole source. Secondly, it is not a storable vitamin, and so must be replenished on a regular basis. Thirdly, a wealth of research confirms that any disease, whether acute or chronic, depletes vitamin C rapidly. Infections and gastrointestinal diseases, in particular, reduce levels of the vitamin quickly.[54] Typhus, relapsing fever, diarrhoea, and dysentery were rife and coupled with the sharp drop in dietary intake of vitamin C, the onset of scurvy is not surprising. More important, the exceptionally high levels of vitamin C in the potato diet operated to the disadvantage of potato dependent populations in times of shortages. People accustomed to saturated levels of vitamin C become depleted of the vitamin more quickly than those used to a low intake because 'the body becomes conditioned to the "de-luxe" treatment, [and] sudden withdrawal … does not allow the physiology of the individual to accommodate immediately to a lower intake.'[55] The potato eaters fell into this trap. A lower intake of vitamin C before the Famine – say between 20 and 30 mg daily – would undoubtedly have delayed the onset of scurvy.

Particularly strong evidence supporting the 'withdrawal syndrome' theory comes from Irish people in Scotland. Christison had 149 scurvy cases in the Edinburgh Royal Infirmary over a period of three months during 1847. All but three were from Ireland. They had arrived in the early summer of that year to work on the railways. All railway labourers had to purchase their food rations in the company's store, and on inquiry it was discovered that potatoes were not eaten by any of the navvies, yet it was the Irish who were experiencing the effects of potato and hence vitamin C withdrawal.

How do fever and scurvy relate to famine and migration? Taking the latter disease first, vitamin deficiency diseases are not usually a conspicuous feature of food shortages, despite grossly deficient diets. The vitamin requirements of famine victims are reduced because of their low level of general and basal metabolism. Nevertheless, deficiency diseases do occur, their prevalence depending to a greater or lesser degree on the customary diet and the duration of the crisis. In the Irish case, the sudden withdrawal of their sole source of vitamin C, the potato, from a population conditioned to saturated levels, proved to be a nutritional trap, into which the potato eaters plunged when the crop failed.

Typhus, on the other hand, was commonly associated with famine, but it was not the lack of food which caused the disease, rather the social conditions associated with famine. In times of food shortages people migrate to urban centres in search of relief and it was this congregating in large numbers which propagated the spread of the infection. Infected lice moved with ease from one body to another, infecting their victims as they travelled. The presence of fever in Ireland is explained, therefore, by environmental factors which fostered its spread. People assembled at food depots, workhouse gates, and soup kitchens. The packet steamers too offered an ideal atmosphere for the disease to spread. Hundreds of immigrants were crammed onto open decks making it easy for the lice to move from one passenger to another transmitting their fatal legacy.

Would these diseases have existed in Britain during 1847-8 without the Irish influx? Dealing with scurvy first; it was not an illness carried from Ireland to Britain, to spread among the indigenous population. The loss of an anti-scorbutic food in the daily diet was the culprit, affecting the poor irrespective of nationality. As to typhus, it was widely accepted that the Irish influx was the principal source of the fever epidemic in England and Scotland by its 'progress, direction and other circumstances.'[56] Murchison expressed the views of contemporary doctors thus:

> fever was imported, to a great extent, by the Irish into the large towns of Scotland and England ... Apart from the circumstances that the epidemic commenced in Ireland, and first attacked those towns of Britain most accessible to Irish immigrants, it is well known that the Irish flocked over to Britain by thousands, that in England and Scotland during the whole epidemic that majority of persons who suffered were Irish, and that at first they were almost exclusively Irish who had but recently left their own country.[57]

This perception twenty years on, however, was tempered. Murchison writing in 1861 maintained that, 'although typhus was more prevalent in Ireland than in Britain, it [was] not imported from the former into the latter country, to the extent commonly believed'.[58] As recent research has pointed out, it is probable that incoming [British] migrants from rural areas and small towns who had little chance to develop resistance to the endemic and epidemic diseases of large urban areas, were particularly susceptible to infection during the massive Famine migration of the 1840s.[59] Furthermore, the congregating of these rural impoverished migrants into urban squalor fostered the spread of disease. Exoneration of the Irish increased following the London typhus epidemics of 1856 and 1862. On both of these occasions there was not an epidemic in Ireland.[60] Murchison thus argued that Ireland's contribution to British epidemics of typhus rested with the overcrowded and insanitary conditions of their habitations and lack of personal cleanliness.[61] The case of the 1847 epidemic was exceptional. Irish immigrants acted as a catalyst adding fuel to an outbreak about to ignite. The preconditions were in position. Poor living conditions in industrial towns and cities, depressed employment, high food prices, and devastation of the cheapest food of all, the potato.

References

1   Cited in W.M. Frazer, *Duncan of Liverpool* (London, 1947), p. 57; T. H. Bickerton, H. R. Bickerton and R.M.B. Mackenna, *A medical history of Liverpool from the earliest days to the year 1920* (London, 1936), pp. 177-8.

2   Letter addressed to Her Majesty's Secretary of State for the Home Department, by Edward Rushton, Esquire, Stipendiary Magistrate of Liverpool, B.P.P. 1849[266]XLVII, p. 1.

3   *First Report for the Commissioners for Inquiring into the Poorer Classes in Ireland (Poor Inquiry ((Ireland))*, Appendix G. Report on the State of the Irish Poor in Great Britain, British Parliamentary Papers (hereafter B.P.P.), B.P.P. 1836[40]XXXIV, pp. 18, 54, 118.

4   Sidney Chave, 'The first medical officer of health: Duncan of Liverpool – and some lessons for today', in Michael Warren and Huw Francis (eds), *Recalling the Medical Officer of Health: Writings of Sidney Chave* (London, 1987), p. 35.

5   Bickerton, Bickerton and Mackenna, *A medical history of Liverpool*, pp.187-8.

6   *Hansard* (Commons), Third Series, XC, 1847, cols 1-3.

7   Charles Murchison, *A Treatise on the Continued fevers of Great Britain*, Third Edition, edited by W. Cayley (London, 1884), p. 49.

8   *Hansard* (Commons), Third Series, XC, 1847, col. 525.

9   For the entire year of 1847 296,231 Irish landed in Liverpool; see F. Neal, 'Lancashire, the Famine Irish and the Poor Laws: A Study in Crisis Management', *Journal of the Economic and Social History Society*, XVI (1995), p. 4.

10 *Hansard* (Commons), Third Series, XC, 1847, col. 526.

11 Ibid.

12 *London Medical Gazette*, 39, New Series IV (1847), p. 878.

13 Ibid.

14 Bickerton, Bickerton, Mackenna, *A medical history of Liverpool*, p. 178.

15 Warren and Francis (eds.), *Recalling the Medical Officer of Health: Writings of Sidney Chave*, p. 31.

16 *Tenth Annual Report of the Registrar General, 1847* B.P.P. 1849[1113] XXI, pp. xxiii

17 *Tenth Annual Report of the Registrar General*, p. xxii.

18 Tuthill Massey, 'Letter on Fever in South Wales', *Dublin Quarterly Journal of Medical Science* (hereafter *DQJMS*), VIII (Dublin, 1849), p. 439.

19 Tuthill Massey, 'Letter on Fever in South Wales', p. 439.

20 Tuthill Massey, 'Letter on Fever in South Wales', p. 440.

21 H.M. Hughes, 'Remarks upon the continued Fever at present existing in the southern districts of the Metropolis', *London Medical Gazette*, 40, New Series, V (1847), p. 972.

22 Hughes, 'Remarks upon the continued Fever', p. 972.

23 Ibid.

24 Ibid. Also see Ruth-Ann Harris, *The Nearest Place that wasn't Ireland* (Iowa, 1994), pp. 173-4.

25 Hughes, 'Remarks upon the continued Fever', pp. 972, 975.

26 M. Flinn *et al., Scottish Population History from the 17th Century to the 1930s* (Cambridge, 1977), p. 373.

27 'Fever in Edinburgh' Medical Intellegence, *London Medical Gazette*, 40, New Series, V (1847), p. 639.

28 Charles Murchison, *A Treatise on the Continued Fevers of Great Britain* (London, 1862), p. 49.

29 Robert Paterson, 'On the Epidemic Fever of 1847-8', *Edinburgh Medical and Surgical Journal*, 70 (1848), p. 380.

30 W.P. MacArthur, 'Medical History of the Famine' in *The Great Famine: Studies in Irish History 1845-52* (eds), R.D. Edwards and T.D. Williams (Dublin, 1956), pp. 265-70.

31 MacArthur, 'Medical History of the Famine', pp. 276.

32 Tuthill Massey, 'Letter on Fever in South Wales', *DQJMS* (Dublin, 1849), p. 439.

33 *The Tablet*, VIII, no.373, 26 June 1847, p. 406.

34 *The Tablet*, VIII, no.373, 10 July 1847, p. 439.

35 *Tenth Annual Report of the Registrar General for the year 1847*, p. xxi.

36 *The Tablet*, VIII, no.374, 20 November 1847, p. 742.

37 See P. Froggatt, 'The response of the Medical Profession to the Great Famine' (ed.), E. Margaret Crawford, *Famine: The Irish Experience 900-1900* (Edinburgh, 1989), p. 148.

38 J.W. Cusack and W. Stokes, 'On the mortality of Medical Practitioners from Fever in Ireland', *Dublin Journal of Medical Science.* (hereafter *D.J.M.S.*), IV (1847), pp. 134-45; idem, 'On the mortality of Medical Practitioners in Ireland; Second Article', *D.J.M.S*, V (1848), pp. 111-128.

39 *The Lancet*, II (1847), p. 320.

40 William Jenner published a three part article entitled 'On Typhoid and Typhus Fevers, an attempt to determine the question of their identity or non-identity, by an analysis of the symptoms, and of the appearance ...', *The Monthly Journal of Medical Science* (hereafter *MJMS*), IX, no. 34, new series (1849), pp. 663-80, no. 35, pp. 726-736; and no. 36, pp. 816-28.

41 C. Murchison, *A Treatise on the Continued fevers of Great Britain*, Third Edition, Ed. W. Cayley (London, 1884), p. 50.

42 An early account of scorbutic symptoms mistakenly diagnosed the ailment as a disease of a 'gastro-enterite' nature. See Dr J.D. O'Brien, 'Cases of a Pecular Form of Gastro-Enterite resulting from the use of Diseases Potatoes', *Dublin Hospital Gazette*, 15 January, 1846, p. 166.

43 T.M. Devine, *The Great Highland Famine* (Edinburgh, 1988), pp. 2, 12-13.

44 *Ninth Annual Report of the Registrar General for England and Wales*, 1846, B.P.P. 1847-8[996]XXV, p. 34.

45 Ibid.

46 Charles Ritchie, 'Contributions to the Pathology and Treatment of the Scorbutus, which is at present in various parts of Scotland', *The Monthly Journal of Medical Science*, New Series no. XIII (1847), p. 40; R. Christison, 'On Scurvy', *The Monthly Journal; of Medical Science*, New Series, no. XIII (1847), p. 6; Henry Lonsdale, 'Remarks on Scurvy in Cumberland and the Southern parts of Scotland', *MJMS*, New Series XIV (1847), pp. 102-3; James Turnbull, 'Observations on Scurvy', *The*

Lancet, 1 (1848), pp. 469-471; Thomas Laycock, 'Purpura or Land Scurvy', *London Medical Gazette*, New Series, iv (1847), pp. 573-4; Shapter, 'On the Prevalence of Scurvy' The Lancet, 1 (1847), pp. 676-7.

47 Lonsdale, 'Remarks on Scurvy', *MJMS*, New Series, XIII (1847), pp. 102-3; Christison, 'On Scurvy', *MJMS*, pp. 3-4.

48 E. Margaret Crawford, 'Scurvy in Ireland during the Great Famine, *Journal of the Society for the Social History of Medicine*, I, no.3 (1988), pp. 287-8.

49 Kenneth J. Carpenter, *The History of Scurvy & Vitamin C* (Cambridge, 1986), p. 246; T. K. Basu and C. J. Schorah, *Vitamin C Health and Disease* (London, 1982), pp. 69-72.

50 Christison, 'On Scurvy', *MJMS*, LXXIX, New Series, 13 (1847), p. 5.

51 T. Laycock, 'A Clinical Lecture on Purpura or Land Scurvy', *London Medical Gazette*, New Series, IV (1847), p. 574; Ritchie,'Contributions to the Pathology and Treatment of the Scorbutus, *MJMS*, p. 77; Lonsdale, 'Remarks on Scurvy', p. 106; Turnbull, 'Observations on Scurvy', *MJMS*, p. 469.

52 Lonsdale, 'Remarks on Scurvy in Cumberland and the Southern parts of Scotland', pp.100-2; Laycock, 'A Clinical Lecture on Purpura or Land Scurvy', p. 574; Turnbull, 'Observations on Scurvy', p. 470.

53 I. Levitt & C. Smout *The State of the Scottish Working Class in 1843* (Edinburgh, 1979), p. 24.

54 John H. Crandon, Charles C. Lund, David B. Dill, 'Experimental Human Scurvy', *The New England Journal of Medicine*, 223, no. 10 (1940), p. 365.

55 Silvia Nobile and J. Woodhill, *Vitamin C, the mysterious radox-System – A trigger of Life* (Lancaster, 1981), p. 69.

56 C. Creighton, *A History of Epidemic in Britain*, vol.II, reprint (London, 1965), p. 205.

57 Charles Murchison, *A Treatise on the Continued Fevers of Great Britain* (London, 1862), pp. 48-9.

58 Charles Murchison, *A Treatise on the Continued Fevers of Great Britain*, p. 57.

59 Marilyn E. Pooley and Colin G. Pooley, 'Health, society and environment in nineteenth-century Manchester', in Robert Woods & John Woodward, (eds), *Urban Disease & Mortality in Nineteenth Century England* (London, 1984), p. 149.

60 Anne Hardy, 'Typhus in the Victorian City', *Medical History*, 32, no.4 (1988), p. 414.; B. Luckin, 'Evaluating the Sanitary revolution: typhus and typhoid in London, 1851-1900', in Robert Woods & John Woodward (eds), *Urban Disease & Mortality in Nineteenth Century England* (London, 1984), p. 115.

61 Charles Murchison, *A Treatise on the Continued Fevers of Great Britain*, p. 57.

The Linen Industry and Emigration to Britain during the Mid-Nineteenth Century

Brenda Collins

THIS PAPER IS ONE OF THE FEW of the volume which does not have the words 'Famine' or 'hunger' in its title. To those who believe that the linen industry in Ireland sustained many families through the 'hungry forties' such an omission may not be surprising. There is certainly a widespread view linking two related ideas fairly closely together – firstly that the linen industry became widely developed as a prosperous domestic industry throughout the northern half of Ireland during the second half of the eighteenth century and early nineteenth century; and secondly, that the effects of the Famine years, especially upon emigration, were felt less severely in the northern counties than elsewhere in the country, especially in the west.[1] A related aspect is the assumption that the transition to the industrialised processes of linen production, the 'industrial revolution in linen' happened without discord or distress. However this paper attempts to tease out these interconnections and takes as its main focus one specific aspect, emigration to one particular town in Britain, Dundee, during the 1840s and 1850s.

Let us begin with two biographical portraits of the period. The first is of Thomas Kennedy who, in 1860, lived near Banbridge in County Down. He started off as a journeyman weaver in 1816 and seven years later set up to work on his own account. He married and settled down on a small plot of land where his wife spun their home grown flax which he then wove and took to Banbridge market to sell. Now, in 1860, he rents his cottage and two looms from a manufacturer, a merchant, for £2 a year. The manufacturer provides him with machine-spun yarn for weaving into cloth. As he says, since the mill spinning came in during the 1830s, he gets more constant work this way though, of course, he is working for wages rather than for himself. It is no longer worthwhile for his wife to spin any more, because the prices at which she could sell her hand-spun yarn have fallen with the competition from mechanisation. A bundle of mill produced 100 leas yarn cost about 2/4d compared to the hand-spun price of 4/10d and took one tenth of the time to produce.[2] However, his wife keeps money in the household budget by winding the weft yarn for the loom, which is a task he would otherwise have had to pay a neighbour to do, out of his wages. The youngest daughter, aged 11, helps her mother at the winding because a constant supply of pirns is necessary for the weaver's shuttle so as not to hold back the weaving. His 25 year old daughter also weaves alongside her father, as did many other young women at that period.[3]

He tells us that if there had not been the weaving work during the Famine years his family would have been destitute. Although he considered that his family's diet was above subsistence, he was so reliant on his meagre wages that when the potato prices rocketed due to scarcity, they could barely afford to buy food. Some of the neighbouring families tried to seek admission to the workhouse in their local town which was intended to provide for the destitute and needy. However, families where there was an able-bodied man were less eligible for poor relief than those of widows or orphans.[4] In his townland, many other hand-loom weavers quit their looms then and went to America and Britain. His son Edward did not go so far but he went to Belfast in 1858 to work in a power-loom factory and now lives there with a wife and family. Both Thomas and his wife miss their son for his presence provided another income to the house and there is no means of keeping in touch as none of them has practice in writing a letter.

The second biography is of twenty year old Mary Clarke who in 1851 was living in a one-roomed flat in a tenement flat in Dundee. She had emigrated to Dundee in the spring of 1847 from her birthplace in County Cavan. There was plenty of work for young girls in the Dundee spinning mills and in 1851 Mary was employed as a reeler in a newly erected flax spinning mill which had a workforce of over four thousand. She tells us how cramped and squalid her home is, for she shares it with her unmarried brother James and sister Ellen, her married brother Owen and his Derry-born wife, Mary McPhail, a married cousin and his wife and a friend, Widow Heany, with her grown up daughter.[5] All of these nine people cooked, washed and slept in one room, two flights up, with a single sash window, sharing a cold water tap and a dry privy (toilet) in the yard below with fifteen other families. For this accommodation, the landlord of the property, who was an elder of the church, charged them two guineas per year, paid at the rate of 9$\frac{3}{4}$ d per week.[6] All of them are Irish and, with the exception of Owen's wife, all were born in County Cavan. The Clarke family had left home together after their father died and their mother took the younger children to the workhouse. Widow Heany and her daughter emigrated with them for company. All the women worked in the Dundee flax-spinning mills and all the men were hand-loom linen weavers.[7]

Very many of the Irish families who settled in Dundee, and in other British towns in the mid-nineteenth century lived in such conditions. Inevitably, the manner of their departure from Ireland was hasty and desperate rather than planned and anticipated; it was a reaction to circumstances, whether those of potato failure, unemployment, eviction or bereavement. Few arrived in Britain with any resources beyond what they wore and could carry. Their poverty encouraged this first generation of famine immigrants to stay together and seek work and lodgings in the company of their fellow country folk.[8]

Both these portraits give some idea of the range of ways in which peoples' responses to the crises of the late 1840s were affected by the wider background of the structure and the changes within the Irish linen industry. In this view, emigration and migration become more than a flight from Famine, rather they become, for the individual or for the family, part of the process of industrialisation and indeed modernisation.

Emigration from Ireland to Britain did not commence in the 1840s. There had been constant to-ing and fro-ing which during the early nineteenth century became intensified into both seasonal and permanent movement. Already, in

1841, which was the first time a national population count in Britain listed the numbers of Irish-born, there were 415,000. It is worth pausing here to reflect that this constituted over three-quarters of all known Irish emigrants world-wide. Between 1841 and 1851 the number of Irish-born people in Britain increased to 727,000. This rise of almost 40 per cent probably underestimates the number of Irish people who arrived in Britain in the 1840s; the real figure may have been nearer 350,000. This increase was of course part of the much wider outmovement which was also to North America and Australasia during the Famine years. So many more people went to North America and Australasia that by 1851 the Irish in Britain were reduced from 75 per cent of all Irish people abroad to about 40 per cent – still, however, a sizeable migrant stream, and one, moreover, which had established patterns of settlement and aspects of chain migration and second generation settlement.

In Britain, during the first half of the nineteenth century, the Irish migration tended increasingly to become one of permanent settlers rather than seasonal agricultural workers. The seasonal harvesters had travelled round the country in gangs, to undertake specific contract work in harvesting grain crops, potatoes or oats. By and large they originated from the west and north-west of Ireland, Sligo, Mayo and Donegal, and they returned to these counties at the end of the harvest season, having earned the money to pay the rent for their small farms.[9] Almost all contemporary opinion considered the young adult men to have the best chance of high earnings in this respect because of their physical strength. In contrast, those who emigrated to Britain with the aim of permanent settlement tended to be either single people with no ties or whole families. For both of these groups the urban work opportunities were the main attraction, because in many of the industrial areas of Britain, particularly in the textile manufacturing towns, there was a demand for women and children to work in factories while their menfolk were labourers.

It is therefore no surprise that in 1851, Dundee, which was the pre-eminent town for linen manufacture in Britain, had the second highest proportion of Irish-born people in Britain (next to Liverpool), and a higher proportion, 19 per cent, than that of any other town in Scotland, including Glasgow. Each of these places were major recipients of Famine-induced emigration.[10] Liverpool and Glasgow were the major ports of entry where many of the Irish stayed on in dock labouring or in construction. Dundee was different. It offered a unique element of continuity in terms of its linen industry and the expansion in jobs for women, men, adolescents and children at precisely the time when the famine conditions in Ireland were putting under strain the structure of the domestic linen industry.

Dundee's economic expansion and population growth began in the 1820s with the impetus given by machine spinning of flax yarn to an established hand-loom weaving centre. In the ten years 1841-51 its population increased by over 25 per cent to nearly 80,000. Over half of all the migrants who came to Dundee in those years were Irish people, not, as might have been expected, Scottish Highlanders or Lowlanders. At this time the linen industry (and from the 1840s, jute) relied on a workforce, some of whom used hand technology and some of whom laboured on powered machines. This combination was most obvious in the hand-loom production of cloth and the steam-powered mill production of yarn and applied equally to the Belfast linen industry as it did to Dundee. The tales of both Thomas Kennedy and Mary Clarke confirm this. As in Ireland, it was not until the late 1850s in Dundee that power looms were widely used. Before that time the expansion in linen cloth production was dependent on the increasing numbers of hand-loom weavers. However, although the hand-loom weavers played an important part in Dundee's prosperity, their numbers were far exceeded by those working in the flax and jute spinning mills, who were mainly women. Between 1841 and 1851 the actual numbers working in the linen industry in Dundee almost doubled, to make up almost one-quarter of the population. Women's employment in the industry increased by a factor of two and a half.[11]

Most of the Irish people living in Dundee in 1851 were first generation immigrant families, like the Clarkes, who had moved there between 1835 and 1851. This is evident from the fact that many of the Irish families identified in the census of 1851 had children who had been born in Ireland in the 1830s or early 1840s. In addition, the numbers of single migrants, adolescents or young adults, was evident in the steady increase in marriages and baptisms recorded in the Catholic parish registers. The Catholic church in Dundee opened in 1836, indicative of the beginning of the substantial Irish presence, while in the late 1840s two more Catholic churches opened in working class suburbs of the city.

Many of the Irish families were no doubt attracted to Dundee by the prospect of their children being able to get paid employment and help the family budget. In rural Ireland, children under the age of about 14 were not usually hired as farm servants. Many young girls, in particular, had completely lost the possibility of earning any money from hand spinning of flax after the introduction of wet-spinning mills into the linen industry in the late 1820s and early 1830s. To work in such mills whether in Ireland or Scotland required migration or emigration. Mill villages in Ireland such as Bessbrook in County Armagh and Gilford in County Down both grew out of such population movements which, though they occurred during the famine years, had their roots in the changes in the viability of rural domestic industry. Bessbrook was founded by the Quaker family of Richardson, who had already a consolidated linen business near Lisburn. It developed as a mill village in late 1845/6 because of the express view of John Grubb Richardson that he had 'a great aversion to be responsible for a factory population in a large town', preferring a location which had 'water power and a thick population around' ... and which 'had, moreover, the desirable condition in my sight of enabling us to control our people and to do them good in every sense'.[12] The workforce began to arrive by the winter of 1846 and no doubt many of the families seeking work in the mill had forsaken their tiny landholdings. By 1852, Caroline Fox, the Quaker diarist wrote that it was a flourishing village which 'five years since had been a wilderness but now contains an immense linen factory, beautiful schools and model houses for workmen.'[13] Gilford grew from a population of six hundred to over 2,800 between 1841 and 1851, clearly due to people moving from the countryside. The naming of 'Keady Row' in the first generation of Gilford's housing certainly suggests a specific place of origin of some of the incomers, just like the 'Irishtown' neighbourhood in Dundee.[14] Wage earning opportunities in the mills opened up with the advent of machine spinning. Children could work in the spinning mills from the age of thirteen, or younger if they were issued with a certificate of age by the mill physician. Girls were particularly sought after.[15] The influx of Irish girls into Dundee completely distorted the sex ratios in the town, especially among the young people. In the age group 15-24 there were twice as many Irish girls as men in 1851.

What were the areas from which Irish people emigrated to Dundee? The evidence is sketchy but various sources, such as the census enumeration books and civil registers, reveal some similar patterns. Over one-third of those in the census whose county of birth was identified came from counties Cavan and Monaghan; 20 per cent from Leitrim, Fermanagh and Sligo, 15 per cent from Donegal, Tyrone and Derry, and 12 per cent from King's County. The civil marriage registers for 1855 indicated a similar pattern.

The domestic production of linen yarn and cloth became widespread throughout these Irish counties during the second half of the eighteenth century and was one of the main source of livelihood for small farmers and cottiers. In the 1780s, Arthur Young described how such farming and cottier families operated as self contained production units. In contrast to some other regions in Europe where the growth of industry stimulated the growth of a wage labour force independent of agriculture,[16] in Ireland the weaver's family combined spinning and weaving with work on the land in growing their food for family consumption or sale. Farm sizes were very small because the farm holdings were merely 'patches for the convenience of weavers' rather than providing a main source of farm income.[17]

This type of family-based linen production was not however a static process because it contained a momentum for change. One important way in which this momentum was evident was in its relationship to the demand for land, particularly in the northern counties of Ireland. This was seen in a changing pattern of land leasing from the late eighteenth to the mid-nineteenth centuries. The rural base of the Irish linen industry was confirmed by the Linen Board's establishment of brown linen markets as a means of facilitating trade between weavers and merchants. Seventy-six towns or villages in the Ulster counties had such markets at one time or another between 1780 and 1820. Hand-loom weavers with land were prepared to pay higher rents for property close to a town with a good linen market. Farming became a means of supplying food for the household and linen production became the main source of income. The price of land around market towns was stimulated beyond the agricultural value of the land because the weavers could pay higher rents and thus when older leases came to renewal of their term the rent levels increased. Because such families were not totally dependent on the land for food, parents were enabled to subdivide their land holdings for the next generation. With the women of the family as spinners and the children required to wind bobbins of yarn, marrying and raising a family was not constrained by established social conventions of thrift and propriety.[18]

In addition, the numbers of cottiers or small land holders grew disproportionately and brought about changes in the social structure. They worked out their rent arrangements for farmers as weavers rather than as farm labourers. Particularly in south Ulster from the early 1800s, farmer-weavers became manufacturer-weavers; that is, as the 1822 Linen Laws Report defined it, they did not work at the loom themselves but they bought the yarn and gave it out to weavers to be woven and then sold the cloth in the public market.[19] The cottiers' means of livelihood became focused on their wage earning rather than on their land resources. The availability of this lifestyle also affected the pace of population growth because journeyman-weavers who previously stayed unmarried as lodgers in their manufacturers' households were enabled to hold a subdivided piece of land, get married and raise a family.

On the eve of the Great Famine the linen counties of Armagh, Cavan, Monaghan, Tyrone and Down ranked alongside those in the west as the most densely populated in Ireland. Twenty years earlier, in the 1821 census, the thirteen square miles of the parish of Urney and Annageliffe in County Cavan supported over nine thousand people, a density of nearly seven hundred per square mile. In such circumstances, the utility of the potato as a nutritious foodstuff was vital. Similarly its scarcity would have undermined the whole system in the 1840s even if there had not been further changes within the structure of the linen industry.

By the early nineteenth century there was a clear regionalised pattern of linen production in three areas of Ulster. Only in one of these, the fine linen triangle between Belfast, Newry and Dungannon was there to be a successful, if protracted, transformation towards industrialisation in the sense that powered mills and factories took the place of domestic production. The timescale over which this transformation took place is illustrated in the life of Thomas Kennedy which was outlined earlier. In his lifetime he saw the impact of machine spinning in wiping out the possibility of his family being able to continue to work in domestic industry 'on their own account', that is, selling their joint production in the market place, and also, later, the further severance of the continuity in the family's joint work when his son left home to work in the power loom weaving factory in Belfast. Thus this success in industrialisation was achieved by breaking the emphasis on the family as the production unit and the substitution of individualist values which encouraged individuals to consider permanent moves away from a birthplace, whether as migration or emigration.

In the regions peripheral to the fine linen triangle in north-east Ulster other changes took place. In the north western counties, flax cultivation and yarn spinning had become the chief output, complementary to the demands for flax from the manufacturer weavers. The advent of spinning machinery in the late 1820s ended the demand for home-produced flax through the market system because the requirements of the spinning mill owners were too great to be met through dealing. Hand-spun yarn was no longer esteemed even by independent weavers because they could buy mill produced yarn more cheaply and therefore get greater returns on the sale of their cloth. In the 1830s, even before the Famine, many emigrated from Derry and Donegal, for it was said that 'the fine sturdy young men who once came to market have now gone out of the [weaving] trade and many have emigrated to America'.[20]

However, in the counties of north-central Ireland – south Armagh, Cavan, Monaghan, Leitrim and Longford – the rural domestic linen industry gained a protracted existence for another generation. The replacement of the market system by the putting-out system where yarn was given out by northern merchants to weavers to 'weave at home and return in web', which was already evident in Monaghan in 1802, meant that family members were required to wind the weft yarn and also to weave.[21] Thus the advent of machine-spun linen yarn from the late 1820s did not destroy the domestic weaving system where it was operated under a 'putting-out' system. Instead it was incorporated into this pattern of 'putting-out' by the manufacturers and by merchants. It reinforced the viability of the weaving households, though of course their wage dependency made them even more vulnerable to changes in the price or availability of their main foodstuff, potatoes. Machine-spun yarn was more even and reliable in quality than that of the majority of hand spinners though the top quality hand spun could not be reproduced by machine. Being even and regular, mill-spun yarn required less strength and skill to weave into cloth, so those whose age or infirmity had prevented them weaving with hand-spun yarn could manage with the mill-spun. Many girls were able to take up domestic hand-loom weaving. 'Even little slips of girls could weave linen of that number (thirteen and fourteen hundred, relatively coarse) with the mill-spun yarn' was a comment of the early 1840s.[22] At piecework rates, youths and girls could earn the same as their fathers. So the changing technology of flax spinning extended the viability of the domestic hand-loom weaving system in south and east Ulster. Multiple loom households became common throughout north-central Ireland and in the linen triangle by the 1830s.

During this time the south Ulster, north-central Ireland counties became integrated into the linen triangle economy and also into the wider linen trade of the British Isles as a whole. Raw flax from north-central Ireland was sent to the spinning mills of Drogheda, Navan and Belfast to be processed while the putting-out manufacturers and agents supplied the rural weavers with machine-spun yarn. Home-grown flax was also sold to the spinning mill owners of Dundee. During the 1830s flax grown in Cavan was exported through Drogheda to be machine spun in Dundee and the spun yarn was then shipped back, via the Forth and Clyde canal, to Drogheda for weaving into cloth.[23] Hence the extension of flax machine spinning both in Ireland and in Dundee benefited those at both ends of the production chain – the flax growers and the weavers who took the yarn from the 'putters-out'. Though the value of linen cloth sales at the markets of south Ulster declined in the early 1840s, the volume of output is said to have increased as weavers tried to maintain their livelihoods in the face of changing circumstances. The availability of two sources of livelihood – linen and farming – hid the potential disaster which would arise from the failure of one or the other.

Thus when the potato blight struck in the autumn of 1845, the loss of about one-quarter to one-third of the crop in the south Ulster counties meant not only food shortages but also the beginning of the collapse of this way of life. By the spring of 1846 there were few potatoes left in store and disease was reported to be prevalent where people had resorted to eating potatoes affected with the blight.[24] Local relief committees were set up to collect money to buy food for the destitute and to organise public work schemes. Despite the reduced planting in the spring of 1846 and the total failure of the seed potatoes which had been planted, the public works schemes were closed in the late summer of 1846 to enable labourers to harvest their crops. The prices of potatoes, rye, oats and barley all rose steeply. People flocked to the workhouses for admission. Public works were restarted in October 1846 for the winter. In County Cavan alone, the numbers on public works schemes rose from 9,000 in November 1846 to 25,000 in February 1847, equivalent to 10 per cent of the entire county population. Soup kitchens were established to give out food rations to those who were not eligible to enter the workhouses. In the spring of 1847 the people in the workhouses were struck by the famine fever and this spread outside as well. The south Ulster counties averaged a decline in population of about one-third between 1841 and 1851.[25] Those who could do so, moved away.

As indicated earlier, some migrant weavers moved within Ireland but for most people the perception was that a journey to Britain was easier. Steam boat sailings across the Irish Sea from Dublin, Drogheda, Dundalk, Newry and Belfast, which were the eastern ports of the linen counties, were twice or three times weekly during the late 1840s. Knowledge of the job opportunities in the linen industries of Scotland and England was widespread among the rural weavers and must have created its own pattern of chain migration. Well before the crisis of the Famine years, in 1835, a Drogheda weaver, Patrick McGray, reported that he had 'heard within the last six months that there is plenty of work in both Lancashire and Yorkshire for weavers'.[26] Indeed, weavers were said to migrate to Lancashire with their families during the winter months because the price of coal was cheaper than in Ireland and to return in the spring time for 'more space and purer air'.[27] Temporary migration turned into permanent flight during the Famine years. During the 1840s factory and mill owners in Aberdeen and Dundee advertised in the press for weavers and spinners. Local agents were used to recruit families for mill work. 'Hands for working in the spinning mills were sent for'. In the 1830s merchants based in Drogheda tried to raise financial support for the construction of a spinning mill in Drogheda by emphasising the better standard of living of the weavers' families in Dundee. One of them said 'their houses are a great deal better, they are also better clothed; as to food I do not know [but] the weavers in Dundee are more regularly employed'.[28] By extolling the benefits of industrialisation such messages carried another code, showing that if industrialisation did not come to Drogheda then the people could make their own path towards it. In 1851, 60 per cent of the Irish men living in Dundee were hand-loom weavers working in small workshops or hand-loom factories where they comprised about two-thirds of the weaving workforce. Their sons worked as weavers too, while their daughters worked in the mills.

By emigrating to Dundee, Irish families were able to continue to maintain a family economy based on the linen industry even if the workplace changed from a domestic to a mill setting. Because of the very specific needs for a female workforce, Dundee also attracted many groups of young single migrant Irish women. It was common for them to migrate in sibling groups of two, three or four and they lodged with other Irish families whose daughters were also mill workers. Widows with families were also sought after by the mill owners and Irish widows made up some 20 per cent of all the Irish heads of household in Dundee in 1851. The typical Irish widow in Dundee had three adolescent children working as hand weavers or mill spinners, whose earnings would have provided a much more stable support than had been possible in rural south Ulster in the 1840s. The decline in south Ulster's population in the 1840s thus came to be a mirror image of that in Dundee in terms of age and sex. It is surely a paradox that, by moving to urban centres of linen production, whether in or outside Ireland, weavers' families were able to prolong their family work economy which had previously linked them so closely to a rural base. It may have seemed, in superficial terms, that such families emigrating, or moving, in Famine times, did so in order to sever their ties with the land and domestic industry. Nevertheless, the ability to maintain the continuities in cultural and family expectations may instead have been the major reason for the selection of some emigrant destinations.

Migration and continuing emigration were two of the enduring Famine legacies to the social structure of rural Ireland. In the north of Ireland the technical and organisational changes in the linen industry defined the form which these legacies took. The most obvious internal demonstration of this interconnection of events is in the post-Famine growth of Belfast as a linenopolis, when thousands of people flocked into the city to work in the mills and factories. Emigration during the Famine to Dundee (and to other textile towns in the north of England) indicates that domestic linen manufacture was not a prop which successfully supported the rural people when the potato crops failed. In the aftermath of the Famine years there was a shortage of hand-loom weavers. Hand-loom weaving wage rates rose by between 20 and 30 per cent between 1848 and 1852. Power looms were adopted to keep pace with the spinning mill output.[29] Domestic hand-loom weaving began to give way to factory-based powered production. The impact of the Famine upon the Irish linen industry, though less graphic than images of starvation, was of long term significance.

References

1   See L. Kennedy, 'The Rural Economy 1820-1914', in L. Kennedy and P. Ollerenshaw, *An Economic History of Ulster 1820-1939* (Manchester, 1985), pp. 1-61.

2   E. Boyle, *The Economic Development of the Irish Linen Industry 1825-1913* (unpublished Ph.D. thesis, The Queen's University of Belfast, 1977), p. 48.

3   This is a composite fictional portrait drawn from verbatim interviews reported in *Children's Employment Commission. Evidence upon the Hand-loom and Hosiery Manufactures in Ireland and Scotland*, British Parliamentary Papers (hereafter *B.P.P.*) 1864(3414)XXII, pp. 215-23.

4   C. Kinealy, 'The Role of the Poor Law during the Famine', in C. Póirtéir, *The Great Irish Famine* (Dublin, 1995), pp. 104-34.

5   This portrait is based on the household enumeration of 12 Lyon's Close, Dundee in the 1851 Census of Scotland. Vol. 215, enumeration book 77, schedule 17. See B. Collins, *Aspects of Irish Immigration to Two Scottish Towns (Dundee and Paisley) during the Mid-Nineteenth Century* (M. Phil. thesis, University of Edinburgh, 1978).

6   J. Myles, *Rambles in Forfarshire* (Dundee, 1850), pp. 80-8.

7   B. Lenman, C. Lythe and E. Gauldie, *Dundee and its Textile Industry 1850-1914* (Dundee, 1969).

8   B. Collins, 'Irish Emigration to Britain during the Famine Decade 1841-51', *Familia*, no.11, (1995), pp. 1-16.

9   A. O'Dowd, *Spalpeens and Tattie Hokers: history and folklore of the Irish migratory agricultural worker in Ireland and Britain* (Dublin, 1991).

10 B. Collins, 'The Irish in Britain 1780-1921' in B.J. Graham and L.J. Proudfoot (eds), *An Historical Geography of Ireland* (London, 1993), pp. 366-98.

11 B. Collins, *Aspects of Irish Immigration*. Chapter 4.

12 Bessbrook Spinning Co. Ltd, *Bessbrook* (Bessbrook, 1945), p. 31.

13 *Bessbrook* (1945), p. 45.

14   D.S. McNeice, 'Industrial Villages of Ulster 1800-1900', in P. Roebuck (ed.), *Plantation to Partition: Essays in Ulster History in Honour of J.L. McCracken* (Belfast, 1981), pp. 172-90.

15   *Factory Inquiry Commission, Supplementary Report of the Central Board, Information on Manufacturing Districts, as to the Employment of Children in Factories, and as to the Propriety and Means of Curtailing the Hours of Labour* B.P.P. 1834(167)XXI, p. 10; Marilyn Cohen, 'Urbanisation and the Milieux of Factory life: Gilford/Dunbarton, 1825-1914', in Chris Curtin, Hastings Donnan, Thomas H. Wilson (eds), *Irish Urban Cultures* (Belfast, 1993), pp. 227-43.

16   S. Pollard, *Peaceful Conquest. The Industrialisation of Europe 1760-1970* (Oxford, 1981).

17   A. Young, *A Tour in Ireland* (Belfast, 1981, reprint of C. Maxwell, 1925 edition), p. 52.

18   B. Collins 'Proto-Industrialisation and pre-Famine Emigration', *Social History*, VII, no. 2 (1982), pp. 127-46.

19   W.H. Crawford, 'The Evolution of the Linen Trade in Ireland before Industrialisation', *Irish Economic and Social History*, XV (1988), p. 45.

20   *Handloom Weavers. Assistant Commissioners Reports, part III*, B.P.P. 1840[220] XXIII, p. 725.

21   C. Coote, *Statistical Survey of County Monaghan* (Dublin, 1802), p. 133.

22   *Handloom Weavers*, B.P.P. 1840[220]XXIII, p. 645.

23   B. Collins, *Proto-Industry*, p. 141.

24   E.M. Crawford, 'Food and Famine' in C. Póirtéir, *The Great Irish Famine*, pp. 60-73.

25   T.P. Cunningham, 'The Great Famine in County Cavan', *Breifne*, II, no.8, pp. 413-37. See also Joel Mokyr, *Why Ireland Starved: a quantitative and analytical history of the Irish economy, 1800-1850* (London, 1983).

26   B. Collins, *Proto-Industry*, p. 144.

27   *Third Report of Inquiry into the Condition of the Poorer Classes in Ireland*. Appendix C, part I, Drogheda,. B.P.P. 1836[35]XXX, p. 42.

28   B. Collins, *Proto-Industry*, p. 145.

29   P. Ollerenshaw, 'Industry 1820-1914' in L. Kennedy and P. Ollerenshaw, *An Economic History of Ulster, 1820-1939*, pp. 73-4.

The Failure: Representations of the Irish Famine in Letters to Australia

David Fitzpatrick

T HE GREAT COLLECTIVE EXPERIENCES of history, such as wars and famines, resist easy representation. How can we hope to convey the sufferings of millions, arising from a common origin yet unique to each individual victim? Poets reach for metaphors (spectre, visitation, scourge, apocalypse, armageddon); moralists make the horror comprehensible by attributing guilt to human agents (politicians, generals, officials, economists); official enumerators and cliometricians construct composite profiles of the dead, the damaged and the dislocated. From Black '47 to the present, the personal experience of suffering has eluded interpreters of the Irish Famine, largely dependent upon the attempts of contemporary analysts to generalise and simplify the chaotic reality.[1] The reports of outsiders such as travel writers, journalists, philanthropists and government officials provide moving but often conventional evocations of suffering, which typically reveal more about the assumptions of the observer than the experience of those observed. The student of individual experience must therefore search for personal testimony such as diaries, autobiographies and letters written by the afflicted rather than their sympathisers. The process of locating and analysing the extant testaments of suffering and survival has scarcely begun.

One obvious but neglected source of inside testimony is the correspondence sent to emigrants by those who remained in Ireland. This was probably similar in volume to the better known reverse flow of 'emigrant letters', which must have comprised a substantial proportion of the three million letters sent annually from North America and Australia to the United Kingdom by 1856.[2] The reduction of postal charges and improvement in shipping during the early 1850s had presumably generated a rapid expansion of transoceanic correspondence in the immediate aftermath of the Famine; yet it is likely that at least a million letters followed the million or so emigrants who left Ireland during the crisis itself.[3] Of these myriad testimonies of Famine only a few hundred have so far become available to historians, although the genealogical obsession of so many Americans and Australians is steadily augmenting the supply.

One might expect such letters to provide detailed and circumstantial accounts of living conditions during the Famine, pinpointing the impact of deprivation and disease on specific neighbourhoods, families, and individuals. As with all semi-private correspondence within fractured family groups, these accounts of the Famine should not be taken as unvarnished statements of perceived reality. Letters to emigrants were instrumental, deploying eloquence and emotion in pursuit of a range of objectives. Peace of mind was perhaps the dominant pursuit, as writers sought and offered consolation amidst disjunction and the erosion of family solidarity. Most letters also had practical functions, such as arranging for further emigration or begging for money. Highly coloured accounts of suffering might therefore have a mercenary motive, although the recipient's intimacy with the writer and the local background counteracted the temptation to spin melodramatic yarns for effect. Personal accounts were also to some extent verifiable, since emigrants were likely to be in touch with others from the same neighbourhood whose parents or siblings could contradict inaccurate reports. Family letters therefore tend to be more reliable than the reports of officials or journalists, whose readers were less likely to have access to conflicting testimony. The letter from home, for all its suspected silences and deceptions, should provide unusually wide-ranging and authentic evidence concerning the day-to-day preoccupations of the Famine-stricken Irish.

Kerby Miller seems to be the only prominent student of the Irish in America to have made even illustrative use of letters from Ireland in the Famine period.[4] Miller's brief extracts from some seven family correspondences serve to highlight the major themes in his analysis of the Irish background to emigration. Several of the selected passages provide reflections upon the Famine's social and economic consequences. A series of letters from a farmer's wife, sent during the last years of Famine in 1849 and 1851, referred to recession ('no circulation of mony … no trade'); depopulation ('one ile of our Chapel would hold our Congregation on Sunday at present'); and foreign help ('were it not for the america provision half Ireland was dead Long since').[5] In July 1850, 'a woman' from Meath affirmed the connection between ejectment and emigration, complaining that 'our fine country is abandoned by all the population, the landlords sending them away from the ditch to the cradle … or out on the roads … We were all ejected in March … I think [we] will see you in America before long.'[6] Personal anguish is expressed in several extracts from a letter sent from Co. Kilkenny in about October 1850, when the worst was already over. Mrs Nolan told her son that 'I cant let you know how we are suffring unless you were in Starvation and want without freind or fellow to give you a Shilling'; 'this is the poorest prospect of a winter that ever I had Sence I Began the world without house Nor home'. She drew a sharp distinction between good and bad neighbours, a moral motif which lingered long in folk memory of the Famine: 'I wood Be Dead long go only for two Nebours that ofen gives me A Bit for god Sake'; 'Mrs lowlor wood not give a penny for godSake if I died Dead on the Street'.[7] The dominant theme in Miller's selection, however, is the desire to escape from the horror of Ireland to an American haven: 'We offin say you had good sucess to leave this unfortunate ireland [and] I often wiched I had gone with you'; 'I think [we] will see you in America before long'; 'what you promised me to take me and little dickey out for the honour of our lord Jasus christ and his Blessed Mother hurry and take us out of this'.[8]

Miller's research has uncovered few extended accounts of the Famine and its consequences, as distinct from disjointed observations and asides. An exception is a letter from John Nowlan, a merchant in Newtownbarry, Co. Wexford, who in September 1847 offered his son in Nova Scotia a graphic account of the disaster – which, so far, had scarcely touched his own family. The Nowlans were surviving, yet 'god but knows not how long for the people the young and old are dying as fast as they can Bury them. The fever is rageing here at such a rate that them are in health in the morning knows not but in the Evening may have taken the infection. Its like a plague the Caus they docters alledge is the kind of food that yellow Corn from america for last year the potatoes were all blasted.' Even so, Nowlan believed that 'were it not for the English Government that sent all that American corn there would not be 100 persons alive and its the opinion of the people that whats in Ireland now will not be alive next year. Theres neither trade nor business of any sort going on. Any person that have the means of going to America but is Either gone or preparing to goe. There went out of this parrish last spring 800 persons. ... If my means was sufficient to take me i should if god permitted have been gone before this.'[9] Nowlan's account is unusual for its blend of general analysis and local observation; yet it lacks the urgency of the staccato utterances of those more critically affected.

At first reading, passages like these seem to provide authentic and irrefutable evidence of the misery of Irish life during the Famine, the inquitous performance of landlords, the uncertainty of assistance from neighbours, and the general preference for emigration. Indeed, the power of Miller's depiction of Irish mentality and the emigrant impulse is largely attributable to his moving deployment of personal testimony. Yet Miller's technique of collage has the potentially misleading effect of attributing general force to particular experiences, whose local and specific connotations are lost in the multitude of illustration. In order to sift general experience from local, and fact from rhetoric, it is desirable to examine entire sequences of letters in local and personal context, with the eventual aim of scanning the diversity of Famine experience rather than reaffirming its apparent homogeneity. This approach is applied to Irish–Australian correspondence in my recent study *Oceans of Consolation*.[10] This book provides the full text of fourteen sequences, with introductory commentaries and a thematic analysis of all 111 letters (including 55 bound for Australia). The writers were selected to represent the major strands of emigration rather than the corpus of surviving correspondence, preference being given to the poor, the unskilled, the Catholic, the female, the rural and the unlettered. Though these letters span more than half a century (1843 to 1906), one might expect extensive documentation – both immediate and retrospective – of the impact of the Famine upon various localities, classes and sexes.

In fact, these sequences make little direct reference to the Famine. Admittedly, only two of the selected letters were sent from Ireland between 1846 and 1852, reflecting the sluggishness of emigration to Australia until the gold fever of the early 1850s. Yet virtually all subsequent writers had lived through the Famine, and the infrequency of later allusions is perhaps surprising. In August 1852, a widow weaver in Armagh remarked dryly that 'there is one thing to Mention and that is the loss of our Potatoe crop in Ireland. I blieve this is the 7<u>th</u> year that the have been taking from us'.[11] The potatoes continued to blacken, and eight years later a small farmer in Fermanagh reported no less tersely that 'the blight is on potatoes as usual'. Yet the Famine, as distinct from the blight, had become a distant event already neatly labelled in the historical chronicle: 'The potatoes was not so scarce Since the year of the Failure as this year. The Turnips is high at present as the year [o]f the publick works when Father sold them out of the under room at 3d per Stone.'[12] Famine mortality was seldom recalled, apart from a pious tribute to a Tipperary priest by Eliza Dalton, wife of a prosperous farmer at Athassel Abbey. In 1853, she wrote to a former servant in Sydney that 'your kind friend the Rev Michael McDonnel caught fever in discharge of his duty Survived only a few days. He was waked and buried in the Chapel of Cashel, amidst the wailings of the poor, for whom he Seemed to live.'[13] Otherwise, the numerous post-Famine reports of farm production, prices and deaths concentrated on the present, with few backward glances.

The depopulation of the country was a major theme in letters from the Daltons of Tipperary, lending imagery and immediacy to a process usually traced through drab census statistics. By May 1851, Golden had 'become a deserted village. Ther is not a house at this Side of the Bridge but one and Mr Dwyers house no one taken with it and the one third is not in the rest of the village. Cloaghleigh is all Deserted there is no one takin with old Cooks part left Idle. Creagh has the most part lying Idle.' Wheat as well as potatoes had become blackened by blight: 'This destroyed all the tillage farmers they are all runing off to america.' Two years later, William Dalton ruminated that 'you Could Not think how lonly every place is here. Every one that Can g[o] to yee and to America are going. Still we hav near enough yet you May Judge. I road by your little Cottage a few days ago and the thisels were growing in the middle of the road.'[14] The Famine had created an impulse for emigration which long outlasted the crisis, causing Eliza to reflect in 1854 that 'although this Country is much improved Strange to Say the remaining few as discontented'. The sense of emptiness deepened, generating the hyperbolic claim in 1858 that 'there is not one house to the 20 in this country that was when you left'.[15]

For more sustained representation of the Famine in correspondence to Australia, we may consult an unpublished sequence of five letters from the adjoining parishes of Aughrim and Croghan in Co. Roscommon, a few miles south-west of Carrick-on-Shannon.[16] These letters were variously signed by Thomas Burke and his mother-in-law Mary Burke, whose daughter Catherine had reached Sydney in December 1841 on a free passage.[17] Internal evidence suggests that Mary Burke's contributions were penned by Thomas and subsequently by an unidentified scribe, and Thomas's voice seems audible even in the passages ascribed to Mary.[18] Unlike the illiterate Catherine, Thomas was presumably a practised if unlearned writer since by 1853 he was 'teaching scholl' (4). Despite occasional lapses of spelling and grammar, and many touches of the local dialect, the Burke letters are relatively sophisticated in their vocabulary and their rhetorical technique.[19] They provide a detailed, thoughtful and intense account of the Famine's disruptive impact on family solidarity, material comfort, and life itself. These letters also illustrate the dependence of those at home on succour from their emigrant connections.

The Poor Law Union of Carrick-on-Shannon, from which the Burkes wrote, was severely affected by the Famine. Though certain unions, particularly in southern and western coastal districts, were still harder hit, Carrick lost almost one-third of its population between 1841 and 1851.[20] By late January 1847, one-fifth of male residents in the corresponding barony of Boyle (and a single woman) had secured public employment on the roads.[21] Up to half of the union's population received free rations from the Commissariat during the period between May and November 1847.[22] When the sole responsibility of relief was transferred to the poor law system in late 1847, Carrick was among only 22 unions to be officially deemed 'distressed' and so exempted from the requirement that all relief expenses be raised locally.[23] The local board of guardians indeed proved incapable of raising sufficient rates to meet its fearsome obligations. Between January 1848 and November 1849, the board's functions were taken over by paid vice-guardians in association with the temporary poor law inspector, Captain Edmond Wynne. Wynne provided the poor law commissioners with an alarming account of conditions upon his arrival, initially to assist the elected guardians, in November 1847. The relief system had just been reorganised following the abandonment of the public works and then the soup kitchens, and Wynne reported that 'there are now wandering about the union about 1,600 persons, most of them have given up their houses and lands, and are only waiting for admittance to the house; and, indeed, they appear to be legitimate objects'. Before long, his prose had lost its supercilious sheen: 'I regret to say, I find that destitution has increased to a fearful extent; in fact, in some localities, it may be said to have reached the entire population.' Wynne believed that less than a score of labourers were employed throughout the union, a fact attributed by the vice-guardians to the refusal of farmers to proceed with tillage.[24] The number receiving poor relief peaked at over 15,000 in March 1848, and again topped 10,000 in July 1849 before the virtual elimination of outdoor relief.[25] In August 1848, the new season's potatoes seemed somewhat less blighted: 'The disease in this district, though as general as that of 1846, is by no means as malignant, at least the progress of destruction is not nearly so rapid.' Yet the sense of crisis lingered on, and in March 1850 the restored guardians lamented that 'multitudes of those persons who had anything left in the Union have fled, and are flying, to foreign countries, to escape from their own, as no longer fit to live in'.[26] Official testimony thus offers a melodramatic backdrop to the personal experience of the Burkes.

Thomas Burke gave a bleak account of the state of potatoes in April 1846: 'As for our Country the potatoes all roted this year in the ridges, and we are in the state of sta[r]ving' (1). A year later, the news was no better: 'So your Father was not able to put down any sort of a crop this year. They are Getting this relief Meal now all over Ireland any family that Has no Land or crop Down they Get one pound of meal in the Day for each person. ... And if you think of coming Home I would wish it was the case But Ireland is a poor place at present although the few stones of potatoes that is planted is Growing well at present' (2). Wynne's optimism concerning the plants sown in 1848 was evidently misplaced, for Burke wrote in January 1849 that 'our Potatoes all failed last year. I had 3 roods of them planted & I never Dug as much as one hundred of them' (3). The loss of the potato was compounded by high prices and punitive rents and rates, as the Burkes often complained. The catalogues of prices were usually allowed to convey their stark message unadorned, as in May 1847: 'The rates of our country is as follows. Oat Meal 3s. 6d to 3s. 9d p stone of 14lb. Flour from 3s. 6d to 4s. 4d p s[tone]. Indian meal from 2s. 9d to 3s. 2d p stone. ... Beacon 10D to 1.0s p lb none of it at that Same[?]' (2). But the consequences of the additional impositions on landholders were made explicit in 1849: 'The Rents & Poor Rates are so very High & no money making of any thing. The Poor of Ireld is all mostly in Poor Houses. There is Land enough now But no one able for to pay the rents of it' (3). Even when the crisis was alleviated, those without land remained vulnerable to poverty. Mary Burke wrote in January 1856 that 'you may judge of the times yourslf that it is very Hard to live without a Holding of Land. That is what reduced my son inlaw Thomas & Ann to be so poor now as they are' (5). Indeed, the Burkes themselves had only narrowly escaped 'the State of Starvation' (2).

Thomas provided his sister-in-law with an unusually detailed account of the Famine's domestic consequences for a small holder who had raised himself well above the potato line. The tithe applotment book for August 1842 indicates that his father had shared an acre and a half of fairly good land valued at £2 10s per annum in Cartron, where Thomas built himself a house (3).[27] If the house resembled the cabins observed in the neighbourhood in the 1830s, it would have offered few luxuries: 'mud or dry stones; pigs best lodged inmates'; 'generally stone-wall houses, thatched, with one or two windows; a dresser, table, few stools: and generally, at most, one bedstead, without comfortable bedding'.[28] From humble origins, Burke had invested quite heavily in short-term lettings of 'conacre' at high rents.[29] As Thomas explained to Catherine in Australia, he had accumulated a satisfying nest-egg by the time of his marriage in about 1844: 'I had fifty Seven pounds in the Bank of Boyle[30] and a good Cow & Heifer worth 20£ when I marr'd Ann. So I am shook out of all By the Land and crop failing' (2). His dozen acres of sub-letting proved to be a disastrous investment: 'I Have spent my money with land. I paid £16 for 3 Acres in the year of 46 that is in the year the Potatoes faild so that was a great loss to me. I likewise took Big Lukes Glancys ground 7½ Acres and Had to pay 20£ for the rents of it. So I am ran out of cash now. Because I built a House in Cartron that cost me 5£' (3).[31]

The letters chronicle Thomas's decline. Having allowed his wife's family to reside in his house at Cartron, by 1849 he found himself 'out of it and all the tenants ejected out of it' (3).[32] After living successively on each of the holdings in Cursiff, Thomas reported his 'Removal' from that townland in January 1852, having been 'Robed paying Rent' and driven into arrears (4). As Catherine's mother explained, Thomas and Ann had 'Had to Give up their land in Cursiff was not able to pay the Rent & taxes of it because the Potates failed these ten years past and even this year itself' (5). Thomas now found other means to restore his shattered livelihood: 'I live with M<u>r</u> Will<u>m</u> Laird. I have only a House from Him & pays him 30s a year for it.[33] ... I deal in a Little traffic such as selling meal & teaching scholl. I thank my God I am more Content than when I Held the Land' (4). Pursuit of property had brought anguish as well as satisfaction to Thomas Burke.

More terrible than the economic devastation wrought by the Famine was the loss of life. In May 1847, Thomas could still discuss death as an outside, if scarcely dispassionate, observer: 'They are Dying like the choler[?] Pigs as fast as they can Bury them & Some of their Remains does not be Burid for ten or fifteen Days & the Dogs eating them some Buried in mats others in their clothes. So thanks be to God there is none of our Family Dying as yet' (2). By January 1849, several Burkes had joined death's procession: 'I now must relate to you the meloncley State of your Mother Brother & Sisters. Your Uncle William Burke Departed on the 25th of May 1848 and your Poor Father Departed on the 3<u>rd</u> of June 1848 & your Cousin Michal Burke that is your uncle Tom<u>s</u> Son Departed on the 5th of Jany 1849' (3). Thomas's dirge was all the more moving for its unadorned recitation of names and dates.

The destructive impact of the Famine, though far from uniform, was arbitrary and subversive of established hierarchies. It placed severe demands upon family solidarity, generating resentment as well as gratitude. The Burke letters exhibit both sentiments within the kinship group defined by Thomas's marriage to Ann Burke. As Thomas portrayed the marriage to Catherine in May 1847, this was a matter-of-fact match. He explained that his father had 'died last march was 4 years so I am his son that is married to your Sister Ann. We had Her in the House after my Father's Death and I fancd Her & Got married to Her' (2). Ann Burke was his first cousin, their fathers being brothers.[34] This did not imply equality within the extended family, for Thomas's father-in-law Edward was a poor hatter from the parish of Aughrim and decidedly his social inferior.[35] Thomas, apparently impersonating his mother-in-law Mary for dramatic effect, emphasised his own generosity to the older couple: 'And only for their Daughter Ann & Her Kind Husband Thos. they would be Dead with Hunger for He always Gave them meal & money to Buy it and He Brought them Down to Cartron to his own House & Land Gave them the Soil of three or four Hundred of potatoes. So they failed and they were perished only for Him & his wife Ann' (2). In his own voice, Thomas expressed anger at the ingratitude of his dependants in Cartron: 'So your Father lives there now and I have only one cow now & if I had money I could Have two. So your Father is Better off than me now for I owe rents of 15£ a year & He pays no rent to me But promsd me work. So they Give no work after How I treated them & robed myself By them in proving so Kind to them when I had the money' (2). Thomas bemoaned the levelling effect of the Famine, exacerbated by the remittance of money from Catherine in Australia: 'Your Father was the poorest of them & He is a[s] rich now as any of them By what you Sent Him & the promise you made Him' (2).

Edward's death in June 1848 enabled Thomas to recover some of his losses, though in a manner likely to have aroused suspicion and resentment in Sydney. 'Your Poor Father Had the comfort of your money for to Bury Him. I preserved it for him although they would Have it spent only Keeping it together for Him. By the time He Recd that Sum of money from you He owed me 30s & more. Only for me they would not Stand it so I Kept my own Because I Had a Deal of rents to pay & every other calls[?] to pay. He Had the pleasure of Dying in Cartron House that is in the House I Built myself in the Land my Father had in Cartron' (3). The Famine had turned the world of the Burkes upside down, with the hatter in his grave probably having the last laugh. Yet these eddies of resentment were not violent enough to unravel the residual ties of kinship, for the widowed Mary Burke was still living with her aggrieved son-in-law in 1856 (5).

The Burke story illustrates the importance of emigration in providing a means of escape from the Famine. The choice of destination was of secondary importance. Catherine was bombarded with requests to help her siblings out to Sydney or elsewhere. 1846: 'If there was a vacancy would you encourage your Brother Thos. or Margret to come to you'; 1847: 'If Thos. or Margret Does not Get an Emigration you might send what would Bring one of them to America next Spring'; 1849: 'Your [Br]other Thos. & Margret longs for you [?to] see you or otherwise to send 6£ or [?7] for to take them to America out of this Poor country & then they might go over to you out of America' (1, 2, 3). In about 1850, Catherine seems to have responded to these demands by lodging substantial payments in Sydney entitling her siblings to free passages under the remittance regulations of 1848. Unfortunately, the additional expense of deposits, travel to Plymouth, and clothing for the four-month voyage, proved out of reach: 'But oh alas they were Not able to go as far as England for they had Not any cost to Bring them there. Tho<u>s</u> wrote to London and rec<u>d</u> all Directions. But then when filled up his prelimanary sheets By all Directions even his Birth day and afterall to no purpose. For Tho<u>s</u>. & Margret should Have each of them two Shoots of Clothes & Half a Dozen of shirts & shemis [chemises] each & Hankerchiefs ½ dozen and Defray their expences from Cursiff to London and each of them Should Have a pound to Deposit at the office of London' (4).[36] After this disappointment, Catherine's siblings confined their reported migrations to the British Isles.[37] In 1856, Mary wrote that 'as for Margret she is in England Married and has one child and Her Husband is Gone to America this year past – did not send for Her as yet. As for Bridget and her Husband they live near Strokestown doing very well. But my son Thomas never left me only one trip He took to engld and done very well' (5).

The elder Thomas himself was strongly inclined to follow the example of numerous neighbours by emigrating to either America or Australia. In May 1847, his desire for departure was frustrated by lack of means: 'So I am in a low situation at present. If I could Go to America when I would reap the crop next Harvest I would go but fear I will not be able. ... So Ann told me that you always promis<u>d</u> her something of relief to Her. So if I Go to America next May I may Go over to you or write to you to come to us as Ireld is a bad place' (2). Six years later, he reflected that 'only for my family was two weak I would Go to America wh[?en] I left the Land. And also I would Go to Sydney only for A[n]n was Pregnant when I left the La[nd]. So there was no free Emigration Si[nc]e 1852 ... or I would apply'(4). Once again, the impulse to emigrate was thwarted by problems of organisation.

For those who could not or would not emigrate, emigrant remittances were often crucial to survival at home. The Burkes in Roscommon were preoccupied with extracting money from the recalcitrant Catherine in Sydney, and deployed an impressive range of rhetorical devices to that end. The heartstrings were tugged vigorously in April 1846: 'Your Father is only medling in Health. As for your mother She is only poorly in Health. But their spirits cheered when they rec<u>d</u> your Letter. They are in expectation of you now performing your promise to them as I understand that is a flourishing Country. So I hope, Dear Catharine that by you leaving them Discontented you may relieve them at their Decline of life as a loving Kind and affectionate Daughter and you in Such Good Earning' (1). Catherine was asked to pass on a similar appeal to her attentive neighbour John Burke, who was to be informed that 'his poor mother is only poorly and if John could send her somthing it would save her' (1).[38] In May 1847 a bill of exchange for £5 was duly delivered, followed (according to the usual practice for foreign bills) by a duplicate in case the first had been lost (2, 3). This caused confusion and dismay in Roscommon, giving rise to repeated requests for a second instalment: 'Your Father mother & Brother likewise your Sisters are all very Happy at you relivg them so I hope when you receive this that you will be up to your promise with them. If you could Send the Bill of ten pounds at once or if not ten you might Send 8£. or more if the Bank would allow it'; 'So you might Send a Letter Before the money with a Small Bill in one & the other in So many days after it'; 'We will be exp[ec]ting your Letter about christmass so we may have Joy & cheer by your letter & so forth' (2). Christmas cheer in the Famine years was conveyed by pounds rather than puddings or honeyed words.

The clamour for support was by no means limited to Catherine's parents, and Thomas worked hard to secure compensation for his family's generosity to the older couple: 'So Ann leaves you to yourself to send Her Daughter Catharine what you like. As for my part I would not ask it only How I treated your Father mother Brothers & Sister when they were starving' (2). Thomas here presented himself not as a beggar but as a moral creditor, a rôle he resumed when explaining his deduction of 30s from the remittance used to meet Edward's burial costs (3). Elsewhere, however, he proved equally adept in the rhetoric of begging, drawing invidious comparisons between Catherine's parsimony and the munificence of neighbours in America: 'As for Nancy Glancys family there is three of them in america. Mick Ann & Catharine the two females sent Home Beyond 10£s. last christmass and Mick will send Home 10£ to his wife and his Brothers again June next'; 'your uncle Willms Thos & Mary Sent Home last spring 12£ to their Father & mother so I Hope you Have the Kindness as well as them'; 'Bryan Dowd Has been in America this 2 years. He remited 19£ to his family and his son Patt & eldst Daughter Mary is with Him. He wrote Home a few days ago & Intends to send Home 20£ to his wife and family to take them all out next March. & your Uncle James Burkes Jeny[?] remited 10£ to Him Last Augst. I never Seen So much Money as came from America this year. We often thought that you & Husband might take a notion of Going to America' (1, 3, 4). For the impoverished victims of the Famine, words and wit were their principal weapons in the struggle for subsistence.

The correspondence received by post-Famine Irish settlers in Australia was likewise preoccupied with arrangements for further emigration, appeals for remittances, and comparisons between Australia and other choices of destination. The Burke letters are remarkable only for the urgency of these appeals, in a period when failure might mean death rather than mere disappointment. Silence from Sydney, with its sinister implications, was a recurrent motif for Mary Burke: 'I am wearied every quarter and every other month & days expecting your long tedious Letter'; 'We thoutht we would not Hear from you that something Befal You or that you were dead'; 'I am Getting no Health Since I lost my old Comrade But I still Have Hopes in you. Indeed only my Kind Daughter Ann I would not be alive now. I Hope you will prove as Kind to me as to your Father as I still Had the Hopes out of you. I am very low in Health But I think if I Heard from you [I w]ould Die easy all in the world' (4, 1, 3). Death could only be postponed: the trick for the Famine Irish was not merely to survive a little longer, but also to preserve the bonds of loyalty and affection which made life worth living.

For Catherine Burke in Sydney, death was postponed until 18 June 1903. She was by then a widow aged 84, survived by only two of her four children. On 7 February 1848, she had thumbed her mark on the register of St Mary's cathedral, to signify her marriage to James White from Co. Kilkenny. James had reached

Sydney as a bounty emigrant on the *Lady Clarke* a year before his bride, on 14 August 1840.[39] Catherine's husband came from a prosperous farm of nearly 100 acres at Ballycarron.[40] The Whites had been wealthy and canny enough to do well out of the Famine, as indicated by a letter sent to James by his father in February 1851: 'You have often heard for the last 4 years that this Country is in a wretched State and so it is, but thank God your friends are still independant. Your Brother Thomas is become a Surgeon which Cost me nearly £[blotted: ?4]00, He is very clever at his profession. your Brother Pat lives at Inchmore holding a large tract of good land – yet unmarried. Martin stops with me. ... If you are still unmarried, and that you find yourself independant, you would find this still a pleasant Country to live in if you did come home. I would provide for Martin and Keep you to manage my affairs as I am now getting feeble. I want nothing from you. You Know I wd rather increase yr Capital, but if you are inclined to marry and in a way of doing well I would be sorry to interrupt you.'[41] Keyran White was evidently unaware that his son had already made his match with that thoroughly unsuitable hatter's daughter from the bogs of Roscommon. The enticements of capital and 'a pleasant Country' were insufficient to draw the emigrant back to post-Famine Ireland. Instead, James White and Catherine Burke spent their long lives in the dreary streets of Redfern, an inner suburb of Sydney. James worked as a proprietor of cabs and drays, and on his death aged 83 in 1898 he was identified as 'late contractor to the Redfern Council, and 52 years a resident of Redfern'.[42] His daughter-in-law maintained the family trade, having just secured a contract for removing house refuse and cleaning street gutters for the Redfern Borough Council.[43] Redfern might be squalid, but it was famine-free.

References

1   For metaphorical approaches, see Christopher Morash (ed.), *The Hungry Voice: The Poetry of the Irish Famine* (Dublin, 1989). Attribution of guilt provides a major theme for many polemicists and historians, ranging from John Mitchel to Cecil Woodham-Smith, *The Great Hunger: Ireland, 1845–9* (London, 1962) and Christine Kinealy, *This Great Calamity: The Irish Famine, 1845–52* (Dublin, 1994). The question of responsibility is also considered by Cormac Ó Gráda, *Ireland before and after the Famine: Explorations in Economic History, 1800–1925* (Manchester, 1988), ch. 3. The most systematic quantitative studies are Joel Mokyr's *Why Ireland Starved: A Quantitative and Analytical History of the Irish Economy, 1800–1850* (London, 1983), esp. ch. 9; and Ó Gráda's Ireland: *A New Economic History, 1780–1939* (Oxford, 1994), ch. 8.

2   The first available UK statistics, for 1856, indicate that the number of letters (excluding newspapers and books) sent to Britain and Ireland was 1,733,745 from the USA, 358,284 from British North America, and 913,733 from the Australian colonies. The volume from the UK to the USA and BNA was 1,547,054 and 396,915 respectively (statistics were not collected for mails to Australia until 1861). American returns indicate a somewhat larger volume of mail to the UK in 1856 (1,997,571 letters). See *Third Report of the Postmaster General on the Post Office*, B.P.P. 1857 [2195 SESS. I], IV; *Annual Reports of the Postmaster General of the United States*, tabulated in Arnold Schrier, *Ireland and the American Emigration, 1850–1900* (Minneapolis, 1958), p. 162.

3   No official returns distinguish between personal and business correspondence or between Irish and British overseas mails; but Rowland Hill stated in 1855 that 'of the letters passing between the United Kingdom and the United States, about one-third are for Ireland': evidence of Hill, Q 74, in *Report from the Select Committee on Postal Arrangements*, B.P.P. 1854–55(445)XI.

4   Kerby Miller, *Emigrants and Exiles: Ireland and the Irish Exodus to North America* (New York, 1985). Letters such as these will be analysed more systematically in the same author's forthcoming *Out of Ireland*, a multi-volume edition of Irish–American correspondence. Professor Miller has kindly checked and amplified the citations given below.

5   Judith Phelan (Queen's County: variously identified as 'one woman', 'country folk', 'a farmer's wife' and 'one Irish woman') to her niece in St Louis or Memphis, 23 May 1849, 24 March 1850 and 24 January 1851; in Miller, *Emigrants and Exiles*, pp. 293, 300, 284.

6   Anne Kelly (Meath) to her brother in Cincinnati [?], 12 July 1850, in Miller, *Emigrants and Exiles*, p. 299.

7   In Miller, *Emigrants and Exiles*, pp. 285, 286, 288, 290–1 (letter attributed respectively to 'one desperate woman', 'a poor widow', 'one of the more fortunate', and 'a starving widow').

8   Judith Phelan to niece, 23 May 1849; Anne Kelly to brother, 12 July 1850; Mrs Nolan (Kilkenny) to Patt, October 1850; in Miller, *Emigrants and Exiles*, pp. 302, 299, 292–3.

9   Public Archives of Canada, Ottawa, MG 24 I 122 (as in my other transcriptions, sentence and paragraph breaks have been inserted, but original spelling and syntax retained). Extracts from this letter also appear in Miller, *Emigrants and Exiles*, pp. 285, 294, 301.

10   David Fitzpatrick, *Oceans of Consolation: Personal Accounts of Irish Migration to Australia* (Ithaca, N.Y., Cork and Melbourne, 1995). A provisional inventory of other surviving sequences appears at pp. 637–41.

11   Mary Devlin and family (Armagh) to Joseph Hammond (Victoria), 8 August 1852 (Ha 5g). Citations in parentheses refer to the sequences reproduced in Fitzpatrick, *Oceans*.

12   William Fife (Fermanagh) to Nixon and Faithy Fife (NSW), 8 August 1860; John Fife (Fermanagh) to Faithy Fife, 11 November 1860 (Fi 2d, 3d).

13   Eliza Dalton (Tipperary) to Johanna Hogan (NSW), 4 September 1853. On 20 August, Eliza's husband William had told her more prosaically that 'your frind Father McDonnell is Dead. He was removed to Cashele got feaver and died' (Da 3a, 2g).

14   William Dalton to Ned Hogan, 15 May 1851; and to Johanna Hogan, 20 August 1853 (Da 1b, 2f).

15   Eliza Dalton to Johanna Hogan, 22 July 1854; William Dalton to Ned Hogan, 17 August 1858 (Da 4b, 5c).

16   The surviving letters to Catherine Burke were kindly made available by Mr Russell Campbell of Griffith, NSW. They are dated (1) 27 April 1846; (2) 29 May 1847; (3) 30 January 1849; (4) 28 November 1853; (5) 15 January 1856. The number of the letter quoted is given in parentheses at the end of each extract.

17   Catherine Bourke, aged 23, a Roman Catholic house servant, unable to read or write, returned as a native of Strokestown, arrived at Port Jackson on the *William Jardine* from Plymouth on 23 December 1841. She travelled under the protection of Pat and Mrs Mullen of Strokestown, Co. Roscommon, receiving character references from three residents of that place. The Colonial Land and Emigration Commissioners had evidently paid £15 from the colonial land fund on her behalf. See entitlement certificate and shipping return (State Archives of NSW, 4/4881 and 4/5220: reels 1339 and 1268 in microfilm edition).

18   The first two letters are signed by Thomas Burke and the other three by Mary Burke, but the first three are in the same hand and the remainder in a second hand. In both the third and fourth letters, the first person singular slides seamlessly from Mary to Thomas and back again.

19   For close analysis of Hiberno-English usage in the village of Cootehall, five miles north-west of Carrick-on-Shannon, see P. L. Henry, *An Anglo-Irish Dialect of North Roscommon: Phonology, Accidence, Syntax* (Dublin, 1957).

20   Only 31 of the 163 unions had greater proportionate depletion than Carrick (31 per cent). The heaviest loss was in Killala (43 per cent), that in better-remembered Skibbereen was 34 per cent, and the loss for Ireland as a whole was 20 per cent. Statistics are calculated from *Thom's Official Directory* for 1851 and 1854.

21   In the week ending 30 January 1847, the relief lists for public road works in the barony included 3,327 able-bodied men, 314 infirm labourers and 494 boys, equivalent to 21 per cent of the male population of Boyle in 1841: *Correspondence ... relating to the Measures adopted for the Relief of Distress in Ireland, Board of Works Series [Second Part]*, B.P.P. 1847[797]LII, pp. 48–9.

22   The maximum number of persons receiving rations on any single day was 32,090, equivalent to 48 per cent of the union's population in 1841. Rationing was still more extensive in 35 of the 130 unions extant in 1847. In the electoral division of Aughrim, where the Burkes lived through the Famine, the 2,015 recipients of rations amounted to 59 per cent of the population: *Supplementary Appendix to the Seventh and Last Report of the Relief Commissioners*, B.P.P. 1847–48[956]XXIX, p. 33.

23   Kinealy, *Calamity*, pp. 176–7.

24   Wynne to Poor Law Commisioners [PLC], 27 November 1847, 5 February 1848, and Vice-Guardians to PLC, 13 March 1848, in *Report from the Select Committee of the House of Lords [concerning] . . . the Union of Carrick-on-Shannon*, app. B, pp. 328, 350–1, 370 (B.P.P. 1850 (725), xi: hereafter, *Carrick Report*); cf. Kinealy, *Calamity*, pp. 198, 202. Wynne's responses to the Famine are further analysed in David Fitzpatrick, 'Famine, Entitlements and Seduction: Captain Edmond Wynne in Ireland, 1846–1851', *English Historical Review*, cx, 147 (1995), pp. 596–619. For an account of the Famine in the nearby Strokestown district, see Robert James Scally, *The End of Hidden Ireland: Rebellion, Famine, and Emigration* (New York, 1995).

25   In the week up to 4 March 1848, 696 paupers were being relieved in the workhouse and 14,821 outdoors; by 30 June 1849, the corresponding figures were 1,744 and 8,560; by 27 April 1850, they were 1,407 and only 33 respectively: *Carrick Report*, pp. 470–2. Comparative returns for the *average* number relieved during March 1848 show that only 18 of the 130 unions had a higher ratio of recipients to population in 1841 (19 per cent in the case of Carrick-on-Shannon's average of 12,930 recipients): *Papers relating to Proceedings for the Relief of Distress, ... Sixth Series*, B.P.P. 1847–48[955]LVI, pp. 1006–13.

26   Wynne to PLC, 13 August 1848, in *Fourteenth Report of the Select Committee on Poor Laws (Ireland)*, app. 4, B.P.P. 1849(572)XV, pt. II, p. 258; *Carrick Report*, p. xxviii.

27   Parish of Killummod (N.A.I., TAB 25/8). The plot, occupied jointly by Thomas (senior) and James Burke, included an acre of first-quality land, half an acre of second-quality, and none of third or fourth qualities. Written testimony to the Poor Inquiry in about 1834 indicated that the average annual rent per plantation (Irish) acre was between £1 and £1 10s in the civil parishes of Aughrim, Killukin and Killummod: *First Report from His Majesty's Commissioners for Inquiring into the Condition of the Poorer Classes in Ireland (hereafter, Poor Inquiry), Supplement to Appendix F*, B.P.P. 1836[38]XXXIII, pp. 36–8.

28   Testimony of William Lloyd, JP (Aughrim) and Rev. Charles Dunn (Killukin), in *Poor Inquiry, Supplement to Appendix E*, B.P.P. 1836[37]XXXII, p. 38.

29 The range of conacre rents reported for Aughrim and Killukin in 1834 was between £3 (unmanured) and £9 9s per acre (manured potato-ground): *Poor Inquiry, Supplement to Appendix F*, pp. 36–8. 'A good deal' of conacre was let out in Killukin, but conacre was 'not extensively' available in Aughrim.

30 Being a small deposit, this would probably have been lodged in Boyle's Savings Bank (established in 1822), where the mean amount lodged in November 1846 by the 1,141 depositors was £36. Boyle also had a branch of O'Connell's National Bank of Ireland, which like all joint-stock banks catered for wealthier clients. See *Thom's Official Directory* (Dublin, 1848 edn.), p. 193; Philip Ollerenshaw, *Banking in Nineteenth-Century Ireland* (Manchester, 1987), pp. 66–7.

31 The tithe returns for Aughrim in August 1842 show that Burke's two lessors in Cursiff (part of the townland of Curries or Corry), Luke Glancy and Bryan Horan, occupied 7.34 and 8.25 (Irish?) acres respectively, valued at £7 15s and £7 13s 9d per annum (N.A.I., TAB 25/19). The Valuation Revision Books for the electoral division of Aughrim East (in Irish Valuation Office, Dublin) record Luke Glancy as occupier of 10.69 statute acres in Corry until 1866, with various Burkes as neighbours. Luke Glancy's nickname ('Big') was one of several used in the Primary Valuation of February 1858 to distinguish between the innumerable Glancys in the vicinity (Big, Little, Sapper, Red, Bawn, etc.).

32 The impact of mass ejectment is reflected in the census returns for Cartron, revealing a decline in population from 164 to 62 between 1841 and 1851 (compared with a decrease of less than one-fifth for the civil parish of Killummod as a whole).

33 The account book for 1855–62 of William Laird, kindly made available by his descendant Mr Arthur Laird of Mullaghmore, Killukin, confirms that Thomas Burke made fairly regular payments of rent equivalent to 2s 6d per month between January 1855 and February 1856. Unlike most of Laird's house tenants, Burke received no payments for labour or services to Laird. For William Laird's career as a stern Wesleyan and intractable relieving officer during the Famine, see Fitzpatrick, 'Famine, Entitlements and Seduction'.

34 The marriage of Thomas and Ann (for whom, being first cousins, a dispensation would presumably have been required) does not appear in the surviving Roman Catholic registers for Roscommon. However, the baptismal registers for Croghan show that their second daughter Mary was baptised in March 1846, suggesting that the marriage occurred very soon after the elder Thomas's death in March 1843.

35 Edward's occupation is specified in the death certificate of Catherine White, née Burke (7627/1903, Registrar-General for NSW). The census indicates that the county had no less than 73 hatters (and 38 bonnet makers) in 1841, compared with only 21 hatters (and 27 bonnet makers) a decade later. The baptisms of three other children of Edward Burke and Mary Caslin appear in the registers of Aughrim for 12 September 1820 (Ann: Thomas's future wife), 23 July 1826 (Margaret), and 5 March 1829 (Patrick). I am grateful to Mrs Mary Skelly, curator of the County Heritage Centre, Strokestown, for her prompt consultation of the relevant indices.

36 These regulations required payment in the colony of £8 for each young adult nominee fulfilling the normal conditions for an assisted passage, an amount reduced to £4 in January 1852. In addition, nominees were evidently required to pay a deposit of £1 and to supply the clothing as punctiliously listed in (4). Remittances were lodged for only 50 emigrants from the United Kingdom to Sydney (1848–50), of whom 10 defaulted. Internal evidence suggests that the proposed arrangement preceded May 1851, and involved the system of remittances rather than 'free' or 'assisted' passages subsidised solely by the state. From May 1851 the clothing requirement differed from that stated, and the contributions required from single men on free or assisted passages invariably exceeded the £1

specified in (4). See Robin F. Haines, 'Government-Assisted Emigration from the United Kingdom to Australia, 1831–1860' (unpublished Ph.D. thesis, Flinders University, Adelaide, 1992), app. 1 and p. 607; correspondence and circulars on assisted emigration to Australian colonies, 14 March and August 1848 (P.R.O.(L.), MH 19/22); Murdoch and Rogers to Merivale, 25 April 1851, pp. 30–3, in *Papers relating to Emigration to the Australasian Colonies*, B.P.P. 1852[Cd. 1489]XXXIV.

37   Another brother, John, lived near Dublin in Dalkey. Bridget, whose husband John Commer lived near Strokestown and 'works every day But is only shifting' (1853), spent part of her married life in her mother's extended household in Cursiff (1, 3, 4).

38   John Burke was clearly a source of support for Catherine in Sydney, as her parents were 'Greatly obliged to him for his Kindness to you since you wen[t] over' (1). John Burke, an unmarried and illiterate Catholic aged 20, had reached Sydney in the *Runnymede* on 30 August 1841, four months before Catherine. It has not been possible to identify his relationship to Catherine or his native place, reportedly 'Moon' in Co. Roscommon. See entitlement certificate and shipping return (State Archives of NSW, 4/4879 and 4/5220: reels 1337 and 1268 in microfilm edition). John Burke also lived in Redfern (also identified as Chippendale) and appears in NSW directories as an engineer or fireman between 1847 and 1873. John and Catherine Burke were witnesses to Catherine's marriage in 1848.

39   He was returned as a literate Catholic labourer aged 25, brought out by J. Marshall. See entitlement certificate and shipping return (State Archives of NSW, 4/4855 and 4/5218: reels 1314 and 1267 in microfilm edition).

40   The Primary Valuation for 1849 indicates that James's father, Keyran White, occupied some 87 acres at Ballycarron (parish of Odagh) and 92 acres at Knockanaddoge (parish of Dysart), as well as renting out seven houses in the mining town of Castlecomer. The corresponding annual valuation was about £144.

41   Keyran White (Ballycarron) to his son James White, 15 February 1851, with Burke Papers.

42   *Sydney Morning Herald*, 18 April 1898. His probate papers record property valued at £663: series 4/15805 (reel 3053 in microfilm edition).

43   Minutes of Redfern Borough Council, 3 March 1898 (Mitchell Library, Sydney, ML 260/70, H 8247). Mrs Ellen White, the successful tenderer, was the widow of James's son Edward. For the development of Redfern, see Shirley Fitzgerald, *Rising Damp: Sydney, 1870–90* (Melbourne, 1987), pp. 27–30.

'The Condition of Our People': William Carleton and the Social Issues of the Mid-1840s

Sophia Hillan King

> At the period of our narrative, the position of Ireland was very gloomy; but when, we may well ask, has it been otherwise, within the memory of man, or the records of history? Placed as the country was, emigration went forward on an extensive scale, – emigration, too, of that particular description which every day enfeebles and impoverishes the country, by depriving her of all that approaches to anything like a comfortable and independent yeomanry. This, indeed, is a kind of depletion which no country can bear long. [1]

WHEN WILLIAM CARLETON wrote these words, the years of Famine had already begun. Moreover, although the novel from which the extract is taken, *The Emigrants of Ahadarra*, was not published until 1848, it had been with a Belfast publishing firm for over a year. Like *The Black Prophet*, Carleton's 1847 novel written to warn the British government of what might happen if they allowed famine to take over as it had in 1817 and 1822, *The Emigrants of Ahadarra* was intended to alert the landlords of Ireland to their responsibilities. In this, the novel is far ahead of its time, and it is curious to read in the light of current thinking. Carleton did not say that famine was the cause of emigration: he rather identified the practices in the management of Irish land which, he believed, predisposed the people of Ireland to consider emigration. Today, his work retains its original note of urgency, and his words take on an extra poignancy when we remember that he was writing at a time when the years of intense emigration had scarcely begun.

The Emigrants of Ahadarra is not Carleton's best work of fiction but belongs, with *The Black Prophet* and some earlier writings of the 1840s, as evidence of his deep concern for social issues touching his own people.[2] His earliest writings were at once joyous and bitter, pouring out in a torrent all he remembered of the Ireland of his youth and, as such, they stand as a testament, social and historical as well as literary, to Ireland in the first thirty years of the nineteenth century.[3] Carleton's friend Thomas Davis, dead by 1845, had described him as 'the historian of the peasantry', writing prophetically: 'Come what change there may over Ireland, in the "Tales and Stories" the peasantry of the past hundred years can be for ever lived with'.[4] Davis did not live to see the great change wrought by the Famine, but his prediction was correct: in the pages of Carleton's early work there remains an invaluable record of life as lived by the peasantry in pre-Famine Ireland. Anyone who has read Carleton's *Autobiography* will recall the vivid immediacy of his description of, for example, an open-air Mass in penal times, or the casual conversation of local people at the cross-roads discussing the likelihood of Bonaparte defeating the English and becoming king of Ireland.[5]

The works to which I refer in this article do not have that edge of excitement and hilarity: they are slower, more reflective perhaps, certainly more given to footnote and digression and, ultimately, not great literature. It seems that, as Carleton's moral sense developed in the 1840s, something of his joyous spontaneity disappeared, replaced by a sober awareness of the burdens under which the Irish tenantry continued to labour. Yet, these works are invaluable to anyone who looks for the authentic voice of the period. Carleton was there: he was highly intelligent, and he was determined that an accurate representation be made to those in positions of power concerning the state of Ireland. 'I have written many works upon Irish life' he wrote in 1845, 'and up to the present day the man has never lived who could lay his finger upon any passage of my writings and say "that is false".'[6]

The influence of Thomas Davis on Carleton's change of direction from chronicler to moralist is considerable. There had always been in Carleton a strain of didacticism, as can be seen in his early, calculatedly anti-Catholic work for Caesar Otway's *Christian Examiner*.[7] The fact that these tales became exuberant celebrations of the people whose ways he had undertaken to correct, is something for which today's readers can be grateful. The tendency to moralise, however, remained and, indeed, was given a new impetus and direction by the work of Davis and his contemporaries. Carleton's biographer, D. J. O'Donoghue, tells us:

> Fired by the awakening of Ireland effected by the Nation, and stimulated by its encouragement and his own necessities into writing for the people rather than the gentry, or for the government, Carleton determined to write a story exemplifying the tyranny and rapacity of the more detestable kind of land-agents, the hypocrisy of those canting attorneys who hung on to the landlord class, the violence of the Orange faction, and the infamous partizanship of many of the grand juries.[8]

The first result of this enthusiastic resolve was one of Carleton's most powerful novels, *Valentine McClutchy, the Irish Land-Agent*, which was published in January 1845. In his preface, Carleton made clear not only his moral purpose but his deep concern, demonstrated since his earliest writings, about the rights and responsibilities of landlords and agents. 'The two great curses of Ireland' he stated, 'are bad Landlords and bad Agents, and in nineteen cases out of twenty, the origin of the crime lies with the Landlord or Agent, instead of the Tenant'.[9]

In the judgement of *The Nation's* reviewer, *Valentine McClutchy* was 'the most complete and daring picture of Irish country life ever executed', and, although Carleton did not write often for it, his connection with *The Nation* was an important one for him.[10] As a novel, *Valentine McClutchy* requires a paper devoted to itself. It is not my intention to discuss it here, my main interest in this article lying in what happened thereafter. For, of course, the year 1845 was also that in which the first signs of the fatal potato blight appeared, and the year in which Davis died. Carleton could not have foreseen these events when *Valentine McClutchy* was published in January 1845 and, until the autumn, this was a good year for him. He was, O'Donoghue tells us, 'depending solely on the writing of books' and 'never worked so energetically either before or after'.[11]

Although he had not carried out his intention, announced in 1839, of writing a kind of sequel to *Traits and Stories of the Irish Peasantry* with the provisional title *The Chronicles of Ballymacruiskeen*, which would 'exhibit such a panoramic view of Irish life, character and manners as may be nearly complete', Carleton embarked in the early 1840s on a new series of *Tales for the Irish People*, intending that these would:

> simply ... improve their physical and social condition – generally; and through the medium of vivid and striking, but unobjectionable narratives, ... inculcate such principles as may enable Irishmen to think more clearly, reason more correctly, and act more earnestly upon the general duties which, from their position in life, they are called upon to perform.[12]

The three tales which were published in 1845 – *Art Maguire, or The Broken Pledge, Rody the Rover, or The Ribbonman* and *Parra Sastha, or The History of Paddy Go-Easy and his Wife Nancy* – are not memorable novels, but remain notable mainly for their indication of the direction of Carleton's work in that productive year. Robert Lee Wolff, in his work *William Carleton, Irish Peasant Novelist: A Preface to his Fiction*, published in conjunction with Garland's series of Carleton reprints, dismisses summarily these three short novels, adding: 'We have not republished any of these fictionalised tracts'.[13] It is a pity, to my mind, that Garland did not republish them. The prefaces in themselves are worth reading, showing us the mind and emotions of Carleton, as he wrestled to express his concern for his countrymen.

Art Maguire, the first of these three works, was dedicated to Father Theobald Mathew, leader of a famous and highly successful temperance movement. The novel sets out to show the consequences of Art's breaking his pledge. Carleton expressed the genuine if rather sad hope that his attempt to alert his countrymen to their duty 'through the aid of truthful fiction', would cause them to look kindly on him, 'to forget his former errors and to cherish his name with affection, when he himself shall be freed for ever from those cares and trials of life which have hitherto been his portion'.[14] The second novel, *Rody the Rover,* was written, Carleton tells us, 'with the same anxious wish to benefit my countrymen that influenced me in the composition of *Art Maguire*' and the last, and arguably the most interesting, *Parra Sastha*, was dedicated to 'the People of Ireland' as a 'feeble attempt to communicate to them information designed to improved their condition and add to their information and comfort'.[15]

Parra Sastha was written in nine days and, indeed, bears every appearance of it. It was written in feverish haste to fill a gap in the Library of Ireland, to which Carleton had earlier contributed, and whose list had promised that its November publication would be Thomas Davis's *Life of Wolfe Tone*: now, Davis was dead. Carleton's tribute to Davis in his preface to Parra Sastha, raw with the emotion of bereavement, and all the more moving for it, is worth reading for its own sake. For Davis's sake, he made a special effort in this work. 'Moved by his example', he writes, 'I have endeavoured to make the following sketch useful to my countrymen. If the perusal of it shall succeed in banishing from them, and from many of my countrywomen also, such habits of indolence and want of cleanliness as I have satirized, I shall feel that I have been the humble means of rendering a humble service to my country'.[16] To his picture of the lazy shiftless Paddy Go-

Easy and his wife Nancy – whose very names tell us most of what we need to know about their characters – he adds '… a short appendix upon agricultural and other matters connected with the house and farmyard, which, I trust, those who reside in remote districts will find to be beneficial.'[17] That appendix is taken from what Carleton describes as 'an admirable little work' by a Martin Doyle, with the title *Hints to the Small Farmers of the County of Wexford*. This work is, we are told, 'directed to The Small Farmers of Ireland – a numerous class, who stand very much in need of sound information upon agricultural matters'. It includes very readable information on such topics as: 'The Condition and Quality of Land; The Preparation of Soil; Cottage Cleanliness; Prudence; Potatoes-Cutting and Planting; Turnips- Seasons for sowing; Wheat-pickling; Manures; and Marl and Irrigation'.

The preface to *Paddy Go-Easy*, dated 28 October 1845, was written at a time when Carleton's concerns with proper husbandry were not yet occasioned by a knowledge of the impact of potato blight. Yet, more than most, Carleton was aware of what was happening in the land. Seeing the warning signs, Carleton remembered his experience of the horror of earlier periods of hunger, notably those of 1817 and 1822, and began to write a moral tale of a significance far beyond that of the three just mentioned. This tale, *The Black Prophet*, serialised in the *Dublin University Magazine* between May and December 1846, and published in book form in 1847, was being written as the horror of the situation became obvious. Appalled, unable to believe that such misery would be allowed to happen again, Carleton described what he had seen in his youth. Want and disease were familiar to him. In an earlier, famous story, 'The Poor Scholar', he had described famine fever, but as a thing of the past.[18] His bitter, ironic preface to *The Black Prophet*, written in February 1847, and dedicated to the then Prime Minister, Lord John Russell, makes clear that he held the government responsible:

> Having witnessed last season the partial and in this the general
> failure of the potato crop, [the author] anticipated, as every man
> must, the fearful visitation which is now almost decimating our
> wretched population; and it occurred to him that a narrative
> founded upon it, or at all events exhibiting through the
> medium of fiction an authentic detail of all that our unhappy
> and neglected country has suffered, during past privations of a
> similar kind, might be calculated to awaken those who legislate
> for us into something like a humane perception of a calamity
> that has been almost perennial in the country.[19]

In his dedication he expresses the ironic hope 'that, as it is the first Tale of Irish Famine that ever was dedicated to an English Prime Minister, your Lordship's enlarged and enlightened policy will put it out of the power of any succeeding Author ever to write another'.[20]

Much has been written on this novel, *The Black Prophet*, I wish only to note that the tendency exhibited in the earlier moral tales finds here its proper home. The melodramatic plot of an old and unsolved murder is, rightly, subsumed in Carleton's anguished and heartfelt appeal to the Prime Minister to rescue the Irish people from disaster. In passages verging on the poetic, interspersed with lurid melodrama, Carleton paints a picture of a stricken land, oppressed even by the weather:

> A brooding stillness, too, lay over all nature; cheerfulness had
> disappeared, even the groves and hedges were silent, for the
> very birds had ceased to sing, and the earth seemed as if it
> mourned for the approaching calamity, as well as for that which
> had been already felt.[21]

He shows a terrible gombeen man, Darby Skinadre, and exposes his ruthless
exploitation of his neighbours; he shows death comparable to that described by
John Mitchel in 'The Famine Year';[22] he abandons his story to explain over
several pages the rationale behind famine mobs and, in one footnote, two and a
half pages long, draws evidence from medical witnesses to the 1817 famine. The
point is emphasised in every way he can devise and, movingly, simply, he writes
at the end of the novel :

> The sufferings of that year of famine we have endeavoured to
> bring before those who may have the power in their hands of
> assuaging the similar horrors which have revisited our country
> in this. The pictures we have given are not exaggerated, but
> drawn from memory and the terrible realities of 1817.[23]

That there was, apparently, no response to this plea must have been a source
of bitter disappointment to Carleton, but he was no longer in a position to take
the government to task, standing in sore need of a pension to supplement his
income. By 1848, having sold his copyrights for very little and with ten children
to support, Carleton was living on the edge of destitution, facing starvation and
threatened with eviction. After many efforts on the part of his friends and
admirers, including Maria Edgeworth and Sir William Wilde, father of Oscar, a
government pension of £200 was awarded to him in June 1848.[24]

Did he then abandon his moral crusade? Was his conscience stilled by the
means of subsistence for himself and his family? It seems not. Before the pension
came through, Carleton had completed, among other works, a new novel. It was
accepted by the Belfast publishers Simms and McIntyre (who had published *The
Black Prophet*), but they did not bring it out until 1848. Carleton, as usual,
disposed of his copyright for a paltry sum. The extract which begins this paper
comes from, *The Emigrants of Ahadarra*. It is a tale of several families, but
principally of the thrifty and well-doing McMahons, one of whom is on the point
of being compelled to emigrate, when a so-called friend plots to have him
removed from his land by planting there an illegal still, and then informing on
him. It is a tale, too, of the careless Burkes, of whom the false friend is the elder
son, a kind of half-educated half-sir, who fits nowhere and is properly
disinherited at the end of the novel. His mother brings to mind the socially
ambitious Lady Clonbrony of Maria Edgeworth's *Absentee*. There is a drunken
hedge-schoolmaster and a villainous poteen maker, who pretends to know no
English; these bring to mind some of the minor characters in Gerald Griffin's *The
Collegians*. As is usual in Carleton, there are beautiful heroines, full of virtue and
spirit – and one virago, redeemed at the end by a spark of goodness. There is a
bad landlord, excused only because he is young and misled by a wicked and
manipulative agent. The agent is duly punished and the young aristocrat comes to
his senses in the end. One good neighbour, a Protestant farmer named Sam
Wallace, emigrates early in the novel, 'finding ... that there was not proper
encouragement given to men who were anxious and disposed to improve their
property'.[25]

Bryan McMahon, the forward looking and ambitious young farmer who is almost driven to emigrate, sums up the condition of the people :

> The landlords in general care little about the state and condition of their tenantry. All they trouble themselves about is their rents. Look at my own case, an that's but one out of thousands that's happenin' every day in the country. Grantin' that he didn't sarve me with this notice to quit, and supposin' he let me stay in the farm, he'd rise it on me in sich a way as I could hardly live in it; an '… to be merely strugglin' and toilin' all one's life is anything but a comfortable prospect. Then in consequence of the people dependin' upon nothing but the potato for food, whenever that crop fails, which in general it does every seventh or eighth year, there's a famine, an' then the famine is followed by fever an' all kinds of contagious diseases, in sich a way that the kingdom is turned into one great hospital and graveyard. It's these things that's sendin' so many thousands out of the country; and if we're to go at all, let us go like the rest, while we're able to go, an' not wait till we become too poor either to go or stay with comfort.[26]

How eerily that voice sounds across a hundred and fifty years, and how frequently have we read similar opinions over the past year in the judgements of history, contemporary and modern, on what was then happening in Ireland. Carleton had rightly identified the essential fact: unless landlords worked with their tenants, their power to influence their own fate was irrevocably weakened. As W.E. Vaughan succinctly puts it: 'Above all, during the period 1848–78 landlords had a chance to succeed'.[27] Elsewhere, Vaughan develops this theme:

> They should have appeared as the champions of the old-world values; they should have appealed to old ties and old ways. They did not introduce the new ways with any thoroughness … The past was captured by their opponents, moreover, and used against them.[28]

It is strange, therefore, to see Carleton's reformed landlord Chevydale proposing, in the mid-1840s, reforms not dissimilar to those retrospectively described as essential by Vaughan in the mid-1990s. In response to the question from another landlords: 'Talking of the country, what is to be done?', the reconstructed Chevydale replies:

> Simply … that we, the landed proprietors of Ireland, should awake out of our slumbers, and forgetting those vile causes of division and subdivision that have hitherto not only disunited us, but set us together by the ears, we should take counsel among ourselves, and after due and serious deliberation, come to the determination that it is our duty to prevent Irish interests from being made subservient to English interests, and from being legislated for upon English principles.[29]

Chevydale does not support repeal of the Union, suggesting instead that landlords as a class may 'find it our best policy to forget the interests of any particular class, and suffer ourselves to melt down into one great principle of national love and good-will towards each other. Let us only become unanimous', he concludes, 'and England will respect us as she did when we were unanimous upon other occasions.' His companion agrees that 'we must identify ourselves with the people whose interests most unquestionably are ours.'[30]

Not content to present his evidence simply through the belated realisations of a fictional character, Carleton sets out early in the novel his own understanding of the causes of emigration. They are, he believes, 'the poverty and depressed state of the country'; 'absenteeism'; 'the general inattention of Irish landlords to the state and condition of their property and an inexcusable want of sympathy with their tenantry'; 'the evil of sub-letting'; 'political corruption, in the shape of the forty shilling franchise ... which led to the prostration of the country by poverty and moral degradation, and for [which] the proprietors of the soil are solely responsible'; 'the use of the potato as the staple food of the labouring classes, in connection with the truck system and the consequent absence of money payments'; 'the high and exorbitant rents at which land is held by all classes of farmers – with some exceptions, we admit, as in the case of old leases – but especially by those who hold under middlemen, or on the principle generally'. His final damning sentence reads:

> By this system a vast deal of distress and petty but most harassing oppression is every day in active operation upon the property of the head landlords, which he can never know, and for which he is in no other way responsible unless by having ever permitted the existence of it, for any purpose whatever.[31]

Of course, as Terry Eagleton reminds us in his recent work, *Heathcliff and the Great Hunger*, 'literary testimony is not, to be sure, hard historical evidence; but it is an odd historical judgement which can run clean counter to such a major body of writing'. 'Perhaps', he continues, with irony reminiscent of Carleton himself, 'everyone from Edgeworth and Banim to Carleton and Moore was simply cursed with too lurid an imagination.'[32]

Perhaps this is so, but there is no escaping the fact that these gifted artists lived through times about which we can only read and speculate. They wrote from the evidence of their own lives. Without them, we would not have the voices of personal experience transmuted through fiction. Without Carleton's impassioned if often melodramatic stories of the 1840s we would not have the wealth of information and impression to remind us of life as it then was. Carleton recreates for us in precise and affectionate detail the people and places of his youth: their implements; their kitchens and utensils; their speech and pronunciation; the custom which would not let a visitor leave unfed lest it damage 'the credit of the house'; their contests of skill and their watchful rivalries; their feasts and wakes. In English literature we find such treasures in, for example, Thomas Hardy. In Scottish fiction, Walter Scott performs the same service; and in Irish writing Carleton and his forebears have left to us this rich repository.

Above all, without Carleton's moral tales of the mid-1840s, we would not have this curious tale of emigration and famine – part history, part economic treatise, part moral tract, part imagination. We cannot dismiss his point of view for, however prolific the documents available to us today, we were not alive during the Great Famine, and he was. He grew up the son of a small farmer and a native speaker of Gaelic; saw yeomen bayonet his sister; joined the ribbonmen and then left them in distaste; set out to travel to Munster to study for the priesthood but abandoned the idea and came back to join in the dances at home; left again for Dublin; wrote there anti-Catholic tracts for Caesar Otway; reconciled himself through his writing with the people of his youth; swore that he needed no government help and then applied for a pension; witnessed murder and disease; suffered starvation and want; described with desperate sincerity all that he had seen and endured; and died in Dublin, of cancer of the tongue, in 1869. Seventeen years before his death, prophetic words, reminiscent of those of Thomas Davis, were written of William Carleton.

> Unless another master-hand should appear like his, it is in his pages, and in his alone, that future generations must look for the truest and fullest pictures of those who will ere long have passed away from that troubled land, from the records of history, and from the memory of men for ever.[33]

As we study these crucial years of Famine and emigration, it may be a salutary exercise to turn to his pages, rediscover his vivid, funny and often terrifying perspective on life in nineteenth-century Ireland, consider his views and then, incensed or exhilarated, make our own judgements in our own time.

References

1 William Carleton, *The Emigrants of Ahadarra* (London and Belfast, 1848), p. 86.

2 William Carleton, *Valentine McClutchy, the Irish Agent* (Dublin, London and Edinburgh, 1845); idem, *Art Maguire; or The Broken Pledge* (Dublin, 1845); idem, *Rody the Rover; or The Ribbonman* (Dublin,1845); idem, *Parra Sastha; or The History of Paddy Go-Easy and His Wife Nancy* (Dublin, 1845); idem, *The Black Prophet: A Tale of Irish Famine* (Belfast, 1847).

3 Carleton, *Traits and Stories of the Irish Peasantry*, First Series, 2 Vols. (Dublin, 1830); Second Series, 3 Vols. (Dublin and London, 1833).

4 David J. O'Donoghue, *The Life of William Carleton*, Vols. II (London, 1896), pp. 78-9.

5 William Carleton, *Autobiography* (London, 1896. Revised Edition, London, 1968), p. 54.

6 Carleton, *Valentine McClutchy*, Preface.

7 For details of Carleton's contributions to *The Christian Examiner*, 1828-31, see O'Donoghue, *The Life of William Carleton*, Vol. 1, pp. 4-19.

8 O'Donoghue, *The Life of William Carleton*, p. 65.

9 Carleton, *Valentine McClutchy*, Preface.

10 O'Donoghue, *The Life of William Carleton*, p. 66.

11 Ibid. p. 72.

12 Carleton, *Art Maguire*, Preface, p. v.

13 Robert Lee Wolff, *William Carleton, Irish Peasant Novelist: A Preface to His Fiction* (New York and London, 1980), p. 107.

14 Carleton, *Art Maguire*, Preface, p. viii.

15 Carleton, *Rody the Rover*, Preface, p. 3; idem *Parra Sastha*, Dedication.

16 Carleton, *Parra Sastha*, Preface, pp. xiv-xv.

17 Ibid. pp. xv-xvi.

18 Carleton, 'The Poor Scholar', *Traits and Stories of the Irish Peasantry*, Second Series, Vol. I (Dublin and London, 1833).

19 Carleton, *The Black Prophet* (Shannon: Irish University Press reprint of 1899 edition, 1972), p. vii.

20 Ibid. Dedication to Lord John Russell, p. v.

21 Ibid. p. 17.

22 John Mitchel, *Jail Journal* (Dublin, 1914), pp. 421-8.

23 Carleton, *The Black Prophet*, p. 406.

24 O'Donoghue, *The Life of William Carleton*, Vol. II, pp. 124-5; Carleton to Charles Gavan Duffy, 1848 (National Library of Ireland, Ms5757, fols. 91-4).

25 Carleton, *The Emigrants of Ahadarra*, p. 58.

26 Ibid. p. 231.

27 W.E. Vaughan, *Landlords and Tenants in Ireland* (Dundalk, 1984), p. 7.

28 W.E. Vaughan, *Landlords and Tenants in Mid-Victorian Ireland* (Oxford, 1994), p. 223.

29 Carleton, *The Emigrants of Ahadarra*, p. 288.

30 Ibid. p. 289.

31 Ibid. pp. 86-7.

32 Terry Eagleton, *Heathcliff and The Great Hunger* (London and New York, 1995), p. 23.

33 *Edinburgh Review*, 1852, in 'National Tintings'; *Illustrated Dublin Journal*, 2 November 1861, p. 132.

Local Relief Committees in Ulster 1845–7

James Grant

L OCAL RELIEF COMMITTEES played an important, frequently a vital, role in coping with the destitution and starvation which followed the heavy local losses of the potato crop in 1845 and the virtually total loss of 1846. Local committees were a spontaneous response on behalf of the needy in a community by those less needy – typically by clergy everywhere and by landlords in rural areas and civic and business leaders in towns. They were not new, given the frequent potato failures in the early decades of the nineteenth century, being used most recently in the failure of 1821–2. We find them responding to the partial failure of 1845, a few forming in the winter, but most in the late spring and early summer of 1846.

Those wishing to avail of government financial support had to integrate into Sir Robert Peel's relief plan under his Temporary Relief Commission, formed in November 1845. Such committees had to follow comprehensive *Instructions to Committees of Relief Districts* for their formation and guidance, published on 28 February 1846. The main requirements were that committees had to be approved by the lieutenant of the county; they had to establish a relief fund; they had to provide townland lists of applicants for relief, especially on public works; they had to submit their subscription lists to the Lord Lieutenant of Ireland, 'together with a list of landlords who do not contribute'. Landlords looking after their own tenants were regarded as contributors. Committees were to encourage agricultural improvement, especially drainage. They were expected to provide local employment if necessary, 'which had to be approved by the Commission'. Gratuitous help could only be given to those unable to work when the local workhouse was full.

Membership of local committees consisted of county officials such as county lieutenants or vice-lieutenants, justices of the peace (drawn from the landed interest), poor law guardians, 'clergymen of all persuasions', an officer of the Board of Works, a coastguard officer (where available) and such other 'active and intelligent gentlemen' as the county lieutenant wished.[1]

Following the total failure of 1846, the *Instructions* were revised.[2] There was one major change of emphasis. The role of committees in providing 'properly scrutinised lists' of applicants for employment on the public works was greatly enhanced because the government's principal relief effort, from September 1846 to April 1847, was to be the provision of work for those dislocated by famine; with the pay earned for work, they could buy food. In some areas where public works were substantial, like parts of counties Cavan, Donegal, Monaghan and Fermanagh, committees seem to have been distracted from their other main function of raising funds. Or, perhaps, many would-be subscribers felt that, with public works providing relief, there was no need for them to contribute; or they felt that paying their county cess was enough. But for most committees the task of providing relief through a local fund, grant-aided by government, remained important. During this period, there were about 240 committees in Ulster in correspondence with the commissariat relief department in Dublin, in contrast to the thirty or so of 1845–6.[3]

The final role of local committees in the months from April to August 1847 was to assist in relief under the Temporary Relief Act (popularly Soup Kitchens or Rations Act), when government finally decided to feed the starving people. In this phase of relief, committees lost practically all control over their activities, for the act was administered within the poor law framework because it was to be financed principally out of the poor rates. For the purposes of the act, all relief districts were to be reorganised into electoral division units and committees rigidly controlled, in each poor law union, by a small finance committee appointed directly by the Lord Lieutenant of Ireland. (Electoral divisions were subdivisions of poor law unions.) One interesting and important feature of this phase of relief is the very full series of statistics for its operation which can be found in the parliamentary papers.[4]

I

Following the partial failure of 1845, local relief committees were active in some parts of Ulster, particularly in counties Cavan, which had about thirteen, and Donegal and Monaghan, each of which had six.[5] In the east of the province, there was certainly one committee in County Down, at Ballymacarrett, 'the poorest suburb of Belfast, ... densely populated by the very lowest class of weavers and other operatives', as its secretary, Rev. John Boyd, described it.[6] There is some evidence for another committee in County Down, at Loughbrickland.[7] In County Londonderry, a committee was formed at Coleraine in mid-April 1846.[8] But the earliest one in the province was in north Antrim.

This committee convened at Ballymoney in December 1845 as a response to the serious potato loss in the four northernmost baronies of County Antrim, namely, Cary, Upper and Lower Dunluce and Kilconway. The average loss for the area was two-thirds, much of the crop having been grown 'on elevated and late situations'; it was a serious loss when set against a national loss of between one-quarter and one-third. The Ballymoney committee was a central one, representing nine sub-committees in the four baronies. It was also a weighty one, containing no less than six justices of the peace and chaired by the formidable George MacCartney of Lissanoure. The committee concluded that it was 'the bounden duty' of government to provide 'the most energetic, prompt and liberal co-operation and assistance' towards providing employment in drainage, road improvements, and other works; to send 'an immediate and liberal supply' of seed potatoes into the small ports of the area and have it distributed through the boards of poor law guardians; and to make loans 'without interest, for one year'. Such a scheme would also ease pressure on the workhouses in the district from labourers, cottiers and small farmers whose plight was a direct result of a serious potato failure. They were '... a class of people the Legislature never contemplated becoming chargeable on the Rates'. Strictly speaking, the committee's view of the poor law was erroneous, but it reflected a widely-held opinion in Ulster as a whole, among both relief committees and boards of guardians throughout the

Famine period, that decent, honest and industrious people should not be forced by the letter of the law to become destitute before being offered relief.[9]

The parts of Cavan affected were in the centre, west and south-west of the county, with a small pocket in the east around Shercock. Average losses for the county were about one-half of the crop, varying from one-third in Kildallan in the west, to three-quarters in the Shercock area. The Shercock committee was the first to form, in early May 1846, followed by others in early June – Cavan, Stradone and Ballyhaise in the centre of the county; Ballyjamesduff and Crosserlough, Killashandra, Ballinagh, Drumlumman and Ballymachugh in the west and south-west.[10]

The main preoccupations of the Cavan committees were fund-raising and the provision of employment. In respect of fund-raising, two points of interest emerge; first, the difficulty of getting subscriptions from absentee landlords and, secondly, the numerous contributions from the small farmers, 'the humbler classes', as Charles James Adams, the Shercock chairman, called them. Nearly every subscription list contained a long recital of names of individuals subscribing sums from one shilling to five shillings. Particularly striking was the Shercock list. Out of a total of £186 15s 6d, seven individuals subscribed £91; there were nine subscriptions of ten shillings and about 86 of £1 each. The extent of contributions from 'the humbler classes' is a reminder how mild were the effects of even a heavy potato loss in 1845-6 in contrast to the state of things a year later.[11]

The employment provided by Cavan committees was mostly in drainage, with some roadworks. There was a preoccupation with roadworks and drainage of bogs, which were seen as facilitating access to fuel. For instance, Ballyjamesduff committee organised drainage of the 'bog of Fraal by which the town of Ballyjamesduff is supplied with fuel' and of 'the lake and river of Cornagrove' by which the bog 'supplying an extensive part of the three parishes of Denn, Lavey and Ballyjamesduff with fuel' would be relieved of its periodic floods and a considerable extent of the lake and river banks reclaimed. Similarly, Crosserlough committee funded 'a new road or pass to Kilnaleck bog'.[12]

The six committees in County Monaghan showed similar preoccupations to those in Cavan, namely, fund-raising and employment. Their correspondence with Dublin Castle gives us glimpses of the liberal conduct of public works under Peel's administration, in contrast to the rigid control of the following season. In June 1846, the county engineer offered the Drumsnat committee 'the recommendation of the labourers and the superintendence of the works', which would have been unthinkable a few months later. In one instance, the committee delegated two of its members, Dr John Moorehead and Rev. Allen Mitchell, to supervise one of the works. Admittedly, it was only 'a footpath for Smithborough', but it required the employment of an overseer and twelve to fifteen labourers daily. The two men further undertook to act as sureties for the expense of the work, the committee guaranteeing them against loss until the monies became available at the following spring assizes.[13]

The Donegal committees were mainly in the west and south-west of the county, at Gweedore, Mullaghderg, Lettermacaward, Killybegs/Dunkineely and Inver; the sixth was at Milford in the north-east. Their great preoccupation was with Indian meal, a reminder of the county's unique position in Ulster, as belonging, in official thinking, to the 'western division of Ireland' which qualified it for direct government intervention in food supplies. Hardly a letter failed to mention meal in one way or another, but the assumption was always that the meal would be for sale, not given *gratis*.[14]

II

The developing awareness, from mid-July 1846 onwards, that the growing potato crop was doomed, brought a sombre mood to the country. 'I have never witnessed anything like the sudden distress that has so generally appeared', wrote the parish priest of Killybegs on 16 July, as he reported the reappearance of 'the destructive rot of last season … as a result, much despondency appears to prevail'.[15] As the alarm spread, committees began to form in every county in Ulster, earlier in the west (typically, September-October) than in the east (typically, December-February).

The material available for the study of relief committees in 1846–7 is very extensive. Just three aspects will be considered here, namely, the organisation of relief districts, the raising of local funds and, finally, the position of committees under the Temporary Relief Act, by which the people were fed in the summer of 1847.

In the relief arrangements following the 1845 failure, county lieutenants in Ulster had formed large central committees, usually presiding over whole baronies, with sub-committees subordinate to them. As arrangements were made to face the new crisis in the autumn of 1846, Sir Randolph Routh was asked to revise the *Instructions* of the previous season for the formation and guidance of committees. Routh was convinced that the large baronial committees had been 'the most successful of all our committees and the best managed'; he cited twelve counties, Antrim and Cavan among them, where they had performed well and he was anxious to retain the concept, believing it would be administratively simpler, as substantially reducing correspondence with Dublin, and would mesh well with the baronial organisation of the public works.[16] He was, however, overruled by Charles Trevelyan, the Whitehall mandarin in charge of Irish Famine relief, whose view was that Routh's plan carried 'serious risk of failure, and of other consequences worse than failure'; what was needed was 'machinery of the simplest kind', suitable for Irish gentlemen and clergy few of whom were practical men of business. His choice was smaller districts of two parishes. In addition to simplicity, they would have the moral value of encouraging gentry and clergy to promote 'the *bona fide* interests of the Public, irrespective of parochial influence'.[17] However, Routh salvaged something of his idea; central committees could be used if county lieutenants thought them 'more desirable'.[18]

In practice, lieutenants of counties could nominate districts as they wished, so that there was no uniformity. For example, the Earl of Erne, lieutenant of Fermanagh, preferred Routh's idea of central baronial committees, appointing one for each of the county's seven baronies; he did, however, accede to local requests for sub-committees which were numerous in the baronies of Lurg, 'as [it] is large', and Tyrkennedy.[19] John Young, MP, acting lieutenant for Cavan, had similar ideas.[20] The preference of Sir Robert Ferguson in County Londonderry was for relief districts based on electoral divisions of poor law unions. It is tempting to assume that Ferguson, as an influential Whig MP, was in touch with the Whig goverment's forward thinking which was already, in the autumn of 1846, eyeing the Irish poor law system as a vehicle for famine relief in addition to 'ordinary' poor relief. Certainly electoral-division relief districts were more numerous in Londonderry than in any other county.[21] In Donegal, Sir James Stewart adhered closely to the *Instructions*, arranging districts of two parishes with few exceptions; similarly, the two-parish principle was followed by Lord Cremorne in Monaghan. However, Stewart soon conceded requests from single parishes and Cremorne agreed with central committees in the baronies of Trough and Farney.[22] Lord Gosford in Armagh seems to have preferred single parishes, though five districts there were based on electoral districts and two on petty-sessions districts.[23] Petty-sessions districts were the preference of Lord Charlemont, lieutenant of County Tyrone; Ballygawley, Clogher, Fintona, Carrickmore, Omagh and Aughnacloy were all in this category. The extensive barony of Dungannon seems to have had two central committees, at Dungannon and Stewartstown, which supervised four and three parochial sub-committees respectively. Finally, all five committees in Strabane barony were parochial.[24]

The two counties in Ulster least effectively organised by their lieutenants were Down and Antrim, probably because their need for local committees occurred, in general, considerably later than elsewhere. The lieutenant of Antrim, the Marquis of Donegall, seemed to be the only one not to reply to Routh's circular to lieutenants of 2 October 1846 requesting them to form committees. As a result, all twenty-eight committees in the county were formed by local initiative and approved retrospectively by the lieutenant.[25] Lack of clear definition by Viscount Castlereagh in County Down caused quite serious local friction for committees in Newry (over the disposal of the government grant) and Rathfriland, where complex relationships among surrounding parishes left the central committee there 'useless . . . [and] totally unmanageable'.[26] Occasionally, local co-operation proved impossible so that no committee was formed. Such was the case in the Crossgar area of County Down, where the electoral division in the Downpatrick union, consisted of

> a number of townlands belonging to different proprietors,
> many of them being subdivided, so that there are about 40
> proprietors in all . . . From these causes it has been found
> impossible to do anything for the relief of the existing
> destitution by voluntary efforts.[27]

The overall result of the freedom given to county lieutenants was that relief districts in Ulster, and in the country at large, formed a chaotic patchwork. The extent of the chaos was not fully realised until the new government policy of relief by food began to be implemented in March 1847, when hundreds of districts had to be redrawn to conform to poor law electoral divisions. There is no doubt that this reorganisation was, together with the forced and untidy rundown of the public works system, a substantial factor in retarding the introduction of relief by food. As a result, the period from February to May was a time of great loss of life. It is tempting, in retrospect, to see Routh's effort to hold on to a central committee system as administratively sounder than Trevelyan's 'machinery of the simplest kind' which authorised the proliferation of local committees, thereby making more difficult the transition to relief by food.

The provision and management of a relief fund was one of the important duties of local committees. Most raised their funds by straightforward public appeal, others by voluntary assessment, usually agreed between tenants and landlords, or among tenants themselves, at so many pence per acre or per pound of valuation of their holdings. Very commonly, funds were raised by the sale of tickets for meal or soup; better-off neighbours could buy tickets according to various and sometimes quite elaborate local rules which they then gave to the less fortunate. The ticket system enabled many committees to avoid giving gratuitous relief which, as a public action, was widely held at the time, by both donor and recipient, to be morally reprehensible. The donation of tickets was also seen as contributing to the 'strengthening of the bonds of society', by which the better-off could practise benevolence and the poor gratitude. The sentiments expressed by the chairman of the Portstewart committee were typical: '... the lower orders are peaceable and well-conducted and appear thankfully sensible of the efforts made for their relief'.[28] A small number of committees undertook a more elaborate system of two funds, one a capital or supply fund, based on local loans to facilitate bulk buying, the other a relief or sinking fund. For example, the Drumholm/Rossnowlagh committee in Donegal established a supply fund of over £1,000 to be 'invested in meal'; it was based on loans from three persons, Archdeacon Fenwick of Raphoe diocese and Colonel Conolly, one of the MPs for Donegal, each of whom provided £400 and the improving landlord John Hamilton of St Ernan's, who loaned £200. Hamilton openly acknowledged to Routh that the committee was interfering in the Donegal grain market against the 'hucksters', which was against the *Instructions*, but this did not deter Routh from recommending a large government donation.[29] Iniskeel and Inishmacsaint committees, also in Donegal, established two funds, as did Portstewart in County Londonderry.[30]

The size of local funds varied so widely and for so many reasons that it is almost impossible to generalise about them. A detailed examination of 181 local funds in Ulster in receipt of government 'donations' or grants-in-aid (usually of 100 per cent) shows that the modal fund was between £100 and £199; fifty-six funds, or just under one-third of the total, were in this band. The next largest groups were in the bands on either side of the mode. Thirty-four funds were under £100 and thirty-five were between £200 and £299. These three groups made up 125 funds, or seventy per cent of the total. To summarise the remainder, there were twenty-seven funds between £300 and £499 and a further sixteen between £500 and £799. Only three, Banbridge, Armagh borough and city of Derry, exceeded £1,000.[31]

Only two secure generalisations about funds are possible. The first is that the major contributors were the landlords, no surprise when one considers their dominant economic and social position in Irish society. The second generalisation is that all of the larger funds were the result of the energetic involvement of the landed interest in rural areas and of the civic and business leadership in towns (often with mixed motives, humanitarian, the desire to maintain control and so on) and by clergy everywhere. Two examples must suffice, the funds of Brookeborough relief committee in County Fermanagh and of Gilford/Tullylish in County Down.

The moving spirit behind the Brookeborough fund, of £579, was the principal landlord who was also an MP for the county, Sir Arthur Brinsley

Brooke. Not only did he contribute £250 himself and other members of his family another £150, but he canvassed widely his political and aristocratic friends in both Ireland and England, as recorded in the committee's long subscription list.[32] The Gilford/Tullylish fund of £602 was made possible by large subscriptions from several local linen companies like Dunbar and McMaster, Dixon & Co., John Smyth & Co., and from the absentee landlord Robert Alexander Stewart of Ards in County Donegal. It also had a vigorous chairman in John Temple Reilly, Lord Downshire's land agent and a substantial landlord in his own right.[33]

Government grants-in-aid of local funds were the next important financial source for committees. From January 1847 onwards, the grant was usually 100 per cent, which was applied to all funds, large and small, irrespective of the extent of distress in a locality. So the irony was that, for example, a large fund, the product of strong local leadership and, not infrequently, less local distress, such as the £1,023 fund of Banbridge committee, with several hundred pounds from local linen merchants, received a further £1,023 from government; while an abandoned community like Drumlumman in County Cavan, where 'The population exceeds 8,000 without any resident proprietors to look after the wants of the poor, or any adequate fund', could raise but £16.12s.3d. from three absentee proprietors and received but £16 from government.[34]

Financial support from charities was substantial only in County Donegal and, to a lesser extent, in County Armagh. A computation from the Relief Commission Papers shows that the total subscribed locally to all the Donegal relief committees was £7,370. The various charities contributed a further £1,665, or 18.5 per cent of the grand total, one-third of it from the largest of the charities, the London-based British Relief Association. The next major charity was the Dublin-based Society of Friends, the Quakers. Others were the Irish Relief Association, the Central Relief Committee (both Dublin), the Calcutta Fund and the National Club (both London), the Belfast General Relief Fund and finally, two ladies' committees, the Belfast Ladies' Committee, which showed a special interest in Donegal and the Londonderry Ladies' Committee, whose efforts were directed solely to Donegal. The success of County Armagh committees in obtaining nearly £1,000 from the charities provides a corrective to the popular notion that the charities were exclusively proactive; they were proactive, but not exclusively; committees had to apply for help. An important advantage for County Armagh committees was the active involvement of a large number of energetic and well-informed clergymen of the Established Church.[35]

III

The Temporary Relief Act was an interim measure which was largely funded out of the poor rates. In effect, if not in name, it was a large exercise in outdoor relief, a dress rehearsal for the handing over, in August 1847, of all extraordinary Famine relief to the Irish poor law system which would be 'extended' to allow it to provide outdoor relief.

Relief by food, directed by a new relief commission under Sir John Burgoyne, was based on the already widespread local relief committees, which were now reorganised where necessary into relief districts consisting of one or more poor law electoral divisions. Its financial arrangements, drawn up by the admiralty accountant, J.C. Bromley, who was on loan to the relief commissioners, were minutely detailed and rigorously applied. Each electoral division committee had to decide how to fund relief; it had also to make careful fortnightly estimates of its needs; both decision and estimate had to be scrutinised by the finance committee of the poor law union, a small group of between two and four men appointed directly by the Lord Lieutenant of Ireland.[36]

Bromley had set out no less than seven methods of funding, of which four were particularly important. The first of these allowed that balances from 'old' committees could be applied proportionately to the new relief districts. Where 'old' committees had large funds, these were often sufficient to carry the district through the temporary relief phase. In regard to the examples quoted above, of Brookeborough in County Fermanagh and Gilford/Tullylish in County Down, it can be said that the Brookeborough fund, with equal government donation, enabled the five electoral divisions associated with the 'old' committee (Aghavoory, Brookeborough, Colebrooke, Derrycrum and Derrycullen) to opt out of the temporary relief act.[37] The same is true of Tullylish electoral division in Banbridge poor law union.[38] The same can also be said for electoral divisions associated with most of the big funds of 'old' committees. On the other extreme, the electoral division of Drumlumman, associated with the 'old' committee of the abandoned community in County Cavan, required almost £700 in rate grant from government and an £800 loan on credit of the rates to see it through the temporary relief phase; this left it saddled with a subsequent poor rate of 2s 10½d in the pound to repay the loan.[39]

Apart from balances from 'old' committees, there were three principal methods of funding: government grants in aid of rates (in extremely distressed areas, particularly in Connacht and parts of Munster, but Drumlumman electoral division was an example), government loans on credit of rates to be raised (the normal funding method) and, finally, government grants in support of local voluntary subscriptions, which were likely to be raised only in less distressed, or more prosperous, areas or where local leadership was vigorous. In fact, the method of funding employed by committees was itself a rough indicator of the extent of distress, or conversely, the economic health of a local community.

Only four unions in Ulster relied heavily on grant-aided rates, Glenties (44 per cent of temporary relief expenditure), Cootehill (41 per cent) and Bailieborough and Donegal (each about 37 per cent). They were also the four Ulster unions most reliant on the temporary relief act, measured by the percentage of their population dependent on issues of rations. In most unions in the province, there was some attempt to fund the act through local voluntary subscriptions, but they were substantial only in half-a-dozen. Downpatrick, Cookstown, Dungannon and Ballycastle raised virtually all their funding in this way and Banbridge and Clogher about one-third of their totals.[40] There was actually widespread confusion among committees about grants in aid of local subscriptions, arising from a lack of clarity in the relevant section of the act. Many did not know that grants in aid of local subscriptions were still available. Despite prominent publicity in the London *Evening Post* in late May which, in the sanguine view of the *Belfast News-Letter*, had an 'electrical' effect throughout Ireland, the matter was not clarified 'until the power of the Commissioners to advance money was expiring'. So most committees relied on government loans on credit of future rates.[41]

The general welcome in Ireland for the temporary relief act was not shared universally in Ulster. The boards of guardians of Antrim, Belfast and Newtownards poor law unions were determined to have nothing to do with it – and succeeded. They were able to convince the new relief commission that the criteria for the operation of the act were not met in their unions, namely, the proven existence of destitution and the absence of adequate means to relieve it.[42] Their success was envied by a number of boards of guardians, anxious but unable to follow suit. Such were, for example, Lisburn and Larne, where minorities on the boards of guardians who urged the act as necessary for their electoral divisions were severely criticised by colleagues.[43] Other unions in which less than half of their electoral divisions used the act were Kilkeel, Gortin, Londonderry, Ballymena, Lurgan, Coleraine and Dunfanaghy. Indeed, only one division in Dunfanaghy union, Creeslough, used the act, but its dependence was very substantial, with a maximum of 52 per cent of its population receiving food.[44]

The case of Lisburn illustrates the thinking of guardians and ratepayers suspicious of the temporary relief scheme. In their view, the adjoining unions of Belfast, Antrim and Newtownards had been exempted from the act, whereas in their union an inspecting officer, a finance committee and twenty-seven local committees, one for each electoral division, had been appointed. Such an arrangement implied 'a suspected dereliction of duty on the part of the board of guardians . . . or a want of suitable exertions for the relief of destitution within . . . the several electoral divisions'. Lisburn was an area in which landlords and those blessed with worldly means had unceasingly looked after their poor. It was a matter of regret that an act, made necessary by the 'culpable neglect of landed proprietors and other men of property' from other parts of the country, should be applied to Lisburn where the work of relief had already been done. Local pride had been injured and wrath provoked, in particular by the 'appointment' of twenty-seven local relief committees. In fact, no committees had been appointed at the time of the public outcry; they had merely been nominated by an over-zealous inspecting officer, anxious to have the mechanism of the act at the ready. In the event, only eight of Lisburn's twenty-seven electoral divisions used the act.[45] The fundamental anxiety of Lisburn, Larne, Belfast, Antrim and Newtownards boards of guardians was, of course, the imposition of an unwanted and, in their view, unneeded burden of taxation.

The Annesley estate papers reveal the attitudes of landlords to the act similar to Lisburn guardians' and ratepayers'. The ideal was to avoid the act if possible. Lord Annesley's agent, Rev. J. R. Moore, was pressed, in June 1847, by the other landlords of Bryansford electoral division of Kilkeel union, Lords Roden and Downshire and Mr Quinn, to join with them in doing so by providing employment for all able-bodied men in the division until November; they calculated a saving of £600 to £700 'among the parties'. Had relief been provided through the act, on the rates, the landlords would have been directly liable for the rates of all holdings valued at less than £4 per annum. In respect of his 'home' electoral division of Castlewellan (Downpatrick union), Moore calculated that his share of agreed voluntary funding cost him £67.10s as against £177.3s had a rate been struck. He supported voluntary assessments towards a local subscription by tenant ratepayers in Ballybrick and Tirkelly electoral divisions (Banbridge union), provided the other landlords agreed an equal contribution. Moore thought it 'most desirable that the landholders should endeavour to take care of their own poor *and avoid having government officers in their district which would entail a great expense on the land'*. He wished other landlords to co-operate 'and prevent the poor falling into the hands of government'.[46] The poor would fall into the hands of government if they were supported by the poor law. Apart from the landlord being liable for the rates of holdings under £4 valuation, poor rates were more expensive than any other form of support because they paid for the system, that is, for such expenses as the salaries of union and workhouse officers and for the maintenance of the workhouse buildings, as well as for the poor.

IV

Pressure of space has led to the omission of extensive discussion on two substantial areas of relief committee activity. The first is the supporting role local committees played in the public works scheme from October 1846 to March 1847. Using their intimate local knowledge, they were required to provide government officials with properly scrutinised lists of applicant labourers. Officials complained frequently that most committees failed in this duty. The only Ulster county whose relief committees were unequivocally praised by an inspecting officer was Tyrone. They were 'indefatigable in their duties in the rural districts and have given great satisfaction'; they were '. . . zealous and . . . disinterested in the discharge of their duties.'[47] The second area is the actual relief which committees provided. Only about a dozen committees offered relief by employment; most avoided it because it was too expensive, but some stonebreaking, digging and farm work were offered for men, and knitting, spinning and various forms of embroidery for women and girls.[48] The commonest form of relief was the offer of meal for sale – usually at reduced prices, in contravention of the *Instructions* – and, increasingly from December 1846 onwards, soup. Of particular interest are several committees, notably Dungannon, Moy and Dunnamanagh as well as others, especially in counties Donegal, Londonderry, Antrim and Down which openly challenged the government's requirement that where committees sold meal they should do so at least at cost price. These committees took the view that the strict application of the requirement would reduce honest, hardworking people – typically labourers with large families whose wages were unequal to current high food prices – to destitution before allowing them to be helped. They further argued that the requirement was absurd in that, if it were rigidly applied, the funds of committees would never diminish, which contradicted their very existence.[49]

V

Local relief committees, despite wide variations in their effectiveness, were a vital element in Famine relief between 1845 and 1847. The partial failure of 1845 was managed in a very matter-of-fact way. The number of committees required was small and their independence of action under Peel's administration reflects the general absence of urgency. Circumstances in the following season were totally different: the potato failure of 1846 triggered an intense crisis, with large numbers of local committees called into operation, earlier in west Ulster than in the east.

Relief committees were a necessary channel of government support; without local effort, government was unwilling to help except in extreme cases. An important condition of official aid was the approval of committees by county lieutenants who were also charged with delineating relief districts. In this task, lieutenants were responsive to local requests, with the result that there was no uniformity in relief districts. When government policy changed, in the spring of 1847, in favour of feeding the Famine-stricken within their poor law unions, large numbers of relief boundaries had to be redrawn, which created serious administrative delay at a critical period.

With 100 per cent grants available from January 1847 onwards, local committees had a great incentive to establish a relief fund or expand an existing one. Their performance in this respect was variable, the largest funds being amassed in places where the leaders of local society were most actively involved and where, ironically, there was sometimes less distress. Some 'abandoned' communities in serious distress failed to raise more than a few pounds and received but an equivalent few pounds from government.

The operation of the Temporary Relief Act from late March to mid-August 1847, organised as it was within the framework of the poor law, deprived local committees of the initiative and control – however imperfect – they had enjoyed under the earlier schemes of relief. In effect the role of the local relief committee, as a willing coming together of community effort across social and religious boundaries, was at an end. The Temporary Relief Act was a major exercise in outdoor relief, a dress rehearsal for the assumption, in August 1847, of all extraordinary Famine relief by the Irish poor law system. The sense of betrayal felt by many local committee members is well summed up in the protest of the joint secretaries of the Banbridge committee when it was displaced by the new committee under the Temporary Relief Act:

> . . . we would deeply lament that the Government should insist on any change being made either in the mode of relief or in the constitution of the Committee.
>
> The Committee are unwilling that some active and energetic members who have hitherto been most efficient in their exertions, and liberal in their subscriptions, should be excluded . . . and that others, who have never taken any interest in proceedings . . . should be appointed in their room.[50]

Such injured feelings cut no ice with an administration determined on economy, efficiency and centralised control.

References

1   *Instructions to Committees of Relief Districts* (Extracted from *Minutes of the Proceedings of the Commissioners appointed in reference to the apprehended Scarcity*), 28 February 1846. Copy in Relief Commission Papers – hereafter Rlf. Com. Papers (Co. Cavan) II/2a/5826, Rev. James Martin, Rector of Killeshandra, to Stanley, 18 Sept. 1846. (National Archives of Ireland).

2   *Instructions for the Formation and Guidance of Committees for Relief of Distress in Ireland consequent on the failure of the Potato Crop in 1846*, B.P.P. 1847(764)L, pp. 104–7. (Hereafter *Instructions*).

3   James Grant, 'The Great Famine in the Province of Ulster 1845-49 – The Mechanisms of Relief' (unpublished Ph.D. thesis, The Queen's University, Belfast, 1986), p. 108.

4   See *Supplementary Appendix Part II and Part III to the Seventh Report of the Relief Commissioners*, pp. 18-21 & 23-81, B.P.P. 1847-8(956)XXIX. (Hereafter *Suppl. App. Pt. II and Pt. III 7th Rep. Rlf. Commrs*).

5   Rlf. Com. Papers for Counties Donegal, Cavan and Monaghan, II/2a & 2b/early numbers.

6   *Northern Whig*, 2 and 9 April 1846; Rlf. Com. Papers (Co. Down) II/2a/19326, Rev. John Boyd to (Commissary General Sir Randolph) Routh, 16 April 1847.

7   Rlf. Com. Papers (Co. Down) II/2a/6440, John Doran, P.P., Aghaderg, Loughbrickland, to Routh, 18 Oct. 1846: '... I applied for the "Acts and Papers" in my former role as a *member* of a *Relief Committee*, sitting in Loughbrickland'.

8   *Northern Whig*, 21 April 1846.

9   Macartney Papers, D572/21/106 (Public Record Office of Northern Ireland – hereafter P.R.O.N.I.). Copy minute book 10 Dec. 1845, 5 & 27 Jan. 1846.

10 Rlf. Com. Papers (Co. Cavan) II/2a and 2b/various early numbers; 2b/D4070, Charles J. Adams, Chairman (Shercock), to T.N. Redington, 6 Aug. 1846.

11 Ibid. 2b/4559, Pierce Morton, D.L., to Stanley, 20 July 1846; D4070, Adams to Redington, 6 Aug. 1846.

12 Ibid. 5193 & 4651, Morton to Stanley, 8 Aug. & 23 July 1846.

13 Rlf. Com. Papers (Co. Monaghan) II/2a/D4007, Rev. Allen Mitchell and Rev. Val Duke Christian, Joint Secretaries., to Redington, 3 Aug. 1846. This interesting document presents a summary of the committee's activities, together with minutes of seven weekly meetings between 13 June and 1 Aug. 1846.

14 Ibid. (Co. Donegal) II/2a and 2b/various early numbers.

15 Ibid. II/2a/4397, William Drummond, P.P., Treasurer for the committee, (no addressee), Killybegs, 16 July 1846.

16 Routh to Trevelyan, 19 Sept. 1846, B.P.P. 1847(761)LI, p. 80. He reminded Trevelyan that in 1845-6 there were about 600 committees in correspondence with the Relief Commission. He expected them to exceed 1,000 in the coming season, whereas in his plan of 'Central Barony Committees' they could not have exceeded 360. He claimed this arrangement would have been 'very useful also to the Board of Works in their references for lists' (since the public works were organised by baronies).

17 Trevelyan to Routh, 12 Sept. 1846, pp. 68-9, ibid.

18 *Instructions*, 8 Oct. 1846 (paragraph 6), B.P.P. 1847(761)L, p. 105.

19 Rlf. Com. Papers (Co. Fermanagh) II/2a/6120, Erne to Secretary of the Relief Office, 6 Oct. 1846; 6426, Erne (n.a.), 18 Oct. 1846. All county lieutenants were requested by a circular of 2 Oct. to form committees. They were provided with printed foolscap schedules on which to return names and addresses of chairmen and secretaries, together with the relief districts; 2a and 2b *passim*.

20 Ibid. (Co. Cavan) II/2a/6284, John Young M.P. (n.a.), 13 Oct. 1846; 6917, Young (n.a.) 31 Oct. 1846.

21 Ibid. (Co. Londonderry) II/2a/6207, Sir R.A. Ferguson (M.P.), D.L. to Routh, 9 Oct. 1846. Trevelyan, writing about this time to Col. Jones, chairman of the Board of Works, cast his mind ahead to 15 Aug. 1847 when the Labour Rate Act would cease and speculated that Parliament might determine 'that the Irish

proprietors [should] support their poor ... by payments out of the current produce of the poor rate ...', – Trevelyan to Jones, 5 Oct.1846, B.P.P. 1847(764)L, pp. 97-8. In fact, the Labour Rate Act, under which the public works scheme was organised, was run down in the spring of 1847, when it was replaced, by the Temporary Relief (popularly 'soup kitchens' or 'rations') Act which terminated on 15 Aug. 1847.

22   Ibid. (Co. Donegal) II/2a/numerous letters for late October and early November 1846, reciting committee after committee named for two parishes; 2a/7727, James Stewart, Bart., to Secretary, Relief Committee (sic), 25 Nov. 1846; ibid. (Co. Monaghan) II/2a/6428 and 6576, both lists of appointments by Lord Cremorne, 18 and 22 Oct. 1846; 2a/6642, Cremorne (n.a.), 24 Oct. 1846; 2a/7429, Cremorne (n.a.) 14 Nov. 1846, appointing the Farney committee.

23   Ibid. (Co. Armagh) II/2a and 2b *passim*.

24   Ibid. (Co. Tyrone) II/2a and 2b *passim*.

25   Ibid. (Co. Antrim) II/2a and 2b *passim*. Eight committees are clearly identifiable as based on electoral divisions and five on parishes.

26   Ibid. (Co. Down) II/2a and 2b *passim* for relief districts; four or five other districts consisted of between one and four parishes. In the thirty-seven or thirty-eight districts in the county, the most common basis of organisation was the electoral division. There were at least thirteen such districts. For Newry see also 2b/9406, Wm Thompson (Chairman of the Newry Rlf. Cttee.) to Routh, 22 Jan. 1847; 2a/10146, Hugh Boyd to Routh, 4 Feb. 1847; 2a/10155, W.I. Corr (n.a.), 4 Feb. 1847; 2a/10249, Daniel Bagot, vicar of Newry (n.a.), 5 Feb. 1847. For Rathfriland, see 2a/13920, Rev. R.A. Agar to the Relief Commission, 12 Mar. 1847; 2a/13888, Rev. Richard Archer to Routh, same date.

27   Ibid. II/2a/11044, Rev. Dr Edward Hincks to Wm. Stanley, 13 Feb. 1846. There was another electoral division of Crossgar in Co. Down; it was near Dromara and belonged to Banbridge poor law union.

28   Rlf. Com. Papers (Co. Londonderry) II/2b/20336, Rev. S. Gwynne, Chairman, to Stanley, 27 April .1847.

29   Ibid. (Co. Donegal) II/2a/6949, M. G. Fenwick (Secretary & Treasurer) to Routh, 2 Nov. 1846. The relief fund was a substantial £485 on which a government donation of £235 was recommended – fifty per cent was the usual maximum donation before Jan. 1847.

30   Ibid. 2a/7421, Rev. Jas Ovens, Secretary (Iniskeel), (n.a.) 13 Nov. 1846; 2b/15884, Edward Allingham, Chairman. (Inishmacsaint), to Stanley, 27 March 1847; ibid. (Co. Londonderry) II/2b/12515: printed resolutions of Portstewart Electoral Division Relief Committee, not dated, but 26 or 27 Feb. 1847.

31   Grant, 'The Great Famine', p. 108.

32   Rlf. Com. Papers (Co. Fermanagh) II/2a/D8342, 2b/7726, 15388, 15708.

33   Ibid. (Co. Down) II/2b/12480 (Gilford/Tullylish). The covering letter for the Gilford/Tullylish grant application was set out on notepaper embossed with the motif of *Dunbar McMaster & Co., Flax Spinners & Thread Manufacturers,* Gilford.

34   Ibid. (Co. Cavan) II/2b/119347 Rev. Matthew Webb (n.a.), 23 Feb. 1847.

35   Grant, 'The Great Famine', pp. 125-7. The local subscription was matched by just under £7,400 from government. By coincidence the figures for Co. Armagh are almost identical, £7,400 raised by local efforts and £7,300 donated by government.

36   Ibid. pp. 218-9.

37   Rlf. Com. Papers (Co. Fermanagh) II/2a/D8342, 2b/7726, 153887 15708; *Suppl. App. Pt. III 7th Rep. Rlf. Commrs.*, B.P.P. 1847-8(956)XXIX, p. 62.

38 Ibid. (Co. Down) II/2b/12480 (Gilford/Tullylish); *Suppl. App. Pt. III 7th Rep. Rlf. Commrs.*, B.P.P. 1847-8(956)XXIX, p. 30.

39 *Suppl. App. Pt. III 7th Rep. Rlf. Commrs.*, B.P.P. 1847-8(956)XXIX, p. 53. The electoral division of Drumlummon was in Granard poor law union.

40 Based on an analysis of *Suppl. App. Pt. III 7th Rep Rlf. Commrs.*, B.P.P. 1847-8(956)XXIX, pp. 23-81.

41 Grant, 'The Great Famine', p. 244; Circular No. 37 – Finance, dated 1 Sept. 1847, in *App. Part I (E) to 6th Rep. Rlf. Commrs.*, B.P.P. 1847-8(876)XXIX, p. 17.

42 Grant, 'The Great Famine', p. 224.

43 *Belfast News-Letter*, 23 April & 11 June 1847; Minutes Larne Board of Guardians, 25 May & 1 April 1847, BG XVII/A/2 (P.R.O.N.I.).

44 *Suppl. App. Pt. III 7th Rep. Rlf. Commrs.*, *passim*, B.P.P. 1847-8(956)XXIX. See p. 45 for Dunfanaghy union.

45 *Belfast News-Letter*, 23 April and 11 June 1847.

46 Annesley Papers, D 1854/6/3 (P.R.O.N.I.), pp. 135, 138, for two letters on consecutive days, 6 & 7 June 1847, Rev. J. R. Moore to Lord Roden, who was evidently pressing for a quick agreement from Moore on a voluntary assessment for an unnamed electoral division. Moore quoted £148 as the expense to the estate of a voluntary assessment and £535 if a rate had to be struck, i.e., more than three and a half times the voluntary assessment. This division may well have been Bryansford. The rate was high because of large numbers of small holders under £4 annual valuation for whose poor rates the landlord was primarily liable; ibid. p. 148, Moore to J. White, Dublin, 25 June 1847. (White was the Annesley lawyer); ibid. p. 130, Moore (n.a.), 26 April 1847; *Suppl. App. Pt. III 7th Rep. Rlf. Commrs.*, B.P.P. 1847-8(956)XXIX, p. 29. The voluntary fund required for Ballybrick was ultimately £195, equivalent to a (voluntary) rate of 8½d in the pound.

47 Extracts journal Captain Oldershaw, inspecting officer Co. Tyrone, 28 Nov. and 12 Dec. 1846, B.P.P. 1847(764)L, pp. 286 & 382.

48 Rlf. Com. Papers (Co. Tyrone) II/2b/D7191, Hon & Rev. Robert Maude to Rt. Hon. Henry Labouchere, 26 Oct. 1846; 8882, Maude to Routh, 8 Jan. 1847; 12241, Chas. Eccles, Chairman (Fintona Rlf. Cttee.) to Routh, 17 Feb. 1847; ibid. (Co. Armagh) II/2b/12483, Rev. W.H. Foster to Stanley, 2 March 1847; 15200, Rev. Henry Disney (Secretary & Chairman) to W. Stanley 8 Feb. 1847; 14716, Rev. James Disney to Routh, 19 March 1847.

49 Ibid. (Co. Tyrone) II/2a/704, Robert. Wray, Chairman (Dungannon) to Stanley, 4 Nov. 1846, with draft reply; 6952. James Eyre Jackson (Moy) to The Commissary General, 2 Nov. 1846, with draft reply. (Letter endorsed: 'Copy for Treasury'); 8989, Same to same, 11 Jan 1847; 9377, Same to same, 21 Jan. 1847, with draft reply; 2b/9758, Henry Cotthurst, Sec (Dunnamanagh), to Stanley, 28 Jan. 1847, with draft reply.

50 Ibid. (Co. Down) II/2a/14456, James Clibbon Hill & John Scott, Joint Secretaries, to the Commissary General, Banbridge, 17 March 1847.

Famine Studies in Schools:
The Northern Ireland and American Experience

NORTHERN IRELAND

Interpreting Famine Emigration with Children at the Ulster-American Folk Park

Evelyn Cardwell

THE ULSTER-AMERICAN FOLK PARK near Omagh in County Tyrone, Northern Ireland is an open air museum which interprets the theme of emigration from Ulster to America through fully furnished reconstructed emigrant homesteads, craft demonstrations, events, exhibitions and research facilities. A particular feature of the museum is its use of costumed interpreters who interact with visitors of all ages.

The Folk Park has, amongst others, four Ulster houses which were occupied during the period of the Great Famine – two buildings from County Tyrone, one from County Londonderry and the fourth from County Monaghan and also a recreation of a 300 ton emigrant ship which is similar to some of the smaller ships which sailed to America during the period of the Great Famine. Useful too in the Famine context is the New York Street Scene in the Emigration Exhibition. It is in and around these exhibits that an educational programme, 'Flight from Famine' takes place. The programme is targeted at 11 year old pupils, since this is where the topic links with the Northern Ireland curriculum (some schools in the Republic of Ireland also participate), and it takes place over a period of two days with pupils spending the night in the Folk Park's residential centre. The 'Living History' approach in general use at the museum has a particular value for pupils who are required to gain an understanding of the past which incorporates an appreciation of the various experiences and perspectives of the period under study. The opportunity to work in buildings that were standing at the time, surrounded by artefacts of the period, brings an invaluable dimension to the technique of role-play by putting the past in an authentic context. It is fortuitous too that this particular age group is one of the most receptive to the idea of role-play, having not yet acquired the inhibitions and self-consciousness that seems to afflict many older pupils.

The use of the site to involve pupils in becoming part of the Famine emigrant movement provides a unique experience which cannot be achieved by drama in the classroom, or by the passive viewing of dramatic presentations by actors.

Much has been written about demythologising the Famine. However, pupils of this age are fortunate in that they are unlikely to come to the topic carrying much in the way of mythological baggage – is there anything there to demythologise? However, it is important that myths are not perpetuated and that everything the pupils do is firmly grounded on evidence. Anchoring the experience on the evidence also helps to ensure that pupils are unable to indulge in uncontrolled flights of imagination. Though imagination must have a place in this programme but only within the confines of the available evidence.

The role-play experience provides opportunities for re-enactment and decision-making within the time period. It also raises many issues which need further discussion and examination of evidence in the classroom afterwards. Since the key aim of the programme is to display a variety of differing experiences in the Famine era, it was decided that Day One would be devoted to the experience of the Famine emigrant, and Day Two would deal with the perspectives of others who did not starve or emigrate.

Day One

The first day begins with an introduction to life in Ireland in 1844 where pupils find out how people usually lived. This is a necessary prerequisite if they are to appreciate the changes resulting from the failure of the potato crop.

Time is moved forward from 1844 to February, 1847 by means of an audio-visual presentation based on contemporary Famine illustrations and extracts from newspapers, until the month of February, 1847 is reached. By this means we also deal with those aspects of Famine which we cannot create in the Park, i.e. disease, death, starvation, and workhouse conditions and it introduces pupils briefly to some of the terms it is useful to know in their role-play scenes following the audio-visual presentation. The programme commences in the period February to September 1847. In an effort to make the break with the twentieth century as complete as possible pupils dress in traditional costume and take on a nineteenth-century identity. Each pupil on the programme is given the name of a Famine emigrant who sailed to America in the summer of 1847. These Famine emigrants form the children of four families for the day and are joined by four Folk Park guides in costume who are in the role of adult members of the family. This reflects the fact that one characteristic of Famine emigration was the preponderance of family groups.

Experiences in the houses vary. It is important that pupils understand that there was not one standard Famine emigrant experience but rather that during the Famine period people found themselves facing different circumstances. They reacted to these circumstances in different ways, and although the choice that faced them was, in some cases, little more than 'Hobson's choice', at other times their future was determined by the decisions they themselves made. For example, the poorest family based in the one-roomed cabin is heavily reliant on work schemes and soup kitchens. A copy of a poster issued by the Earl of Caledon in December 1846 provides the stimulus for this work.[1]

In contrast, the existence of the linen industry in the north and the further introduction of fine needlework skills helped in some way to ameliorate the condition of the hungry – this proves the focus for another activity and is developed from an account from Tartaraghan parish in County Armagh where the local rector reported in 1847:

> . . . weavers are sitting up three nights per week, in order by
> any means to procure food for their families . . . I have seen
> them, in returning to my own home, from visiting the sick
> at 2, a.m. working as busily as in the day-time.[2]

The American link is dealt with by another family – they cook and taste Indian meal stirabout and receive an emigrant letter from America. A local contemporary newspaper provides a number of recipes for cooking Indian meal and a suitable emigrant letter was sourced from the Emigration Database at the Ulster-American Folk Park.

At the height of the Famine about 3 million people were being fed at the soup kitchens. This figure is often used as an indication of the scale of the disaster in Ireland but it also indicates that many people did not starve. One family, therefore, was selected to lead the life of a fairly secure tenant farmer whose main concern was the threatened increase in rates rather than the fact that his potatoes had failed. This class of person emigrated too. 'From every part of Ulster the middling or small class of farmers are leaving in hundreds for the purpose of seeking a secure home on the other side of the Atlantic'.[3]

Throughout these activities the Folk Park guides and pupils are in first person role as they discuss their situation with other members of the family. During the conversations, information is fed in about deaths, workhouses, the plight of neighbours, as well as other more abstract ideas such as the respect expected by landlord and constant fear of eviction.

Since the theme is Famine emigration, each family has to be prompted to emigrate. This is achieved by means of a neighbour who calls to deliver various pieces of information to the different houses ranging from an emigrant letter and the news that the local landlord is offering assisted passages to America, to the fact that linen prices have declined further or the poor rate is being raised yet again! These issues provide opportunities for each family to discuss the negative and positive aspects of emigration and to decide on the best course of action.

The concept of differentiation between families is continued as each family with its luggage [or lack of it] travels to the seaport by a variety of methods. These differences are emphasised again in the booking office where some families pay their own fares but others have their passages pre-paid by the landlord or by an American relative. Pupils also witness a scene where a potential emigrant is advised to go to Liverpool where passages are less expensive since he cannot afford the fare for the direct journey from Ireland to America.

The synchronisation of the arrival of all the families at the quayside leads to the complete confusion that would have been typical of a busy nineteenth-century seaport at the height of the Famine. Pupils on the quayside then share their previous experiences with each other as they wait around for their ship to be prepared for the journey to America.

During the journey across the Atlantic on the reconstructed sailing ship, two points are addressed – firstly, emigrants had very little control over what happened to them and secondly, not every emigrant had the same experience. Pupils and their leaders are initially somewhat taken aback by their treatment by the ship's captain, partly because of his rude and uncaring nature and the fact that he is no respecter of persons, wealth or class. The shipboard experience proves to be a great leveller of persons. Very few privileges are available to anyone, unless they can buy them.

Regarding the events on the journey pupils select experiences from a series of chance cards which contain quotations from emigrant journals about actual voyages. While there is a strong probability that a family will draw a card referring to death or disease it is by no means certain. This approach removes the idea of the inevitability of death on every emigrant voyage. Depending on the cards drawn, the staff who lead the groups can introduce into their role-play relevant discussions about hopes, fears, fever, hunger, storms and death.

The emigrants are still at the mercy of others as they are checked for disease on arrival at New York harbour and run the gauntlet of the infamous New York runners as they emerge into the American Street.

Having inspected their new living quarters they then regain some control of their lives when they go job hunting.

Coming from the politically correct society of today pupils are usually horrified to read a job advertisement which says, 'No Irish need Apply'. This raises the general issue of prejudice and tolerance – topics which receive a very high profile in the curriculum of Northern Ireland schools.

Opportunities which are open to some of the immigrants are the possibility of finding work in a cotton mill, enlisting in the 1st New York Regiment to fight in the war against Mexico, going west to work on a canal, or to purchase a farm in the Territory of Wisconsin. In order to make these decisions pupils have to recall their various earlier experiences and choose the one best suited to them.

Music is one way of addressing the theme of cultural continuity and adaptation – Famine emigrants generally retained many of their songs and much of their music in America but were also in contact with the music of others. Exposure to American culture for our pupils comes in the form of the singing of Stephen Foster's new song 'Oh Susannah' first performed in public in the fall of 1847.

Day Two

While it was important to appreciate that it is difficult to define a standard emigrant experience during the Famine, it was equally important to realise that many people in Ireland didn't starve or emigrate. How did these people react to the events around them?

Having spent the previous day with the thought of the dreaded eviction hanging over them, some pupils now turned their attention to the perspective of the landlord and his agent. A request arrives from the landlord for a report about the condition of his estate and the agent's recommendations for improving the situation. As part of the response, pupils assist the agent's wife to prepare soup for the hungry tenants – something which is frequently referred to in the documentation of time. Ynyr Burges, landlord of Parkanaur Estate, near Dungannon, County Tyrone wrote:

> My lady instituted a kitchen with every apparatus and convenience for feeding the labourers all of whom were fed daily – they got the best beef, potatoes and pudding which sustained them while many were starving – they all paid a portion, to prevent them thinking they got it for nothing and 'Cut the head' of idleness.[4]

While the food is cooking, the pupils are given part of the rent roll and some background information on each of the tenants. Decisions are then made on the basis of this information, as to whether eviction, reduced rents, food or continued tenancy should be the appropriate recommendation.

Another group adopt the role of reporters and artists from *The Illustrated London News* and gather information on the varied housing and living conditions in Ireland for presentation to its readers.

How can 11 year old pupils on a short visit to a museum deal with the government perspective? Even revisionist and post-revisionist historians of the Great Famine cannot agree as to the degree of responsibility that can be apportioned to the government at the time. Can it be pursued in a museum context or is it better left to the classroom where documents can be studied and analysed in detail?

In the Folk Park we introduce the idea of a government perspective by concentrating on the emigrant experience and pupils in the role of shipping inspectors are asked to compile a report on the emigrant ship to be submitted to the Prime Minister, Lord John Russell.

Another point we wish to illustrate is the fact that for some people there were increased financial opportunities. From a number of possible role models, we selected the shipping agents and owners, who not only needed more crew members for their ships but also provided the printers with increased work. Pupils print posters and shipping tickets and the new crew members are taught how to splice ropes, tie various kinds of knots, scrub decks and sing sea shanties to assist them in their work.

The theme of voluntary aid to the starving Irish is also considered. We know that Hugh Campbell, a middle-class emigrant who left Ireland in 1818, and whose ancestral home is in the Folk Park, sent back flax-seed to his tenants in the Famine years to assist them. John Joseph Hughes, whose boyhood home is also in the Folk Park, worked tirelessly as Bishop of New York in the late 1840s to assist newly arrived Irish immigrants and to collect donations of cash and food to send to Ireland. The archives of the Society of Friends have numerous references to fund-raising for Irish relief in many small towns and villages in the USA, such as Steubenville in Ohio.

> This town is seventy miles by water below Pittsburgh, on the Ohio river. Its population is about 6,000. We have raised about 350 barrels of flour . . . for distribution to the sufferers by famine in Ireland. Some of the contributors are from the north of Ireland themselves, or descendants from those who emigrated from that quarter of Ireland; and therefore it would, perhaps, be gratifying to them if our donations could, consistently with your general plan, go to the north of Ireland.[5]

Pupils discuss various methods of fund-raising and work on compiling a quilt of a traditional American pattern to 'illustrate' American links to the Irish Famine.

Museum education programmes by their nature have pupils for a short period of time, and should give pupils an experience which is object linked and cannot be achieved in the classroom. In this instance the experiences are designed to expand the pupils understanding of famine emigration and to provide pointers for further research and discussion on their return to school. The process of sharing with each other the different experiences they have had over the two days is a valuable educational tool in itself which will enhance their oral and aural skills. The ways in which teachers capitalise on this programme are varied – it can serve as an introduction to the topic, as a midway addition or as a consolidation of the study.

Wherever it is slotted in to the teaching programme [and the museum advises that it should be quite early in their study] we trust that the experience they have is thought-provoking, memorable and novel and introduces some of the main issues of the period in a way that pupils of 11 years can handle with confidence and a meaningful degree of understanding.

References

1   P.R.O.N.I., RLF COM 11/2b Barony of Dungannon, County Tyrone.

2   *Transactions of the Central Relief Committee of the Society of Friends during the Famine in Ireland 1846 and 1847* – (Dublin, 1852), p. 192.

3   *Derry Sentinel*, April 1847.

4   P.R.O.N.I., T 1282.

5   *Transactions of the Central Relief Committee of the Society of Friends*, p. 243.

AMERICA
Ireland, Famine, Emigration, and Boston

Lawrence Bickford

Conference presentation by:
Tyrus Houston, Middle School coordinator and history teacher
Lawrence Bickford, computer coordinator and teacher
Anna Zimmer, grade 12 student
Carl Hampe, grade 12 student

AT THE HOPKINTON MIDDLE SCHOOL, New Hampshire, U.S.A. a unit on Ireland, Famine, Emigration, and Boston entitled *Immigrant* is taught to 8th Grade Students (13 and 14 year olds). What is this unit called *Immigrant*? *Immigrant* is a nine week course of American history that asks students to assume the role of a real person and to write that person's story. Immigration is a major theme of American history, and one we choose to teach in an intense, and highly engaging way. All students spend one quarter of the school year studying this unit, which borrows from an approach called Drama in Education to bring life to the issue of immigration to the United States. Each student plays the part of an actual Irish emigrant who travelled from Ireland to Boston in the 1840s whose name is found on an actual ship's passenger list that has been transcribed into a computer database.

Our two dozen or so students work to absorb some history of the 1840s, both Irish and American, then convert what they have learned into a journal of historical fiction. They listen to descriptions on what life was like at the time; they ask questions; they discuss what they have learned; they play roles in our little dramatizations; but most of all they write. The focus of their writing is a journal of historical fiction, in which they chronicle a year in the life of the person whose part they have chosen to play. By the time the nine weeks are over, each pupil has written, carefully revised and polished, compelling and historically accurate journals of twenty, thirty, forty and more pages in which they chronicle a year in the life of an Irish immigrant. This cycle repeats itself four times a year as four history classes take part in the unit.

Immigrant is taught in the school's computer laboratory. Every student is assigned to a computer, which serves our students well as a writing tool. They are taught both the *use* of a word processor and the importance of revising one's writing. The word processor certainly makes the revision process easier, and we would like to think that the quality of the writing speaks for itself. In addition, the computers serve as storage for a collection of primary-source documents, a collection similar to, but far smaller than the Ulster-American Folk Park's database in Omagh, County Tyrone, Northern Ireland. These include the passenger lists of several sailing ships. It is from the database that each student selects the name of the person whose story he or she will write. Somehow, knowing that they are writing the stories of real people lends credence to the work. In addition, letters, diary entries, pictures, advice to emigrants, and eyewitness accounts of the hardships of the Famine era – all dating back to the 1840s – are stored on the computers for easy access at any time.

In part because of the attraction of computers, in part because of the dramatization and role-playing, in part because of the hands-on nature of *Immigrant*, our students are drawn into this unit and become deeply engaged. They work hard. They ask if they might be allowed to come into the computer laboratory before or after school to work on their journals. They ask if they might be allowed to work on them at home. Because the students are so engaged in the work, they take great pride in what they write. The result is the quality of writing as presented below.

> *Yesterday was a day that I will always remember. Late yesterday evening John returned from a neighbour's house. He was late for our dinner (small though it was) and Ellen was firm in her belief that we should always eat together, so a quarrel immediately began. They went on arguing, each trying to make his or her point. Ellen got a crimson face and her eyes turned to blue ice. They were drowning each other out with their voices, shaking the dark house with all the noise, until John took out a paper from his pocket and brandished it before Ellen's face. She glared at him suspiciously for she can't read, but I stepped forward and read it aloud. It was an advertisement for a ship that was to sail to America. Boston was the name of the city. John explained that while he was at the neighbour's house he was shown the paper.*
>
> *'The neighbours are going', he said as we sat down to eat. He lowered his voice and added uncertainly, 'Perhaps we should, too'. The silence that followed was like a blanket suffocating all of us. I ceased to think clearly. My mind raced with thoughts mingled with rising panic and excitement. Such an idea had crossed my mind, but I had never imagined the possibility that we might go. Then suddenly, the room exploded with talk and questions. Ellen was shocked. Leave Ireland?! Sail? On a ship? Us? How? When? Her face was a strange mix of snow white and blood red as she rolled off the reasons why the trip was impossible.*
>
> *'Oh, the terrible things I've heard', she said urgently. 'People falling overboard and shipwrecks and sharks! Sea serpents! Out on the water in the middle of the sea! No land in sight! Fevers that take whole boatloads of people! I hear they call them coffin ships! Coffin ships! And leave my home? My country? . . .'*
>
> Angela Meehan

> *There is a place where there is no endless cry of hunger, no wild lament of those in mourning for loved ones. People walk on strong legs and wear clothes that fit perfectly. Laughter and merriment fill the air and work is plentiful and good. Bellies rumble with pleasure at the large meals served every day and children in perfect health play*

in the streets. No one has ever heard the cry of a nation of people in destitution. No one has felt their own voices join the chorus in a cry for help and a plea for life. There are no bodies heaped in holes and left to rot, and there are no walking bones that can barely be called human. The smell of decaying bodies is a foreign one to these people, and the taste of the last bit of food or a rotten potato does not linger in their mouths. God smiles on these people and on this place. I wish it were Ireland, but it is not.

Rebecca Russell

Another important point our students learn in depth is that making the decision to leave their homes in Ireland led people to a most difficult challenge, the dangerous voyage across the North Atlantic.

Cork Cove, better known as the 'Bay of Tears', of southern Ireland is calm and beautiful. The bay has a mysterious peacefulness to it that I can't explain. The air smells of saltwater and I hear the sound of waves washing on the shore and the cries of seabirds in the distance.

The S.S. Davis Browne is a massive, black ship. I have never seen anything as huge and beastly before. Working on several of the sails that fluttered in the breeze of the bay, sailors climbed the three masts that seemed to reach up touch the sky. The hard-working men were busy loading, unloading, and repairing the ships. Feeling very small compared to this mighty ship, I glanced around at the many others in the port. To my surprise, they all looked very much like the Davis Browne. Many were much bigger and even more frightening than our ship. They were huge! I can't compare the size of these sailing vessels to anything that I have ever seen before in my life!

Before we boarded the ship, I chose to buy my eating utensils. I bought a small bowl and a spoon for one pound and twenty pence. It was very costly, so now I only have six pounds and sixty pence left. I suppose I could have bought from another of the many vendors, but this man had the shortest line. With the hustle and bustle of the port, I wanted to make sure that I made it to the ship as soon as possible. The first mate met us at the dock, blew a whistle, and commanded all English aboard. After they boarded, we Irish stepped on board one at a time to give our names to the captain.

I fear that this might be a difficult journey. As we filed into our dwelling for the voyage, the 'tweendecks, the air instantly became polluted with the smell of the many bodies crammed into this small, dark place. With no portholes for sunlight and the only source of fresh air being the hatch, our quarters are not very healthy or comfortable. There are so many people on this ship, all of us anxious to make it to America, yet regretful for leaving Ireland. I just hope we make it there safely.

Beth Watson

Death stalks this ship now and we are doomed. Like a shadow he is always watching us. He haunts us in our sleep and picks his victims one by one. Already he has claimed the souls of two people I knew. First he claimed a four-month-old infant, and after that Michael Laughlin, the father of Bridget. To make matters worse, the bodies of these dead are dumped into the cold, dark ocean by a bloody Protestant! The captain has not a care of what happens to us Irish and makes the funerals as brief as he can. Sometimes he does not even show up!

As for myself I am also condemned to my bed. Day upon day I lie here in my bed of sickness and breathe in the vapors of the ill and sweaty. How I long to climb up the hatch and expose my body to the top deck. I dream of the sun shining on my face, and the wind whipping through my hair. But alas I am stuck in this awful hole, where a person dying is not big news.

I also dream of my homeland, of Ireland. I dream of the beauty of the land, and of the brisk spring mornings I spent with my father. And then sometimes I dream of awful things. I dream of sea monsters devouring our ship in one small gulp. Or the dreaded ship's disease breaking out and everyone dying. Worst of all, I once dreamt that we did make it to the new world. But in the new world we found exactly what we had left; corruption, poverty, and starvation. I hope that in the new world I find a new and better life.

Jared White

Here is another excerpt, as Lauren Detwiller brings her journal to a close:

And as soon as I finish signing my name, I will store you in a box, hidden far from my view, never to be touched again by me, the author. Decades will pass, and one day deep into the future, another generation will find you, still in your original place, eager to be discovered. As I look at you now, I have to smile. Your leather case is worn and tattered, the binding slashed, and the pages torn and faded. Your appearance is far from appealing, but yet you are. These are the signs of love; the love I had as I carefully wrote each precious word onto your surface. Each word is now cherished and preserved beneath your shabby cover, shielded from the hardships that most definitely will follow.

And that is how I will end this journal. I am closing a chapter in the book of my life and starting another. My closing line will be spoken in two words, words that have much more meaning than I can begin to describe, yet when I think of these words, I think of extreme gratitude. The power of them will never be known to human beings. These two minute words of great importance are . . . thank you.

A student a year or so ago finished her journal on a similar note. When our nine-week unit ended, she proudly handed in a 45-page work, wrapped in a scrap of linen and tied with ribbon, just as it might have been a hundred and fifty years ago.

The completed journal is divided into four parts:–

- **Life in Ireland:** Here the student journal, a piece of accurate historical fiction, begins. Students write of themselves, their families, the land, landlord, the gale, cottages, work, the community, diet, changing times, and more.

- **The decision to emigrate:** the 'push' and 'pull' factors used to describe the forces that drive emigration. Our students explore the many pushes and pulls that were involved in the movement of people in the 1840s. They role-play family discussions and write about why they went to America: he might have been evicted, or might have a sister in Boston, and so on.

- **The voyage:** At 3:00 p.m. on a Friday afternoon, after seven hours of school, *Immigrant* students board a mock sailing ship in the school's computer laboratory, created using stage flats, props, tape loops, and a great deal of imagination. Eighteen hours later they will set foot in Boston. During the voyage students experience cramped quarters, poor food, a mean first mate and a hard captain, storms, sickness, boredom, music, burial at sea, and more. Some of the students' best writing will come from this eighteen-hour overnight experience.

- **Life in Boston:** Here students must apply for work from a database of actual jobs available in Boston and face 'no Irish need apply' discrimination if their application is for the 'better' jobs. They find housing, shop for food and dry goods, and design a budget. All of this involves working with actual data from the 1840s. Also, lurking behind hidden corners lie life's little fates, such as the loss of a job, an injury, or the arrival of unexpected relatives. Sometimes fate, plus hard work of exceptional quality, might bring a promotion, a new baby, or the arrival of a loved one from Ireland.

To truly understand the power of *Immigrant* we would like you to hear from our student presenters, Carl Hampe and Anna Zimmer.

Carl Hampe 12 Grade Student

It is certainly not a requirement for an *Immigrant* student to have an Irish background. In fact, the majority of students do not. But this programme had special importance for me as the great grandson of Patrick Moran and Mary Curran of Dingle, County Kerry, who emigrated in the late 1800s to Boston, Massachusetts. I never had the chance to get to know my grandfather and so I found myself wondering about my elusive Irish ancestors. Through the *Immigrant* programme, I got the chance to understand my Irish heritage and to experience the kind of life my family led.

I remember searching through the ships' logs on our computer database (similar to the one found at the Ulster-American Folk Park) looking for Patrick Moran in the listings. Unfortunately I did not find him. The closest name I found was William McNamara, of County Cork. The importance of my Irish connection was not lost, however. Although I didn't find my actual relative, I did find an identity. Through this identity, I created, over the next nine weeks, my own history based on the factual history received in class.

For a thirteen-year-old, nine weeks is a long time. But after a week of writing I became completely engrossed in my character. Ireland began to develop from the mythical and mystical land of St. Patrick's Day hype into the tangible, if somewhat less desirable homeland of the cottier.

A huge part of *Immigrant* is the overnight stay which we use to simulate the long voyage to America. The atmosphere is created with theatrical props: a plank for boarding, a bell to call passengers 'on deck', tape recordings of babies crying, simulated portholes, etc. These props help shape the voyage into something students never forget. Listening to a recording of babies crying in a dark room may not be the same as living on a ship for 8 weeks, but these effects help bring a realism which can be seen in our journals. For example, my own 8th-grade journal talks of the emigrant's first day aboard ship:

> *The ship we are taking is called the Oregon. It's quite a majestic ship: three whole masts, giant square sails; and a beautiful banner they call the American flag. We gathered our money, paid our passage, and signed the log. As I climbed aboard, I saw two sharply dressed men. One, the meaner of the two, was Mr. Hatcher, first mate. The quiet one, I learned, was Captain John Mayhew. He gives the orders and when he says jump, you best jump. Personally, I don't like either of them; they're quite ornery folk.*

> *The first mate led us down to our quarters, a big room with a low ceiling he called the 'tweendecks. It is not a very pleasant place. I hit my head on the low roof several times. The room reeked with the smell of mildew and rot.*

> *Tonight we had a fair dinner of potatoes and water. The potato was hot and the water was cool, which is better than most of our recent meals. The cook, however, was not as good as the meal. He was something from hell.*

> *We were allowed to walk up and down the deck for a moment. When we went back down to the 'tweendecks, I saw several rats scurry across the floor.*

Although the majority of students who take the course are not of Irish descent nearly every American has descended from one group of immigrants or another. Whether Chinese, Polish, English, African, or Iranian, we all have ancestors from somewhere outside of the New World. Therefore, just as the identity of William McNamara became important for me with my Irish background, it can become important for any student with any background.

In April 1995 I came to Ireland for the first time, along with twenty other students from our school, all of whom had been through *Immigrant*. On that trip we travelled throughout western Ireland. In Dingle, I was able to walk through the fields of my great grandfather, and visit the church where he worshipped. It was a powerful experience for me. We also stopped in Cobh. At the Queenstown Heritage Center, Director Michael Collopy pointed out a powerful part of what we were doing. Our trip to Ireland had taken our immigrant characters' lives full circle. I had returned to Ireland and found my great grandfather's land. I had returned when he could not. Everyone else on the trip had also returned, having brought their immigrant identities back home to Ireland. Their 1840s counterparts had never had that opportunity.

Not everyone in the programme gets the chance to travel to Ireland. However, everyone does carry a piece of *Immigrant* with them for the rest of their lives. The *Immigrant* unit has seen to it that these people are not forgotten, we have brought some dignity to their memory, and we let them live on.

Anna Zimmer, 12th grade student

For me, *Immigrant* was an enlightening unit. It made such a big emotional impact on me as an eighth grader that, two years later, I wanted to experience the indecision, the frustration, and the final joy of getting to America all over again. I approached Mr Bickford and asked him what I could do about helping him or getting involved in the class. He had received requests like this before, and was prepared to offer me a few options.

It was too soon for me to 'sail' again (that is, take part in the overnight re-creation of the sailing voyage), as there was only one summer between me and my maiden voyage. The honour of 'sailing' a second time was reserved for juniors and seniors only. He offered that I could sell plates and cutlery on the docks, or I could 'stow away'. The latter entails hiding in the 'tweendecks of our makeshift ship while the immigrants board and stow their baggage. As the first mate checks the 'tweendecks and discovers the stowaway, the action starts. The stowaway makes as much noise as he or she can and resists capture, gaining the attention of the paying passengers and the captain. A grovelling session ensues, usually ending in the deposit of the poor stowaway on the dock: ten minutes of excitement followed by a long walk home from school.

Ever the actress, stowing away appealed to me most. On the day of 'sailing', there I was in my skirt and shawl, grovelling in the best Irish accent I could muster. It came out sounding rather British, but the faces of the immigrants as they watched this exchange reminded me that it isn't the accent that counts. The action is what's important. This little drama was reflected in many of the journals from that group, and I was excited beyond belief to experience my run-in with the captain and crew through the eyes of the *Immigrant* students. The creativity of the students amazes me every time I read through an excerpt. What began as a simple, dramatic improvisation became, through their eyes, an embellished production, complete with tears and high drama.

Since that first wild performance, I have been thrown off the ship two more times, and I finally sailed once more, in my junior year. It was just as enthralling as it had been the first time. I helped to add colour to the scenes played out along the voyage, and had a chance to write some myself. I got a feel for how much work goes into creating the entire voyage, not just the opening scenes. Also, I found the experience of bringing life to my character a very moving one, given my experiences with the unit. The feelings I mentioned earlier – indecision, frustration, and joy – poured out onto the computer screen with little resistance. I'd have to say my foray into historical role-playing has been as beneficial to me as to the students themselves.

Each year a few *Immigrant* graduates help with the sailing or in the classroom, and it enhances the unit for everyone. Virtually every class has a high school student assisting the eighth graders in some way. There have been a long line of memorable student aids who have helped to make *Immigrant* what it is today. It has been well worth my time and effort, and ensures an experience for the eighth-graders that none will forget.

Mr Houston and Mr Bickford

Allow us to begin with a few questions. Why would we, as teachers of American history, wish our students to learn about the Irish Famine of the 1840s? Why would we be interested in spending weeks studying Irish immigration to the United States? And why would we spend a quarter of the eighth grade school year so tightly focused on a single theme: Irish emigrants of the Famine years?

The answers are these. The United States is a land of immigrants, and, as teachers of American history, we have a strong interest in the movement of peoples from other lands to the United States. The roots of those people remain strong even today. In addition, we want our students to understand famine, past and present, and the impact of such terrible hardships on the people who make up a population.

We subscribe to an approach sometimes called 'less is more'. Less breadth of coverage allows time for more depth. And so we focus our study of immigration in American history on a single group, the Famine Irish. Our students gain a deep understanding of the people, life in both Ireland and the United States at that time, and the forces that drive people to leave one country for another. Thus, one of the key points we wish our students to learn during their time in the *Immigrant* unit is this: what were the forces that pushed the Irish from their homeland?

So, *Immigrant* is history, writing, and computers, combined in a way that our students find both attractive and challenging. In teaching about our history and about immigration to the States, we have found it important to teach about Ireland's history as well, to help them to understand the forces that brought – and continue to bring – people to our shores. Using computers, dramatization, and role-playing, we try to make the unit as engaging as possible. Our students respond with the kind of powerful writing you have heard.

There is one more benefit to *Immigrant*. We believe our students come away from the unit with an increased sensitivity to famine and such hardships in today's world. Wrote Julie Davis in her journal:

> *It was dawn and the sun was coming up right behind our bakery. The air was cool and brisk. I looked at the people with the first morning light on their faces and I was aghast. The people outside on the street were starving and clawing at the window and door. Their faces were downcast and their cheeks were hollow. Their eyes seemed to be set back in their heads, and when I looked into them, it was like I could see their whole lives before me. I could see all the problems that they had gone through.*
>
> *Among the throng of people I saw a child hanging onto her mother, now a skeleton for lack of food. The little girl started crying. Suddenly William turned me from the dreadful scene and embraced me. I started crying. Couldn't England see what was going on here? Couldn't they see what was happening? I know why William turned me away from the awful scene, to protect me. But it was too late. I already had the horrid scene engraved in my mind. I will never forget that as long as I live.*

We hope that all of our students will remember what they have learned for an equally long period of time.

INDEX

D

Dalton, Eliza, 164
Dalton, William, 164
Davis, Thomas, 175, 176, 177, 182
Dawson, John, 83
De Vere, Stephen, 27, 28, 29, 30
Delaware, U.S.A., 23
Denn, County Cavan, 187
Denver, U.S.A., 57
Derry City, *see*
    Londonderry, City of,
Derrycrum, County Fermanagh, 192
Derrycullen, County Fermanagh, 192
Derrylavan, County Monaghan, 76
Detroit, U.S.A., 26, 57
Devine, David, 91
Devon Commission, 87
Diaspora,
    African, 11-12
    Chinese, 12-13
    Cornish, 13
    Greek, 13
    Irish, 7, 41
    Korean, 13
    Russian, 13
    Sikh, 13
Dickens, Charles, 51, 54
Diner, Hasia, 61
Disease,
    cholera, 26, 36, 51, 55, 104, 122, 123
    diarrhoea, 130, 138, 141, 145
    dysentery, 2, 29, 31, 32, 55, 118, 130, 138, 141, 145
    fever, 2, 21, 25, 27, 28, 30, 31, 32, 33, 34, 36, 54, 104, 115, 122, 123-4, 128-31, 137-46, 158, 163, 164, 178, 180, 202, 206
    plague, 34, 105, 111, 115, 116, 131, 163
    relapsing fever, 2, 141, 145
    scurvy, 141, 143-6
    smallpox, 138
    tuberculosis, 55
    typhoid, 129, 141, 143
    typhus, 2, 29, 118, 138, 141, 145
    vitamin deficiency, 141, 145
Doehne, Rev. J.L., 44
Donegal, County, 94, 153, 155, 156, 185, 186, 187, 189, 190, 191, 192, 194
Donegall, Marquis of, 189
Douglas, Dr George Mellis, 26-7, 29, 30, 31, 32-3, 34-6
Douglass, Henry Grattan, 94
Dowd, Bryan, 169

Down, County, 89, 151, 154, 156, 186, 189, 190, 192, 194
Downpatrick, County Down, 189, 192, 193
Downshire, Lord, 193
Doyle, John, 50
Doyle, Martin, 198
Drogheda, County Louth, 83, 84, 104, 120, 157, 158
Drumholm, County Donegal, 190
Drumlumman, County Cavan, 187, 192
Drumsnat, County Monaghan, 187
Dublin Quarterly Journal of Medical, Science, 139
Dublin University Magazine, 178
Dundalk, County Louth, 81, 83, 84, 158
Duncan, Dr William Henry, 123-4, 129, 130, 137, 138
Dundee, Scotland, 2, 140, 151, 152, 153-5, 157, 158-9
Dunfanaghy, County Donegal, 193
Dungannon Union, 94, 156, 189, 192, 194, 202
Dungiven, County Londonderry, 41
Dunluce, County Antrim, 186
Dunlop, Nancy, 91
Dunnamanagh, County Tyrone, 194
Dunphy, Eamon, 5

E

Eagar, Edward, 43
Eagleton, Terry, 181
Earl Grey, 94
Edgeworth, Maria, 179, 181
Edwards, R.D., 5
Elgin, Lord, 29, 34
Elliott, James, 95
Elliott, Mathew, 95
Elliott, William, 95
Ellis Island, 42
Elphin, Bishop of, 31
Emigrant letters, 3, 42, 52, 61, 161, 206
Emigration,
    assisted passage, 44, 72, 85
    Database –
        Ulster-America Folk Park, 201
        New Hampshire, 205
    European, 17, 18, 20, 22, 63
    female, 3, 41, 45, 54, 61-8, 91, 93-5, 105, 106, 107, 127, 130, 144, 152-5, 158
    free settler scheme, 96
    landlord sponsored, 72
    passengers, 25-9, 30-1, 32, 34-5, 77, 80-4, 92-3, 110, 124, 131, 146, 205, 210-1

Tyndale, William, 7
Typhoid *see* Disease,
Typhus *see* Disease,
Tyrkennedy, County Fermanagh, 188

U
Ulster-American Folk Park, ix, 199-204
Unemployment, 64, 120, 138, 152
Upington, Thomas, 41

V
Van Dieman's Land, 44, 45, 96
Vaughan, W. E., 180
Virginius, The, 31
Vice-Guardians, 165
Vagrancy,
  geographical distribution, 103, 108
  Irish, 87, 103, 106-8, 115-22

W
Wales, Irish paupers in, 2, 105, 109, 137,
  138, 139
Ward, Hugh, 76
Ward, Peter, 77
Waterford, County, 102, 104, 106
Westport, County Mayo, 72
Wexford, County, 102, 162, 178
Whately, Richard, Archbishop, 87
White, James, 169, 170
White Keyran, 170
Whyte, Robert, 25, 28, 32-3
Wilde, Sir William, 101, 179
Williams, T.D., 5
Willoughby, Rev. Mark, 33
Wilson, Susan, 95
Wiltshire, England, 106, 107

Wolff, Robert Lee, 177
Women's emigration, 3, 45, 54, 61-8, 94-5,
  106, 127-8, 152, 153, 154, 158
Woodham-Smith, Cecil, 5
Workhouse,
  assisted packages, 91, 92, 93, 96
  children, 1, 88-9, 93, 95, 96-7
  orphans, 1, 90-7
  population, 88, 90, 93
Workhouses,
  Armagh, 94
  Cavan, 94
  Carrickmacross, 75
  Coleraine, 89, 92, 97
  Cookstown, 94
  Donegal, 94
  Dublin, 94
  Dungannon, 94
  Enniskillen, 94
  Inishowen, 91
  Kenmare, 73
  Larne, 95, 193
  Letterkenny, 91, 92, 93, 97
  Lisburn, 96, 193
  Lisnaskea, 94
  Londonderry, 88, 91, 92, 94, 97
  Skibbereen, 94
  Strabane, 91, 92, 93, 97
World War I, 12, 65
Wray, Ann, 91
Wynne, Captain Edmond, 165

Y
Young, Arthur, 155
Young Irish Movement, 44
Young, John, 188

Printed in Northern Ireland by Nicholson & Bass Ltd